# Homeschooling by Heart

## A MOM'S ROAD MAP

## FOR MAKING IT ALL WORK

by

Kristina Sabalis Krulikas

This book is surrendered to the most perfect Holy Family:
Jesus, Mary, and Joseph.

It is also dedicated to all
homeschooling parents and their children.
May the Holy Family always be your model
and the Lord's graces rain down upon you!


My thanks to my children Viktorija, Giedré,
Gintaras, Linas, Katryte, and husband Richie,
who encouraged me each and everyday.
I love you!


A very special hug to two dear friends,
Cynthia and Felice,
who inspired, edited, suggested, and critiqued.
Without the two of you there wouldn't be
a mom's road map.
Your homeschooling expertise is a true treasure!


Andy - thank you
for being my personal computer guru.
This book would still be in computer land without you!

Kristina

Homeschooling By Heart

All scripture quotations taken from **Ignatius Revised Standard Version** (CA: Ignatius Press, 1966) or **The New American Bible** (NY: Catholic Book Publishing, 1992)
Poetry selections taken from:
**Favorite Poems Old and New** by Helen Ferris (NY: Doubleday & Co., 1957)
**Treasury of Best-Loved Poems** edited by Christopher R. Moore (NY: Gramercy Books, 1992)

Cover design by David Frantz, Home Based Publishing
(homebasedpub@earthlink.net)

Edited by Rhonda Howard and Clare Ulik

ISBN 0-9714935-0-2

Published by
Solomon's Secrets
1264 Alhambra Drive
Fort Myers, Florida 33901
e-mail address: Sudievu@aol.com
http://www.solomons-secrets.com

# TABLE OF CONTENTS

# LIST OF CHARTS, TABLES, AND SCHEDULES:

## CHARTS & SCHEDULES

I've included charts, schedules, lists, tables, and outlines in the book wherever applicable. These are only guidelines. Please take them and use them, as you will : revise, delete, and add. Make them yours. Or...don't use them at all. They are included as an aid, not as a handicap!

# INTRODUCTION

*Two roads diverged in a wood, and I -*
*I took the one less traveled by,*
*And that has made all the difference.*
"The Road Not Taken," Robert Frost

*Life is so short and our time with our children here on earth is even shorter. When our firstborn enters this world, it seems that our future is endless; no limits bar the possibilities in store for our child and us. Soon the days pass, in a flurry of diapers and sleepless nights, and if we are blessed, our hands are once again full with a precious new life. Before the coming of our second, we question whether there will be enough love in our hearts for two – and of course there is. The days begin to whir by even quicker now, and in the twinkle of an eye it's time to think about school...*

When my oldest was three, I joined a moms' group at our church. I specifically went because I heard that there would be a speaker talking about kindergarten. (Could you believe that I was worried about school when she was only three??) Well, the speaker never showed up, but I happened to sit down next to an expectant lady and her mother and we got to talking. (I was drawn to them because her mom had a rather heavy accent. Since I was raised bilingual, I thought we might have something in common.) Eventually our conversation turned toward school and kindergarten. This expectant mom told me "she has no plans for school at all and is going to homeschool all her children!" (She was pregnant with her third.) Thus began a long and lovely friendship. The two of us eventually were chosen to run the club; for one of our meetings we found a lady willing to speak to the group about homeschooling. To make a long story short, about eight of fifteen moms in that group eventually homeschooled, with seven of us still at it. Not bad!

I had always been convinced that kindergarten was totally unnecessary - that its sole reason for existence is to allow kids to socialize and play, not learn formally. Of all the schools I visited, only one had a three hour kindergarten. There was no way on earth I was going to send my child to a full-day program, and I didn't like the school that offered the shorter version. On top of which I was already contemplating the future – I was pregnant with my third child and I knew that we could not afford private school for three children. Additionally, the public schools – were public. (I attended public high school and am quite aware of the difference between a public and private education.) Therefore, homeschooling became our alternative.

My husband was all for it. He, like me, didn't think much of kindergarten, so there was no worry that we would educationally "ruin" our child. He had great faith in my teaching abilities, and he was frugal enough to realize we'd be giving her a great education at a minimum cost. We had only one living grandparent, my mom, who didn't utter a word of dissent. She, being well read in the daily news, was quite aware of what was taking place in the schools and thought homeschooling seemed a very safe alternative for her oldest, darling grandchild.

This is how our journey began. Luckily, God sent friends along that were all in the same boat - just starting to homeschool. There was a lot of handholding among us. We all joined our local support group and started schooling. Our family's homeschooling odyssey has come a very long way since that first day almost nine years ago. We now have five children ages 13,11,8,5, and almost 2. During our journey, our emphasis has changed from merely striving to give them the best possible education, to building Godly character and raising them in Christ's image. In fact, it's only by the graces God pours forth on me each and every day that I am able to keep on homeschooling.

During the years, a group of us started our own private school for homeschoolers (one of the two legal ways to homeschool in the state of Florida). This has been a blessing to us because we have met so many wonderful and interesting families, who have tremendously enriched our lives. As administrator of the school, I have had to learn to become more organized, knowledgeable about homeschooling, familiar with curriculum, and aware and assertive about my own life goals.

We are still a bilingual family trying to speak only Lithuanian at home (English when necessary during school). My two older daughters have played Suzuki violin since they were four and piano since about seven; my son plays cello and piano. They're also two belts away from receiving their black belts with Dad. As our family has grown, we've turned our hearts more and more toward home in an effort to feel more connected and in tune with one another. When the kids were babies, and being new in town, I would go out to the mall almost every day so that I could interact with other people. I was lonely. Now I can barely drag my kids to the store, and I am quickly becoming "store phobic" myself.

One of the major turns our journey took was when I attended my first state homeschooling convention in Orlando. I came home with the neatest books for the kids that I shared with my husband. It was these Usborne books that led him to becoming a sales rep, travelling to all the homeschooling conferences within a 1000-mile radius. Because he sells books, we have one of the finest libraries imaginable. (It also has to do with the fact that I'd rather buy a good book over a dress any day!)

And so that's the story of my family in a nutshell. There will be lots more about them coming up later as I try to explain ways to make homeschooling your children the most memorable experience you and your family will ever undertake.

This book was written for those of you who are just beginning your homeschooling journey; it's written for those who have been homeschooling for awhile and are "burning out" and thinking of putting their children back in school; it's for those who are just dreaming about the possibility of schooling their kids at home and want to know how to prepare; and finally, it's for anyone who has the slightest desire to school at home. My sincere hope is that by reading this book at least one parent will realize that they can do it; and perhaps someone else will reconsider putting their child back into an institution. God willing, some of the ideas found within these pages will help organize and orient your family so that your journey becomes easier, more relaxed, and fun-filled.

Obviously, a large portion of this book is geared more toward the mother than the father, as most commonly it is the mother that bears most of the homeschooling and household burden. I encourage both dads and moms to read this book together so that the two of you can work toward the same goals and become more involved in the actual schooling and sharing of the household responsibilities. Homeschooling children is not a one-person job meant to be slung onto mom's shoulders; both dad and mom need to discuss goals, aspirations, and responsibilities. The entire family needs to be involved in some of the decision making, as well as in the day-to-day field duty. If one person is left to do everything, fatigue will soon set in and all will be lost.

Put the kids to bed, sit back, throw off your shoes, sip a cup of tea, and share a few moments with me. I've spent many years working with my children, as well as gleaning ideas from all the parents that I have had the privilege to know and work with. The discoveries that I have made along the way are the basis of this book. When we are the ones experiencing the problem, it seems as if no one else could possibly ever have gone through the same situation and that it is specific only to our family. However, as an objective observer to other people's problems, as well as having experienced most of the same difficulties firsthand, I can tell you that most families who school at home share the same experiences and hardships. The problem is that they have no one to confide in, and so they begin to feel overwhelmed and stressed. Their lives seem to come unglued and consequently the first thought is to quit homeschooling. In their minds, homeschooling is the source of all their family's woes. It's my opinion that homeschooling is just the easiest target to shoot at and eliminate; in reality, there are many other influential factors that are causing the difficulties.

I realize that this book may not be a solution for all your life's woes; each of us is an individual with very different concerns and cares. Choose and pick solutions for your immediate difficulty. Also, be aware that the only constant in life is that there is no constant – our lives change from moment to moment. Therefore, what may work for you this week, may not work the next. (This is especially true when your children are very young.) If you suddenly find that your daily schedule is no longer working, stop and reassess! Be intimately aware of the rhythm of your family's pulse; if it starts missing a beat or racing too quickly, you may need to change gears again.

It's my hope and prayer that you find this book to be a road map to *"homeschooling by heart!"*

*Kristina Krulikas*

*What is a family?*

*But God has so adjusted the body, giving the greater honor to the inferior part, that there may be no discord in the body, but that the members may have the same care for one another. If one member suffers, all suffer together; if one member is honored, all rejoice together.*
*1 Corinthians 12:24-26*

# PART ONE

## REFLECTION

## OR

## "READING THE ROAD MAP"

# CHAPTER
## ♥ 1 ♥

## THEY'RE HOME! NOW WHAT?

The phone rings. I answer it. On the other end someone breathlessly says, "I took them out of school Friday. They're home. What do I do now?"

You can't imagine how many times I've heard these words from deeply concerned, but rightfully nervous, parents.  They're so frantic to remove their children from school, that they don't consider the consequences of their actions nor the journey they're about to embark on with their kids.

Then you have the parents who make their decision to homeschool when their firstborn is somewhere between the womb and five-years of age (like me). These parents plan, search, consult, and buy…sometimes before their child even speaks!  They're the ones that turn their spare bedrooms into replicas of the schoolrooms they're striving to avoid (oh yes, I did!).  All this, so that homeschooling would feel "legitimate."

Somewhere in the middle are the parents who start considering homeschooling and take months or years to begin the process. They're cautious, curious, well informed, and nervous.

It doesn't matter which of the above applies to you.  Taking the homeschooling plunge is all that matters!  Now that you're on the road you may be feeling a bit nervous and need some help.  You've come to the right place, because this is what my book is all about.  Let's go on a journey.  Let's delve into this homeschooling business and try and see how we can make it the best adventure your family will ever take together!

We need to begin at the very beginning.  Sit down with a pencil in hand and relax.  Jot down answers to the questions as you consider what's being asked.

The reason I ask these questions is so that you can analyze your own feelings about homeschooling and pinpoint which area of your life is causing you the most trouble. In order to fix these trouble spots, you must determine what's not working well.  Sometimes I am so rushed and tired that I can't take the time to even sort out what's troubling me. How can I expect to come up with a solution, or ask for help from anyone, if I don't know what to ask for? It then becomes a vicious circle: the more tired I become, the more hopeless the situation looks; the more hopeless the situation, the more readily I become exhausted. Nothing gets accomplished!

Please consider each of these questions seriously. Try writing down your answers, and then we can move forward and make it all come together!

**Now, try and recall why you wanted (want) to homeschool.**

_____

_____

_____

_____

_____

_____

_____

**Think back and try to remember what you thought (or think) homeschooling your children would (will) be like. Describe your "dream day."**

_____

_____

_____

_____

_____

_____

_____

_____

**What are your feelings about homeschooling now? Are you content, or do you feel that there's some room for improvement in your life? What area of homeschooling gives you're the most trouble – in other words, what doesn't work? (Skip this question if you're just starting out!)**

_____

_____

_____

_____

_____

_____

_____

**Does a dirty, cluttered house bother you or can you blissfully ignore the mess by working around the piles?**

_____
_____
_____
_____
_____
_____
_____

**What are your feelings about cleaning?  Do you enjoy cleaning?  Are you organized?  Do your kids help willingly, or only when coerced?**

_____
_____
_____
_____
_____
_____
_____

**What do you think would help you make it all work?  Do you want more help from the kids or your husband, a babysitter or housekeeper, money, more books and equipment, someone to plan your curriculum or schedule?**

_____
_____
_____
_____
_____
_____
_____

**Do you have time for yourself, or do you run around from one job to another?  How do you feel about this?**

_____
_____
_____
_____
_____
_____

**What do you think your role is while you school? Mama, teacher, or...?**

_____
_____
_____
_____
_____
_____
_____

**Are you content with your children's behavior? Are they well-behaved? Would you be proud of them if you took them out in public?**

_____
_____
_____
_____
_____
_____
_____

**If you feel that your children aren't well-behaved do you have a plan ready with which to discipline them? Name or describe it.**

_____
_____
_____
_____
_____
_____
_____

**Are you confident about teaching them? If not, why?**

_____
_____
_____
_____
_____
_____
_____

**Are there any character flaws in yourself or in your children that you can pinpoint as roadblocks in your homeschooling?  What are they?**

_____

_____

_____

_____

_____

_____

_____

**Are you having fun homeschooling?  Are your children having fun most of the time?  Do you think you should be having fun homeschooling?**

_____

_____

_____

_____

_____

_____

_____

**Do you think of homeschooling as "school at home" or as a way of life, a lifestyle?  Why do you consider it a lifestyle?**

_____

_____

_____

_____

_____

_____

_____

**Do you praise God each and every day for allowing you to homeschool your children?  When?  How?  Should you praise God with your children?**

_____

_____

_____

_____

_____

_____

_____

**Do you beg God each day to guide and lead you in educating your kids? When? How? Do you think that you should do this with your husband?**

_____
_____
_____
_____
_____
_____
_____
_____

My guess would be that no matter what you wrote down - be it you took your kids out of school because you feared for their safety, or you felt that your child would receive a better education at home, you homeschool for religious convictions, or you live too far away to send your kids to school - that the real reason is (or was) because you love your child and want the absolute best for him. Am I right?

Because we homeschool our children, love them so much, and desire the very best for them, we need to do everything humanly possible to make this odyssey work. So let's keep contemplating....

Did you have this wonderful fantasy of all your children sitting around the table quietly doing their schoolwork while the toddlers play with their blocks in the corner and you bake bread? At noon all of you tranquilly share lunch and then you whisk the toddlers off to their nap while the others continue working till the clock strikes 2:00PM. Perhaps you would then take a trip to the park and let the younger children play while the others quietly listen to a book being read aloud by you. Then, you return home and let the children do whatever it is children do, while you prepare the evening meal and cheerfully greet your husband at the door at 5:00, looking ravishing. By 8:00PM all the children are bathed and in bed and you sit down, relax, and have a leisurely conversation with your husband.

Is this reality? The answer is a definite **NO**! You start to school and not only does reality hit, but it hits hard. You have trouble getting through the schoolwork, and the kids aren't cooperating; the laundry is piling up, the dishes aren't washed, the beds are unmade; you're sitting and wondering how any normal homeschool mom ever gets anything done when your husband walks through the door! You turn to him and whimper, "Where are you taking us to dinner?"

## REFLECTION:

Many of us jump into homeschooling headfirst. This is probably a real blessing, because if we knew beforehand how much our lives would change, half of us would run away. Use this chapter questionnaire to really delve into why you chose homeschooling and see if that original motivation has changed at all. I believe it's necessary to train ourselves to constantly keep that motivation dangling like a chocolate treat before us so that we never lose sight of our objective. When we face hardships or discouragement along the way it's always a blessing to be able to say, "There's such a good reason for doing this." And when you have a great week, pat yourself on the back and say, "It is worth everything in the world to be able to do this."

Even though we may have changed along the journey, grown or matured in our educational and religious convictions, that original reason for schooling our kids at home is probably still as important, if not more so, than it was when we first began.

If you're just starting out, these questions will help you anticipate areas which may be a source of difficulty in the future. Now, even before you begin to homeschool, you can smooth things out so that your future journey's not too bumpy!

# Prayer For This House

May nothing evil cross this door,
And may ill-fortune never pry
About these windows; may the roar
And rains go by.

Strengthened by faith, the rafters will
Withstand the battering of the storm.
This hearth, though all the world grow chill
Will keep you warm.

Peace shall walk softly through these rooms,
Touching your lips with holy wine,
Till every casual corner blooms
Into a shrine.

Laughter shall drown the raucous shout
And, though the sheltering walls are thin,
May they be strong to keep hate out
And hold love in.

By Louis Untermeyer

# CHAPTER
## ♥ 2 ♥

## HOMESCHOOLING...A LIFESTYLE

You've made the decision to homeschool. You've either taken the kids out of school or will just be beginning with your firstborn.  For the record, it is much easier to incorporate the children's education into your family lifestyle if they've never been to school because you, or the kids, have no preconceived notions and no set routines.  If your kids have been in school awhile, then your family is used to doing things a certain way and every time you want to make changes there'll be resistance.

Why do most parents, especially moms, consider homeschooling a tremendous stress and burden?  Put simply in a nutshell: it's a great responsibility and lots of work. Isn't merely raising a family enough stress, without having to add another dimension? Take a moment.

**When we decide to homeschool our kids, are we adding another dimension or responsibility to our already full lives? If so, how would you describe this new dimension?**

_____

_____

_____

_____

_____

_____

_____

_____

The answer for most parents should be yes...**by today's standards.** Modern society says that the kids in school should be taught by a "professional" and that mom should either be doing her own thing or working.  Must it be this way**? A definite resounding NO!** Homeschooling our kids should be as natural as nursing our babies or caring for our children's hurts.  If we prioritize our lives, and re-consider what's really important, each and every one of us should be able to make it work.

None of us gave a second thought to teaching our children to talk, walk, or go potty. None of these are easy to teach.  They require a lot of patience on our part, but all can be accomplished usually by the age of three. We just did it because it had to be done. Yet, when it comes to teaching them to read symbols, or learn their multiplication tables, or the countries of the world, we freak out. "We're not trained to do that! Only certified teachers can teach!" I say, **"Anyone can teach a child."**

My kids' Karate teacher keeps telling them that they need to have "a fire in their belly " in order to get their black belt. In other words, without an intense desire and an overwhelming longing, they'll never get it. I say that each and everyone of us needs that "fire in our belly" for homeschooling in order to make it work. **If you want to teach your children, if it's that important to you, then you can do it!** Yes, it takes time and patience, but tell me, what job is more important than educating your kids? The dishes can wait, dinner can be late, the beds unmade, clothes unwashed, if that's what it takes to educate your child. Those jobs will still be there waiting for you when your children are heading out the door to begin their own lives. Don't let chores come in the way of raising your children.

What you need to consider now is whether this formula will work for you:

**Family + Education + Daily Living - Daily Stress =
Homeschool Lifestyle**

**Are you willing to try and change your personal expectations and family schedule in order to allow this new lifestyle to blossom in your family? How are you going to achieve this?**

_____
_____
_____
_____
_____
_____
_____
_____

**Are you willing to simplify your life in order to reduce stress? What are you willing to change?**

_____
_____
_____
_____
_____
_____
_____
_____

In my opinion those people who incorporate homeschooling into a lifestyle are those who are the most successful. What do you mean by that, you ask?

Well...homeschooling does not mean replacing traditional school with "school at home." To really homeschool means making schooling, or education as I prefer to call it, a 24-hour commitment, thereby totally combining it into your family's schedule or life(style).

"The law says I only need to school **5** (fill in the blank) hours! You've got to be kidding! If that's what it takes to homeschool forget it, I'll send them back to school!"

Stop! Please realize that a 5 hour day in school is **not** five hours but a mere fraction of that. I've heard so many stories about how little actual instruction is given at school. Some say that the kids are lucky if they receive ten minutes of school for every hour of their school day. This means that for every five hours, students are perhaps being taught about fifty minutes. Maybe, just maybe, fifty whole minutes the entire school day! As told to me by one mom, a public middle school in our area has a "fun day" every Friday. This means that **no** schoolwork is being done on Fridays. Nowadays the schools are closed frequently for "teacher duty day." This is a day where the teacher can catch up with her paperwork. (Does it mean that in our day the teachers were never caught up? How is it then that we received the superior education?) Another parent, who helped out in the classroom, noticed that a video would always be turned on for those kids finishing their assignments quickly. What about those kids who were just struggling to finish their assignments?!

Another of my pet peeves is forced busing. This means that instead of your child going to your neighborhood school they are bused all over town. (Think of all the wasted time on the school bus and the potential trouble that can come about! One of our neighborhood kids told us that last year her school bus had a TV/VCR. All the kids would bring videos with them to watch while travelling back and forth from school. Wonderful!) Locally, the middle school kids begin their school day at 9:30AM. Half the day is done! Another local school was sending the kids home at lunch every Wednesday so that the teachers could catch up on their work. What happens to the kids whose parents work?

Now consider whether **your** children can contain their "school day" in five hours. Think about all the extra hours that your child reads or spends building something that really interests him. Do they sew a dress, cook, or become engrossed in the encyclopedia or Internet looking up some interesting tidbits? Do they sometimes dig outside for snails or worms, or make drawings of trees and birds? What about the hours spent at the library searching for information or just "neat" reading material? Also, what about the time they spend communicating with your retired next-door neighbor or the postman or the grocer? What of the hours that they're able to think and daydream and formulate a vision for their tomorrow?   Hours that might otherwise be spent commuting back and forth to school or doing homework at night to make up for all the hours they weren't being taught in school!  Is this wasting time, or is it part of a person's "real" education?  Are these the components that make up a "real education," the type that we adults have been carrying on ever since we **left** school?

**Think about what education means to you.**

_____
_____
_____
_____
_____
_____
_____
_____
_____

What is education? According to **Noah Webster's American Dictionary of the English Language** (a reprint of the 1828 edition) education is: _"The bringing up, as of a child, instruction; formation of manners._ **_Education comprehends all that series of instruction and discipline which is intended to enlighten the understanding, correct the temper, and form the manners and habits of youth, and fit them for usefulness in their future stations."_** (My emphasis).

Education is the ability to refute the "over-population myth." It's knowing where to go when one wants to know how many people there are in this world; and what one needs to do to find out if, in fact, the entire world population could fit in the state of Texas, each person having about 1,000 square feet of his own. (When I was told this I didn't believe it, and so I took out my **World Almanac** and did the calculations myself.  Guess what?  Everyone in the world could fit in the state of Texas and each would have about 1,200 square feet of space!  I've heard it said that this housing situation can be compared to living in Brooklyn.)

An education is being able to clearly and succinctly debate about the rights of the unborn without becoming emotional, knowing exactly where to go to find more facts, and realizing that in order to debate the issue you must be aware of what your opponents will use as an argument. An education is going to the library - heading for the computers, knowing how to look up a subject, and knowing where to find the shelves for the books that you need.  An education is knowing when to talk and when to listen.  An education is being able to wash your own laundry without dying everything red and knowing when to use a hot iron and when to use a cool one.  An education is knowing how to boil water and what to do with it after you've boiled it. (An even better education is knowing how to boil water in the wilderness when you have no matches and what to look for to eat.)  **An education is realizing that you'll never know it all, but then, no one**

**ever does. An education is the knowledge that you can always find the answer if you really care.**

That's the secret...**if you really care**. This is what we need to instill in our children. We want them to care about their education; we want them to love the learning process. You don't need to be a rocket scientist to accomplish this goal. However, you do need to be passionate, or have a "fire in your belly" for education. If you live a passionate life, this passion will someday be transmitted to your children by osmosis. Don't give up. If you persevere, it will happen. Don't lose faith. It's a fire; it will spread!

## REFLECTION:

Consider the importance of incorporating school into family life. When you homeschool, the line which separates home life from school is very indistinct. Its edges are extremely blurred and you don't know where one begins and the other ends. Should this homeschool lifestyle be a goal to strive for in your family?

Do not love the world or the things in the world. If any one loves the world, love for the Father is not in him. For all that is in the world, the lust of the flesh and the lust of the eyes and the pride of life, is not of the Father but is of the world. And the world passes away, and the lust of it; but he who does the will of God abides for ever.

John 1:15-17

# CHAPTER
## ♥ 3 ♥

## MOTHERHOOD: EVERYTHING ELSE IS A JOB!
## OR
## HOME SWEET HOME

So what's your role in this new lifestyle change that I'm encouraging?  Are you still going to be your kids' mother or are you now their teacher?  Or better yet are you mom-teacher or teacher-mom?  In order to untangle this web, we need to back up a bit.  Let me ask you a question: **How do you feel about your home? Is it a home or is it a house?**

_____

_____

_____

_____

_____

_____

_____

Do you feel that your home is "home sweet home" or just a place to hang your coat and spend the night?  Do you think of it merely as a place having four walls and a roof, or do you really enjoy being at home?  Is it your family's sanctuary, a haven, a place of warmth, well being, and love? Do you enjoy entertaining at home?   Or would you rather be out shopping or running around?  **Is your heart at home?**

_____

_____

_____

_____

_____

_____

_____

My mom says, "Everywhere is nice, but home is best," which probably is the Lithuanian equivalent to, "Home is where the heart is." It's nice to travel and sightsee, but "home sweet home" is the place I desire. You may feel the same way, but I don't believe society would condone it. Society would say you need to be out in the "real world" working 60-hour work weeks, entertaining in restaurants, taking exotic vacations, and keeping the kids in daycare. Society would not approve of a stay-at-home mom that likes being a stay-at-home mom. You may love it, but don't you dare say it aloud or brag about it!

Now let's get back to the original question. We all need to reconsider our role as mom. Are you just going through the motions anxiously waiting for the kids to go to bed or grow up and be out of the house, or do you **love** being a mom and having a family to care for? If you're the former, then you should start thinking of each act you undertake throughout the day as having a deeper significance in your life, and your family's, than merely a job that has to be done routinely. Wake up in the morning giving praise to our Lord; work toward a closer relationship with Him. Do this each and every day with every action you perform. Our role as mother is a vocation that we have chosen, or have been called to by God. It is up to us to live up to our motherhood vocation to the best of our God-given ability. When making breakfast for our children, we are nourishing the bodies of God's children; when teaching, we are helping souls come closer to the kingdom of heaven; and when sewing, baking, carpooling, or reprimanding, we are doing God's work on earth.

Mom – stop and smell the gorgeous roses. They're growing right in your own home under your very own nose!

It's your job (vocation) to be the best possible mom (parent) that you can be. Think of each chore that you do, no matter how trivial or tedious, as an act of love for God. If the chore you need to accomplish is especially arduous, unite your suffering to the Lord's as He carried the cross to Calvary. The path you'll follow will not be an easy one. There'll be plenty of peaks and valleys, but knowing what the purpose of all this is will help you make that walk – the walk up to heaven. When you're discouraged and ready to give up, cry out to Jesus; ask Him, beg Him to come and help you, and I'm sure that soon you'll find yourself ready to once again take on the "motherhood challenge."

Know that your vocation is just as important as any other calling because you are helping lead souls to heaven. Now you need to make sure that everything done in your home is conducive to your calling. You need to make that house a home - a pleasant dwelling place for all that reside under its roof. You need to focus on what's most important: your spiritual relationship with our Lord, your relationship with your husband, your children, and their homeschooling. Most importantly is making sure that they keep maturing in wisdom. You need to stop any interruptions and superfluous activities. You need to radically simplify, thereby eliminating stress. You need to make sure that enough time is spent at home and forget about running all over town. If you're not home during the day, very little learning will be accomplished. If you're running around to various activities in the afternoon, you won't have enough time to make supper. If supper's not on the table, how will your family ever have an opportunity to talk to each other, share, and learn what was done that day?

When I stay home all day, I have dinner on the table by 5:00 and sufficient time to do the various odds and ends that I couldn't accomplish during the day. I may even have an opportunity to relax for a few minutes and gain some "quiet time" before my sweetheart comes home from work. The home is run more smoothly with mom spending the majority of her time nurturing everyone **within** its walls. The kids aren't stressed out running around; they are able to relax and play, go to bed at a respectable hour, and wake up refreshed. The same applies for mom and dad.

Another wonderful blessing of staying home is the money that's saved. Cooking and baking at home saves money, and not to mention the food is far more nutritious than found in a restaurant or "ready-made" in a supermarket. (Have you ever looked over the ingredients on a cake purchased from the bakery? There are about twenty ingredients, most of which you can't even pronounce!) The less you spend, the more you save; the less your husband has to work because the fewer bills he has, ergo the more time your family has to share. The less you spend, the less junk you pile up in the house that clutters your living space… that needs to be cleaned, stored, and organized…that makes you a nervous wreck while you're teaching because there's no time to clean! **So by staying home you're a calmer, saner, more relaxed, and fulfilled person!**

Have you ever considered making Sunday a true Sabbath (Sabbath means "to rest")? Not doing anything on Sundays that isolates family members from one another? My kids encouraged us to practice what we preach by coming up with this plan months ago, and we've been fervently trying to keep to it. On Sunday, no one can read a book that isn't religious. (We have a tendency to go off in corners and just spend the day reading.) There's no television, no computer (most important!), no playing with neighborhood friends, and we try to do at least one family group activity. This all began because we felt Sunday was becoming just another weekday, and this is not right. It should be a day to give thanks to the Lord and be together as a family, and the fruits of this have been marvelous. I would like to eventually reach the point where our main meal is prepared the night before and there's no "real" cooking that day. Now please don't misunderstand. We are human, and there are Sundays that we have to go into a grocery store to buy milk or bread because there's none at home, or we watch television because there's something wonderful on, or because we're exhausted and just want to relax. Those are the exceptions, and not the rule. This new Sabbath day that we've created in our home has brought us together, encouraged us, and brought us closer to the Lord. **Sunday has begun to feel**

**like it's the Lord's day, and not ours.** We're building a holier lifestyle, which will hopefully extend to future generations and be a witness unto others.

Motherhood is even more than creating a pleasant, loving home and tending the hearth. A mother, first and foremost, should be her children's prayer warrior, praying daily for each of their needs. She must set the example and instill discipline and Godly character because she is the one with the children all day long (assuming dad has a job that takes him away from the home daily). Hopefully, all behavior, both good and bad, is reported each evening to dad, who as head of the family makes necessary corrections and adjustments. Since mom is the one who is usually alone with the kids for the better part of the day, she must be ready to meet all challenges headlong and not have to wait till evening for rewards and punishments to be distributed. Mom needs a working system that she can have readily at hand. Finally, mom needs to be a cheerleader, constantly encouraging the children to do their best work.

Because you're already going against the flow by homeschooling, keep flowing and make your home the center of family life and unity. Keep a loving home! Years from now when the children are all gone they won't remember, and neither will you, how many weeks passed between "real" cleanings. What they'll remember is how lovingly their mother created their home, all the wonderful experiences they had there, and all that their parents taught them. Enjoy what you already have – your children, your husband, your home – the grass is always greener on the other side, but perhaps not so lovingly tended as yours! Be happy with what you have and work at making it the best!


### REFLECTION:

What role do you want to play in your family? Do you want motherhood to be seen as merely a chore, a duty that must be fulfilled in order to have children, or as a vocation that is cherished and nurtured? Is it a role that will be seen in the future as one that is deserving of praise and imitation?

Do you see yourself as merely a law enforcer or as a cheerleader, prayer warrior, guiding hand, enabler, and provider?


### FURTHER READING:
**Women Living Life on Purpose** by Kym Wright (FL: AlWright Publishing, 1998)
**Women Living Life on Purpose Study Guide** by Kym Wright (FL: AlWright Publishing, 1998)

# MOM'S KIDS' JOURNAL

This diary is inspired by the book or movie **Little Men,** and my friend Cynthia. It's purpose is to record your children's character strengths or flaws so that you could share your observations with them. Try and write in it at least once per week. Take a blank notebook and divide it into as many sections as you have children. At the top of each section write your child's name. Record your thoughts here and once a week read your memos to each child individually. Have fun!

Child's Name_____

Date_____

(Your goal is to record their strengths and weaknesses sometime during the course of the week.)

How did he shine this week?

What specific praise reports do you have?

Which areas does this child need to improve in?

End with a special prayer for each child.

(Ask each child to come into your room once a week, and begin by asking him some questions like the following:)

> Do you feel like you're struggling in any particular areas (for example: school work, prayer life, relationships, virtues,...)

> How are your relationships with your brothers and sisters?

> Is there anything I can do to help you?

> What has your thought life been like lately? (Has he been having any troubling or reoccurring thoughts?)

After you completed the discussion, read your weekly journal entry to him. If you decide to undertake this exercise, God will surely bless you and your children! This journal will provide a wonderful opportunity for an open and communicative relationship with your children. You will be providing them with a working example of a caring, nurturing parent. May God reward your endeavors eternally!

# MOM'S GOALS

If we don't schedule priorities, we would never get anything done. This is a list of things that perhaps you would like to accomplish during the day, week, or year. Prayerfully consider the different activities and decide which is most important to you. You must then make time to do it. If it's reading a book, plan on reading only a few pages a day for a few months. If it's a date with your husband, set a time and get a babysitter!

| MY DREAM LIST | SUN | MON | TUES | WED | THURS | FRI | SAT |
|---|---|---|---|---|---|---|---|
| PRAYER TIME: | | | | | | | |
| SPRITUAL READING: (NAME BOOKS) | | | | | | | |
| | | | | | | | |
| BOOKS: (PLEASURE) | | | | | | | |
| | | | | | | | |
| SEWING/CRAFTS: | | | | | | | |
| | | | | | | | |
| PLANNING SCHOOL YEAR: | | | | | | | |
| | | | | | | | |
| | | | | | | | |
| CORRECTING ASSIGNMENTS: | | | | | | | |
| | | | | | | | |
| | | | | | | | |
| DATE WITH HUBBY | | | | | | | |
| | | | | | | | |
| TIME FOR FUN ACTIVITY WITH KIDS: (CRAFTS, SEWING, NATURE WALK, ETC.) | | | | | | | |
| | | | | | | | |
| | | | | | | | |
| INDIVIDUAL JOURNAL TIME WITH KIDS: | | | | | | | |
| | | | | | | | |
| | | | | | | | |
| | | | | | | | |

# CHAPTER
## ♥ 4 ♥

## FIRST SIMPLIFY

If you agree that homeschooling is a lifestyle, and that your children need to be a part of this lifestyle that you are creating, it's time to consider simplifying your life.

"What? Simplify? Why? How?"

Our society has become so complex and demanding, that in the process it has turned us into fast moving automated beings, running from one job to another and trying to accomplish as much as is humanly possible! Society expects us to taxi our kids to soccer practice, music lessons, ballet, gymnastics, and this activity and that activity. If we refuse, we're considered negligent parents. According to statistics, society expects us to have about two kids per family - not five, six, or even more. Society has set up certain expectations that fit the general populace, and expects us to conform to their mold. Well...sorry! No way!

**We break the preconceived mold just by homeschooling.** There's no putting it back together again. It's shot, broken to smithereens, just like poor 'ol Humpty Dumpty! When we have more than two kids, we blow away most everyone's mind (except, of course, the majority of homeschoolers who are in reality a minority). How can a "normal American" possibly desire more children? Stay-at-home mom? Ha! Forget it, we're all goners! Don't even bother trying to "fit the mold," flow with the mainstream, or be politically correct. You might as well face it, your children will also be viewed by the majority of school children as not normal, or in their terminology, "geeks." Now that you understand the thought processes, I hope that you feel liberated enough to "do your own thing" and "be your own person."

The very first thing you need to do is simplify your life. How is this done? **By s...l...o...w...i...n...g   d...o...w...n...** How do you slow down? Do not take on more than you can handle. Learn to say **"No!"** to outside activities. We're not super moms; we're plain old moms that can do only so much. The problem is that many moms start homeschooling and never change their pre-homeschooling speed. They keep the same pace as before and slowly the Energizer batteries wear down and the bunny flops! **SLOW DOWN!**

Slow your thoughts down. I don't know about you, but my mind has the tendency to be in constant motion - thoughts and ideas whizzing by at the speed of light. If I don't write things down, I never remember them. How many times have you gone to another room only to look around, dazed, wondering what in the world brought you there? We do this because we're not concentrating on one thought, one action.

Learn to concentrate. I know that we've all heard it said that moms can do three things at once. Yes, we can – but should we? How well do we really do any of these three things, and is it good for us to be under so much daily stress? By focusing all of our attention on one problem or thought at a time, we're cultivating our new slower pace. Don't rush decisions; take the time that is needed and think them through. Most of the time we make a snap decision as if our lives depended on it. Our kids are on to that one: catch mom when she's frazzled and she'll make a quick decision, hopefully in their favor!

Always pay attention to the person you're talking to by looking them straight in the eye and listening to what is being said (and teach your child to do the same). How many times have you given your kids an answer to a question that you didn't even hear? Eye contact shows the other person that you're listening and that you truly care about what is being said.

It is very important that we live life intentionally, not spontaneously or mechanically. This means that everything we do, is because we choose to do it and not because things just fell together that way haphazardly. We choose to wake up at 6:30AM and pray; having the doorbell wake us up at 8:00AM and knock us out of bed is a spontaneous reaction. We choose to eat a nutritious breakfast; we eat on the run because there's no time and then we mechanically reach into the fridge and grab anything. We choose to play with our children; we miss a special field trip because we forgot to sign up. Do in life what you choose purposely, not mechanically because you live by the seat of your pants and don't make intentional choices.

Always remember that time spent with your family is the most important activity. When you say yes to raising a family, you need to make intentional choices. When you say yes to doing something, you're actually saying no to something else that you're already doing. We only have so much time that can be spread around.

In a family of small children, you need to make the decision that your apron strings are tied to your children and home. Life is much simpler and more pleasant when you choose to stay home with the little ones, instead of running around. They become tired and cranky, loud and exuberant, and in turn you become tired and cranky, and lose your patience. Young moms, please realize that your little ones are much happier at home playing, rather than out on the town being pushed from one activity to another. Stay at home. When you feel the need for company, go to the park or invite friends to your house. Make your present surroundings your "exploration place." Soon the children will be older and then they'll enjoy field trips and excursions – or at least they won't tend to be so cranky! For the present, stay home and slow down!

Concentrating on one thought at a time and one activity at a time leads to a slower physical response. Making the conscious decision that you are going to live life intentionally and not spontaneously puts you in control of the situation. You aren't forced into doing or missing any activities. You will have succeeded in slowing down. Here are some concrete ideas on how to slow down your pace.

Begin by waking up early, leisurely praying, walking, reading – whatever it is you like to do - then shower, dress, and make your bed. (If you do this every morning routinely, you'll feel like you've accomplished quite a bit even before breakfast!) Now you're ready to take on the world. You're not rushed; you're not behind the eight ball before you even begin the day. In this fashion, you can be ahead of schedule the entire day. Always plan ahead. It's when we're rushed and falling behind schedule that we become stressed and lose it. Never get to that point. Slow down. Make time for yourself and God. Greet your kids in the morning with a smile on your face. The first five minutes of our day determine how the rest of the day will go. Make yours cheerful and peaceful.

Practice patience. Patience shows love. Try to be patient with yourself, your children, and your husband. The more you slow down the more patient you'll become. Don't let the smallest tidbit frazzle you. Let criticisms and negativity slide like water off oil. Each time you encounter something that may set you off, say a quick prayer. Let God be the person you turn to all day when you start losing it. As you slow down, each day will become more enjoyable; your patience will grow. Don't allow the world to place you on the fast track again!

I heard a very interesting talk show recently about modern technology and its significance. Decades ago it was thought that the computer age would be so efficient, quick, and monetarily rewarding that only one spouse would need to be employed, with most of the work taking place in the home. Furthermore, our work hours would be much shorter because computers would make us so much more efficient. Did this happen? I would say that we are definitely living in the computer age. Presently all of America is wondering and hypothesizing what is going to happen as the clock ticks away and we move from 1999 to 2000. What will those computer chips do? No one knows for sure. Doesn't sound too efficient or reliable to me. Can most families support themselves on one paycheck? No way! Are we working less hours? Ha! Where are all the benefits of this technological age in which we reside?  Where are all the extra hours that we were supposed to have gained?

Instead of simplifying our lives, I believe that technology has created a greater mess. We now have telephones, answering machines, cell phones, and beepers to keep us wired to everyone else, keeping us from escaping an avalanche of calls.  We have computers that make our typing, research, and communication so much more easy, but heaven help us if they crash!  There are microwaves, dishwashers, trash compactors, and ice machines in our kitchens, as well as televisions and VCR's and CD players in our living rooms (and our cars).  If you notice the school kids, many of them are carrying beepers and cell phones! Do we have more spare time because of any of these conveniences, or **have they just made more time for us to be able to do more things?** (Some may argue that beepers and cell phones are a great safety feature.  This is not true if they merely replace a parent being at home and they make the kids even more independent from their parents.)

In the past, you'd eat dinner and two or three kids would clear the table, wash and dry dishes, and put them away.  This work created and enhanced relationships. Now we have a solitary figure in the kitchen doing all those tasks and sticking dirty dishes in the dishwasher so that everyone else can run off and do something else. Do you know how many neat stories, songs, and confidences were told while cleaning the kitchen?  Meanwhile are the other family members forming more intimate bonds? No!  TVs came along and have taken away our reading time, quiet talks, card and board games.  The VCR makes sure that we don't miss any spectacular program.  The answering machine cattily blinks at us when we come home and seems to snicker, "Just turn me on and listen to all the calls you need to return!" (If it's that important, they'll call back!  We can't even spend a peaceful evening at home without being bombarded by telemarketers.) Also, don't you love the lady that's shopping and hanging on to every word over the cell phone?  How can we talk to our neighbor if we're so busy gabbing on the phone while we maneuver the shopping aisles?

All of these are great inventions and conveniences, but do we need them to live meaningful lives?  Couldn't we live without them?  How necessary are they?  Do they simplify our lives or just complicate them by giving us more time to do "important things"?  How many of them could you eliminate so that your life wouldn't be so overloaded?

I think that there are quite a few of us that wistfully think of bygone days and wish that we could live like that once again. What I wouldn't do for 10 acres, some chickens and cows, perhaps a horse or two, a garden, and enough isolation so that I wouldn't be tempted to hop in the car and run to the nearest McDonalds or supermarket every time I have a yen.  I dream of all of us being so content on our little farm that we willingly work it and grow tired together each day.  We wouldn't need to travel far for company because we would be surrounded by fun-loving, caring neighbors.  Additionally, there'd be a small country store within walking distance where all the neighbors could meet and gab.

Yup, it's a dream all right.  I don't see it coming true in my very near future. I guess our family was put in this particular spot for some special reason that only God knows.  I can't have the idyllic setting, but I can try and live the idyllic life.   I need to create a lifestyle for the environment that I was put in.

So…we turned off our answering machine, put "locks" on our television, discourage telephone interruptions during the day by not calling others during school and disturbing them.  I hide the car keys so I'm not tempted to stray away, and plan my meals so that I don't need to go to the supermarket as often.  I no longer use the dishwasher because the dishes aren't very clean anyway, and because I want my kids to have fun in the kitchen talking to each other while they wash the dishes. This, in turn, promotes healthy responsibility and diligence while they're working together.  We sold the microwave because it took up too much room, and in the bargain, discovered how much better food tastes that's warmed in an oven.  Much more planning is needed, and so patience and foresight are fostered.  There's now a time limit on the computer for every child and outdoor recreation is not only encouraged, but also required. We've given away a television, decided against an extra VCR, and are seriously considering losing the cable service.  In reality, this virtually means the end of TV - **Y…E…S!**

All of this was done in the hopes of simplifying our lives and creating a more stress free, down-to-earth lifestyle.

**REFLECTION:**

Do you need to slow down?  Is your mind in fast motion?  Try and concentrate on one thought at a time today.

Do you give your undivided attention to the person you're speaking to? Do you make eye contact?

If you're a young mom, are you willing to make this your season to be at home?

Have you been intentionally living your life, or spontaneously and mechanically?

Do you believe that when you say yes to one more commitment, you're saying no to something else that you presently do?

Do you see homeschooling as just one more commitment or as a "lifestyle change?"

What are your feelings about voluntarily simplifying your family's lifestyle?

*And all who believed were together and had all things in common; and they sold their possessions and goods and distributed them to all, as any had need. And day by day, attending the temple together and breaking bread in their homes, they partook of food with glad and generous hearts, praising God and having favor with all the people. And the Lord added to their number day by day those who were being saved.*                    *Acts 3: 44-47*

**FURTHER READING:**
**Hearth & Home** by Karey Swan (Colorado: Singing Springs Productions, 1996)
**The Lessons of St. Francis** by Michael Talbot with Steve Rabey (NY: Penguin Group, 1997)
**Take Your Time, Finding Balance in a Hurried World** by Eknath Eastwaran (NY: Hyperion,1994) Please note that a Buddhist English professor wrote this book. It's definitely worth reading; he has a wonderful way of approaching simplicity and slowing down your life's pace. He does not try to convert. In fact, he stresses the importance of relying on God and the beliefs of your own religion.
**The Simple Living Guide** by Janet Luhrs (NY: Broadway Books, 1997)

# CHAPTER
## ♥ 5 ♥

## BUILDING COMMUNITY
### (A Group of People Sharing a
### Common Bond or Location)

What is probably most sorely neglected these days is community. We all cry out that we need and want it, but how many of us have actually reached out and tried to get to know our neighbors? How can we expect to build community when we don't make the effort to meet our neighbors? Sometimes it can be an exasperating ordeal because many people in this day and age don't seem to want to meet! Either they're scared, or they're so rushed that they don't have time to work on relationships. When you decide to homeschool, it's important to make an effort to build community. You're going to be spending a lot of time alone at home with your kids; you need the friendship and support of both your neighbors and the homeschooling community.

I've found that the easiest way to get to know my neighbors is to be conspicuous by spending time outside my house in the front yard! (What about those front porches in days gone by? I would love to have one with a couple of rockers!) Ever since I began walking in the mornings, I've had more opportunities to talk to people than ever before. It seems like everyone who owns a dog is outside around 7:00 AM. (And didn't you always think that you were the only one that had to take your dog out so early in the morning?) If they're not walking Fido, then they're heading off to work and I get a chance to wave and say "Hi!" Last Christmas, my children and I baked a loaf of bread for each neighbor. Boy, were there some surprised people on the block! My favorite was the lady who suspiciously asked how much she owed us and was so pleasantly surprised when the kids replied, "Nothing! Merry Christmas!" Quite a few of the older people felt that they had to return the greeting and gave Christmas gifts to the kids. The best was an elderly man who invited all of us over for a visit and a taste of his chocolate. What really surprised me was the thank you note that the kids received from one neighbor lady who said their visit and loaf of bread made her holiday. We received the note almost two months after Christmas! We were still on her mind. What a blessing to all of usl!

The benefits of building community are new friends and people that you can rely on in a pinch. You're provided with extra eyes and ears to watch the home while you're in or out; keeping an eye on the kids while they're playing; opportunity to have impromptu chats as neighbors come by and even borrow a cup of sugar; and having someone to reach out to when the necessity arises, and vice versa. **We all need to develop community so that we become part of something larger than just our families**. No longer do we have the days where the entire family from Grandpa to Aunt Myrtle lived within a few miles of us. Now our extended and immediate families are sometimes scattered throughout the country, perhaps the world. We need others to depend on, to share, celebrate with, and help us out.

Another important aspect is that our neighbors get to know us and our children, and see first hand that homeschooling is not something to fear. If you're just starting out homeschooling, you want your neighbors to be supportive. They're going to be seeing a lot of you and the kids; they need to know that you're not neglecting your children. If you have a large family, your neighbors can learn to appreciate again the fruits of a large family. Perhaps your neighbors aren't Christians, and you are able to witness to them by just being there and reaching out. There are so many benefits to building community in your neighborhood; do it and enjoy!

The importance of building community goes beyond mere physical location. Community means developing relationships, which take lots of time and patience. These ties are what give us roots, define us as people, and connect us to something larger than just ourselves. We all need relationships to make us feel like we belong in time and place, help us mature, grow in virtue, and place value on life.

Homeschool support groups should be our community. Every homeschooling family needs to feel the support of the larger homeschooling community; every mom, especially one that's brand new to homeschooling, needs the support of other moms. You should be able to find some like-minded people that you can relate to and share feelings. I can't stress enough how important it is to have other homeschooling moms to communicate and build strong relationships with and to depend upon when the need arises. When we're down in the dumps, and can't seem to climb out of the hole we've dug ourselves into, we then need to be able to call another homeschooling mom, share our problem, and seek advice. You may be surprised to learn that they've already gone through what you're now going through and can help you, or they may know of someone else that can help. A community of friends like this may be what keeps you afloat homeschooling. (The best way to find homeschooling support groups is as follows: ask your church office if there's a homeschooling group in your church, question your school board's homeschool liaison, or contact your state homeschooling association and they should be able to direct you to groups near you. Of course, there's always the Internet.)

Find yourself three or four moms that you feel a kindred spirit with and have a mom's night out. (If you can't find any other moms – pray! I have a dear friend that was looking for like-minded friends and she started to pray. God sent her an abundance!) Everyone comes over to one mom's house and brings a dessert or appetizer, and you can bring up a topic of discussion or just decide to share with one another. Plan picnics or dinners for all the families; have fellowship together as frequently as time permits. You'll find that not only will this be a support for you, but your husband will get to know the other dads and may get the support that he needs. Also the kids will have other homeschoolers to play with and make friends. Remember that older children especially need to see other homeschooled kids. One of the reasons so many go back to a school institution is because they miss the socialization. If your religious convictions are mutual, may I suggest that you plan times of communal prayer. This is a great way to help someone who's floundering in his or her faith come closer to the Lord. (Remember, "For where two or three are gathered in My name, there am I in the midst of them." Matthew 18:20) Have educational fairs to display the kids' work, plan a commencement celebration at the end of the year, or try co-oping. You do not need to plan hundreds of activities or invite lots of people. Actually the fewer families involved, the more fulfilling the event.

Another source that many isolated homeschooling moms are reaching out to is the Internet. You can get into some great chats on the homeschooling sites and learn a lot. The computer has opened up a whole new world for moms at home with kids. But remember, don't become addicted to the Internet, as it is addictive. Set a time limit for yourself at a certain time of day when you're not taking time away from your family, and stick to it. Many moms use naptime for online time. However, if it's your only time for prayer, a quick clean up, or reading a good book, then perhaps split the time. Don't spend it all online!

Something that my group of moms came up with this year is a Mommy's Loop. All the moms that were interested in talking to each other, on a more-or-less daily basis, created a Mommy's Loop on their email. You can start a conversation and send it instantaneously to all the moms with the flick of the mouse. They in turn can respond to everyone with their comments, or go off on different tangents. This has led to lots of sharing of ideas and philosophies. I was hesitant at first because I didn't know what to expect, but I really anticipate hearing from the other moms, and the subjects that are broached are fascinating. I've really learned a lot! (It's like getting a letter everyday from your best friend!)

Just as it's important to build family unity, a close knit community is just as necessary in this day and age. A homeschool community is the icing on the cake and will make your homeschooling odyssey an easier and more pleasant one. Find friends!

## REFLECTION:

Community is important in this age when families are spread out throughout the world. Do you have family nearby? If not, do you sometimes feel lost and lonely without them?

Try to make yourself visible in your local community. Meet your neighbors and develop relationships. Think of different ways that will foster better community ties.

Work on your relationships. Nurture them like you would a garden. Don't take friends for granted! Invite someone over that you haven't see in awhile.

Are you sometimes feeling overwhelmed homeschooling? Do you have some sort of support? Join a support group or start one.

If you're online, check out the web for homeschooling sites. If you can't get out of the house this is a viable alternative for homeschooling support.


*Let brotherly love continue. Do not neglect to show hospitality to strangers, for thereby some have entertained angels unawares.*
*Hebrews 13:1-2*


## FURTHER READING:
**The Lessons of St. Francis** by Michael Talbot with Steve Rabey
　　(NY: Penguin Group, 1997)
**Take Your Time,Finding Balance in a Hurried World** by Eknath Easwaran
　　(NY: Hyperion, 1994) See note on page 42.
**Web Sites:** I'm hesitant to include specific ones because Web Sites are
　　notorious for being here today and gone tomorrow. The best method is to
　　look in the Web directory, or your carrier (for example, AOL: Keyword),
　　under homeschooling and check each site until you find the one that suits
　　you. Here's one to get you started:
　　http://www.home-school.com/ (Homeschool World)

# CHAPTER
## ♥ 6 ♥

## DON'T COMPARISON SHOP!

If you want to be happy as a wife and mother and enjoy your homeschooling journey, don't ever compare yourself to others or their methods. This would be just as bad as looking at your neighbor and saying their grass is greener and I want it! You are you. You'll never be the person that you may envy – and yes, we're all prone to doing it. She may seem to have it "all together," but appearances can be deceiving. What appears to you to be the perfect role model may have problems that you would never expect, or in reality, she may be pretty close to perfect after all. When you meet someone and feel that they're doing the absolutely best job of homeschooling their kids, don't try to duplicate their style! What works well for her and the kids, may not work at all for you and your family. No matter what her attributes, you still can't be her. God made you who you are, and you need to work with what you've got. Concentrate on your good points, and work on those areas of your life that need improvement. Situations and ideas change as we grow older and gain more experience. No one ever stands still in a vacuum; the world around us keeps changing, and so do we and our families.

We need to stop relying on ourselves. If you believe, rely first and foremost on God. Pray daily for His graces. Turn to Him when you're not feeling strong enough to go on. He will help and protect you; He will show you the way. Next, start relying on your husband. Perhaps he's not too good at that role because you've never relied upon him before. Give him a chance. Pray for him; ask God to make him the spiritual leader of your family. Ask your husband for advice; turn to him when you don't know what to do with the kids. Eventually he'll gain confidence and be your partner in homeschooling. If your husband isn't an eager participant in this homeschooling journey or if he lacks confidence, the more you rely on him, the more you ask him for his advice and his opinion, the more he'll grow self assured and confident.

If your husband already is the head of the family, then let him be. What a relief it is to have someone else in charge. Yes, you do want to confer and share ideas and respect each other's point of view, but ultimately someone has to make a decision and be in-charge. Let it be him. And make sure your kids see that you rely on your husband. Let them know that you both share the burden and responsibility; that it's not mom making all the decisions. The best example that you can give your kids is showing them how much you love their dad and rely on his judgement and guidance. Try not to argue in front of the children and never belittle him in front of the kids. Every time you do this, they will follow your example. You can be sure of this.

Always expect the unexpected. Be prepared! (A good Scout!) Have a backup plan for emergencies. That's why God allowed the VCR to be invented. Stick in a history flick. (Remember the library is full of wonderful videos that are educational! Though you may want to be in earshot in case there's something unsavory on it.) Let your older kids (even if they're only eight) teach the younger ones for awhile.   Have some educational cassettes around, or have them play games. (They can learn to count playing **Monopoly!**) Have a drawer full of fun coloring books or worksheets ready for those pinches. Take a day from your busy life and spend it planning for those times when you just won't be able to teach.

When you have to cancel school because you're in bed with morning sickness, you won't be frazzled.  If it's a different type of unforeseen occurrence, like having to take the kids to the doctor or going away for a family emergency, don't worry or fret. If a relative or neighbor is sick, take the time to fix meals, watch their kids, buy them groceries – learn to serve others as family. Don't we all want to be able to help others in their time of need? Their time of need usually occurs at the most importune times when we are overwhelmed. So we don't make that casserole to take over, or we don't volunteer to help watch their kids. Yet we want our children to grow up serving others.  How are they ever going to learn to do this, if **we** don't stop and make the time to serve others?  We can't do this only for our bosom friends. We need to help anyone who calls out. It's easy to help our dear friends, but it's not quite so easy to help mere acquaintances. **This is real life.** Homeschooling is part of your lifestyle and life does not revolve around "doing" school. (Do you think that a lot of learning goes on in school when a substitute takes over for the day or week?  Ha!)  When you get a lemon, make lemonade!

Enjoy what you have – time is so short.  What is a lifetime, in contrast to eternity? What seems to be forever now will pass with the blink of an eye and all your little ones will be gone.  Concentrate on actions that build character and holiness. Don't be consumed with getting it all done. The children are little only once. Enjoy them while they're growing.  Soon there won't be a baby to hold in your arms.  If they're older, remember to spend enough time talking and sharing. Those are the moments that true wisdom is nurtured and bonds are made that will not be broken. If your teen spends all his time trying to avoid you (or vice versa), you'll never get a chance to know the "real" person your child has become.  What will the point have been?

Don't ever think that your kids would be better off in school than home. It's a lie! Don't let yourself think that you're incompetent. This is the devil himself at work on you. Your kids love you. Do the best you can, and God will do the rest. If you truly love them and care for them, they'll always be better off at home. **Home is where the heart is, and no one can duplicate a parent's love.**

## REFLECTION:

Do you find yourself studying other moms and trying to find out how they homeschool? Reflect upon how different you and your kids are from her and her family. Think of ways to stop yourself from comparison shopping. Learn to pray when the desire takes over.

Learn to rely on God and your husband. Think of at least one question that you could ask your husband about homeschooling, which would require his opinion.

Let your husband take the lead in your family. Show him how much you value his opinion and direction.

Next time you're tempted to argue with your husband in front of the kids, stop, pray, and think of something positive to say!

Expect the unexpected. Be prepared! Take time right now to think of at least two activitiies your kids could do if an emergency came up and they would have to be on their own.

Think about all the great things you do with your family and how thankful you are for them. Praise God for giving you the opportunity to raise them.

Think of three reasons why your kids are better off at home than in school.

Think of all the wonderful things you can do for and with your kids that a school cannot.

## FURTHER READING:

**All The Way Home, Power For Your Family To Be Its Best** by Mary Pride (IL: Crossway Books, 1989)
**The Way Home** by Mary Pride (IL: Crossway Books, 1985)

## The Character
## of A Happy Life

How happy is he born and taught
　　That serveth not another's will,
Whose armor is his honest thought,
　　And simple truth his utmost skill!

Whose passions not his masters are,
　　Whose soul is still prepared for death,
Untied unto the world by care
　　Of public fame or private breath;

Who envies none that chance doth raise,
　　Nor vice; who never understood
How deepest wounds are given by praise;
　　Nor rules of state, but rules of good;

Who hath his life from rumors freed,
　　Whose conscience is his strong retreat,
Whose state can neither flatterers feed,
　　Nor ruin make oppressors great;

Who God doth late and early pray
　　More of his grace than gifts to lend,
And entertains the harmless day
　　With a religious book or friend.

This man is freed from servile bands
　　Of hope to rise or fear to fall:
Lord of himself, though not of lands,
　　And, having nothing, yet hath all.

Sir Henry Wotton

# PART TWO

MAKING IT ALL WORK

"THE JOURNEY"

# CHAPTER
## ♥ 7 ♥

## WHERE DO I BEGIN?

Begin at the crack of dawn.  Set your alarm so that you have plenty of time to start your day leisurely before the kids are up and around.  I like to pray morning, noon, and night. I try to wake up at 6:30AM. I jump into my clothes and go outside to walk and pray.  This is a great time of day to be outside, especially in southern Florida.  It's cool; the sun isn't up yet, but as you walk, you can slowly see dawn slip away and the sun mount the sky.  Along the way, I'm serenaded by birds, squirrels, and frogs. (I live near a river.)  Even my cats follow me partially along the route.  As I walk up and down the street, I pray for everyone that I know including the neighbors.  What a wonderful way to start the day!  My motivation for getting out of bed is the time I have to spend with the Lord and the knowledge that if I don't get up and walk, I'm going to have a very difficult day.  Sometimes my eldest daughter joins me to pray.  Almost always I get to see and greet my neighbors as they are leaving for work.  What a way to build community!

Offer all the good and the bad to the Lord and you'll be amazed at the peace you'll be blessed with.  When I make time for prayer, calamities still occur, but I have a calmer and more pleasant attitude. My time alone with God prepares my spirit and mind for the unexpected.  Next time you go into the laundry room and find that the hose blew off and there's water pouring everywhere, Praise the Lord!  When your daughter does an unexpected somersault, hits the fireplace, and you're off to the hospital for stitches, Praise the Lord!  When the phone won't stop ringing all morning long – take it off the hook, and Praise the Lord!  Finally when you're ready to put the roast in the oven for a very special dinner and find that the oven's broken, Praise the Lord! (and make reservations at McDonalds!)  There's nothing like prayer mixed with a very healthy sense of humor.

Prayer doesn't guarantee that you won't get upset, or blow up at the kids, or get grumpy.  But I feel that I'm much calmer and more patient with prayer than without it!

After you've set the above in motion (and like any new task it takes about a month for a habit to form), you're ready to proceed to step two.

## SUMMARY:

1. Begin each day with prayer…and don't stop!

2. Try and see the funny side of trying situations. Humor is the best medicine available for both the receiver **and the giver!**

*Count it all joy, brethren, when you meet various trials, for you know that the testing of your faith produces steadfastness. And let steadfastness have its full effect, that you may be perfect and complete, lacking in nothing.*

*James 1:2-4*

## FURTHER READING:

**The Holy Bible,** especially the "Psalms" and "Proverbs"

**The Imitation of Christ** by Thomas A. Kempis (New York: Catholic Publishing Co.,1993)

# CHAPTER
## ♥ 8 ♥

## GOAL SETTING

**Goals**: objectives; or for the sports minded, the end of the race!

Before you do anything (other than pray), before you plan your curriculum or school schedule or any other detail, you and your husband need to sit down and plan your family's journey together. This adventure encompasses everything – your lives together as a couple and your lives together as a family.

Oh sure, you could plod along day to day without a plan, but then how will you know when the journey is coming to an end? Life is easy...when you're dead, you're done. Physically raising kids is another fairly easy one...when they've flown the coop, you're done. Your husband's, perhaps your own career, is finished when you retire. There's more to **really** living life than that.

Don't you want objectives for your kids' education? Do you want them to go to college? If so, then you need financial or scholastic objectives - ensure that they study their best to perhaps qualify for scholarships. Do you want to live in the same house forever, or do you want to eventually move? Does your husband want a different job or career? All these are goals or objectives that need to be considered thoroughly. Now don't misunderstand me. I know perfectly well that the Lord could take me home to heaven at any minute, but then again, he may not. I want to be prepared either way. I want to be prepared spiritually, physically, and financially. I need to talk things through with my husband so that I have some clue in which direction our journey's headed.

Goal setting may actually be one of the most difficult tasks that you'll have to accomplish in organizing your life. This is the case - for me. I have many goals; the problem is fitting all of them into my life. Most people feel like failures if they can't meet every goal, therefore, be realistic when considering your goals. Do not take on too much, too fast. Take it easy. You're like that little baby who's just learning to walk. You have to take one step at a time and be very careful as you toddle along. One wrong step and you'll fall, and it might take you a long time before you lift yourself up and try again. So take it easy and take tiny, tiny steps.

Remember, if you don't have a plan, you don't have direction. How will you know where you're going?

Some people are good at keeping track of almost anything in their head. Good for them! That's great. However, I'm not like that. I need to sit down, think of a plan and write it down, re-think it, discuss it with my husband or friend or kids, finalize it, and put it into action. I'm a visual learner. I think that you should start out that way. Somehow it feels more binding when it's in writing.

**This is what you need to do:** (It's best to do this with your husband so that you're both working toward the same goals. It will take some time so allot a leisurely afternoon with no disturbances, or perhaps take a weekend get-away without kids!)

**First, plan long-term goals – 15 years from now:**
1) How old will your kids be?
2) Where will your kids be living?
3) Where do you want to be living?
4) What will your finances be like?
5) What is it that you will have hoped to achieve by then:
   A) Physically?
   B) Spiritually?

For some reason it's easier (perhaps because it's so far off in the future) to plan for 5, 10, and 15 years from now. Fifteen years? Yes siree, we need to consider what our goals will be in 15 years. Take me for example. I'm forty-three years old as of this writing (don't tell anyone!). My oldest is thirteen and youngest is one. There are three others sandwiched in between. In 15 years, four children will be out of the house and the youngest will be ready to do something constructive with her life. I'll be (gulp!) fifty-eight and my husband (chuckle,chuckle) sixty-two. By then, we hope to be retired and living somewhere in the mountains perhaps raising sheep and llamas, and there might even be some grandchildren bothering us (oh, that really hurt!). I hope and pray that all my children will still be as close to the Lord then, as they are now.

**What are your goals for 10 years from now (same questions)?**

In 10 years, three children will probably be out of the house and my husband should be retired (our plan is that he leaves his government job by the age of fifty-five at the latest). Hopefully, we'll be somewhere in the mountains just starting our little ranch. Richie, my husband, will perhaps have another job (self-employed) because we'll need to supplement our income for a few years until our IRA's kick in.

**What are your goals in five years (same questions)?**

In 5 years we'll just be sending our oldest off to college. We'll be heartbroken and not know if we'll be able to carry on without her. Of course our others will keep us so busy that soon we'll adjust. We'll probably still be living in Florida (sweating!) in the same house. Each year we'll be trying to build up our little business that we presently have, so that by the time Richie retires, his business - selling books to homeschoolers - will be full-blown. We'll be trying to live frugally so that we could save a little on the side for retirement and other expenses. (Did you notice that I never mentioned college and its expenses? This is because I'm brainwashing my children now, telling them they have to study hard and obtain scholarships in order to go to college. With five children we don't even dream of paying for their college education. Actually, I've always felt that they would need to pay their own way to fully appreciate the education they would be receiving. Anything that's given freely is quickly taken for granted.)

**This brings us to the very near future. What are your goals for 1 year from now?**

Now it becomes much harder to set goals. It seems to be harder to agree with your spouse too. It's much easier to picture yourself a year from now; each of you might see a different future. My goals at 1 year from now are to: keep simplifying our home (and lifestyle) so that it runs smoothly and efficiently; lose thirty pounds (please, oh Lord!); pray diligently every day and teach my children faithfully about the Lord; save money; cut back on extra curricular activities. As you can see, my husband and I could have difficulty in agreeing with some of these goals.

**What are your goals for 1 month from now?**

In 1 month I'd like to have lost ten pounds (OK, I'd settle for five at this point); have the school year basics completed (meaning math and English); have my household running smoothly; and have the girls cooking more meals alone.

**What are your goals for next week?**

In 1 week, I'd like to be settled into a real diet (no cheating); have my house completely de-cluttered and organized; and have completed twenty more pages on this book.

**What are your goals for tomorrow?**

Tomorrow I'd like everyone to wake up cheerful and ready to take on the world; have a few minutes all to myself; and read a good book to each of my youngest.

**In 1 hour I'd like to be in bed!**

Are you catching on?  I thought it would be easier to give you concrete examples, rather than just alluding to them. I've also included a sample Life Goal Chart.  A place for the kids' names and ages is included so that you can see what their ages will be and the probability of them still being in the house. Whether they are home or not will affect your financial picture. Now, sit down and set your goals and be sure to do it with your husband.  Remember, these are life goals.  Don't worry about school goals just yet.

P.S. Oh yes...and have fun!!

## SUMMARY:

1. Sit down with your husband and contemplate your family's future. Talk about how you see your life in 15 years (and less).  Use the Life Goals Chart to help you.

2. Remember, these are not carved in stone.  They're merely guideposts for your future journey together as a couple and family.  Without some direction, you'll get lost!

*I press on toward the goal for the prize of the upward call of God in Christ Jesus.*

*Philippians 3:14*

DATE:_____

# LIFE GOALS

| | KIDS | AGE | PHYSICAL | SPIRITUAL | FINANCIAL |
|---|---|---|---|---|---|
| **15 YEARS** | | | | | |
| **10 YEARS** | | | | | |
| **5 YEARS** | | | | | |
| **1 YEAR** | | | | | |
| **6 MOS** | | | | | |
| **1 MO** | | | | | |
| **1 WEEK** | | | | | |

# CHAPTER
# ♥ 9 ♥

## DISCIPLINE
## Or
## O-B-E-Y YOUR MOM AND DAD

*Children, obey your parents in the Lord, for this is right. "Honor your father and mother" (this is the first commandment with a promise), "that it may be well with you and that you may live long on the earth." Fathers, do not provoke your children to anger, but bring them up in the discipline and instruction of the Lord.*
*Ephesians 6:1-4*

*For the moment all discipline seems painful rather than pleasant; later it yields the peaceful fruit of righteousness to those who have been trained by it.*
*Hebrews 12:11*

<u>DISCIPLINE</u>: Education; instruction; cultivation and improvement, comprehending instruction in arts, sciences, correct sentiments, morals and manners, and due subordination to authority. (<u>Noah Webster's 1828 American Dictionary of the English Language</u>)

This next step of our journey is essential: your children's discipline training and your relationship with them. You can make mistakes along the way, which is allowed and expected, but it's crucial that you always correct these mistakes. In fact, this area is so important to your homeschooling endeavors that it warrants its own goal chart! Your family's future homeschooling success or failure depends on how much effort you put into your children's training. Needless to say, both you and your husband have to be in agreement as to how you will proceed. This is an area of family life where you **must** have each other's total support and commitment! It will not succeed if one of you disciplines and the other rebukes the disciplining spouse for disciplining. You need to work as a team toward the same goal: Well behaved children that make you proud!

Take a look at Noah Webster's definition of discipline. Discipline does not mean punishment. Discipline is the training or development of your children's character so that they submit to authority. It sounds severe, but it isn't. Don't we need to submit to God's authority over our lives, to our husband and parents, to our commanding officer or boss, and to our teachers? In order to live life civilly and humanely, we submit to others many times throughout the day! We don't necessarily do this because we are subservient to them, but because someone needs to be in charge. You can't have all chiefs and no Indians! If we don't train our children well, they are going to have a very difficult time when the time comes to work with others.

How do you discipline? At the very simplest level, the answer is by teaching a child to obey the first time.

This idea of creating a lifestyle revolves around the idea that your children are willing participants and helpers. If they won't obey, how are you going to get them to help you clean, cook, and learn? There are a lot of good books that address obedience. One of the best and most succinct I've ever read is **To Train Up A Child**, by Michael and Debi Pearl. I strongly encourage you to read this very simple and small book that's packed with wisdom, encouragement, and very straightforward advice. The authors point out how devastating lack of obedience can be. If you were in the front yard and saw your child run into the street, that child needs to know to obey when you say stop. He shouldn't answer back with a why, and continue to run. The child needs to stop instantly. Otherwise he may be run over by a car (or, in the case of the above mentioned book, by an Amish buggy). If you see your two or three-year old reach for a hot pot and you say stop, that child better stop or he will be burned. Children need to know that when you tell them to do something, it should be done at once and not an hour later (or as in most cases, upon the third request).

How do you train your child to obey? Well, it's a lesson in parent patience. You need to be committed to the task and never waver. You need to follow through with your promises or threats. If you tell a child to do something or else he'll be punished, you better carry through with that promise, or else that child will not listen to you the next time. Children want clear-cut rules: obey me the first time I ask you, or you will be punished in some manner. Be consistent. If chewing gum in the house is forbidden, then don't say no two times and then ignore the bad behavior the third time.

Children, no matter how young, are very astute; they're born gamblers. They know exactly how to push your buttons; they know exactly how long they have before mom or dad will carry through on a threat. They're masters of parent psychology. An average parent will give their child at least two or three chances before they'll discipline. Believe me, the child will wait that long. He knows how long to wait before he needs to submit. Action must be taken before the child can rebel.

What would happen, if the next time, you give him only one (or no) warning? You better believe that that child will be much more careful from then on…until he sees that you've become "lazy" again. That's the bottom line. We, as parents, are lazy. It takes energy to be on top of our kids. If that child doesn't go and clean his room, I have to reprimand, punish, and then make sure that the job is done properly. I also have to make sure that I do whatever it is I threatened to do, such as no playing games on the computer for a week. The next day, when that child starts whining that he wants to play on the computer, I need to remember to say no, and then come up with an alternative. If he continues to whine, I must not condone the behavior. As you can see, child training is a very time consuming job. We need to be consistent 100% of the time or else that child will keep pushing our buttons!

You're probably thinking to yourself, "But they're only children!" But as the Pearls mention in their book, what you have at the age of two is what you'll have at the age of fourteen **unless** you train them otherwise. We are all "trainable." If you can teach a pet to obey, there's absolutely no excuse for a child!

I have found that spankings work best with young children (up to the age of about seven or eight). The punishment is swift, and you can both carry on with your lives. Always spank calmly, not when you're agitated. If necessary, send the child to his room while you calm down. Hug and talk after the spanking. Discuss with the child why his behavior was inappropriate and why you had to give the spanking. Always have the child ask for forgiveness from the person he offended; forgive them for their wrongdoing. Be sure to tell the him that you love him. For those with older children the best punishment is taking something away from them: computer time, TV, special books, playtime, etc. You need to find out exactly what it is they care about the most. It has to be important to them, or else it won't be effective as a punishment.

It's very important to realize that you must remain calm and in control when you punish, especially spank. One reason parents "lose it" is because we wait so long before anything is done. At first, we may ignore the bad behavior hoping that it will stop; we then warn them once, twice, and perhaps a third while we're quickly losing our cool and patience. We spontaneously take action instead of intentionally (remember?). By now, we're furious and lash out at the offender. Instead, we need to purposefully take action when the child disobeys the first time, calmly saying, "It's time for a spanking. Let's go." Or "No computer (fill in with whatever they love) for today because you didn't listen." If they don't care about anything enough to "take it away" from them, have them work above and beyond their normal chores. Have them clean out the garage, the attic, or the basement all day. Your child will really be impressed!

Remember that the best teacher is a good role model. If you expect courtesy from your children, be courteous; if you want them to be polite, act politely; if you want kids that don't curse, then watch your language. Whatever bad habit **you** have, be assured that your child will pick up and imitate that action. Always try to lead by setting the best example that you possibly can. Of course sometimes, in extreme irritability, a choice word may slip through your lips or you may act out of character yourself. Apologize! This shows them that you know you did wrong and are willing to acknowledge it publicly.

**Praise** your children lavishly when they deserve it. Sometimes we're so intent on forming their characters that we forget to praise them when they do a job well. If we consistently praise them, they'll try harder to be good.

Require respect. Don't ever let your children talk back to you, or to any other adult. In fact, they also need to speak respectfully to their brothers and sisters. (If they aren't polite at home, they won't be polite when they go out.) Always request that they apologize and perhaps give a hug or kiss. It's so easy to dismiss sarcasm, anger, or back talk. But practice your parent patience and correct this very disrespectful behavior immediately. Don't overlook physical disrespect either - the posture that says, "I don't care what you say," or the clothing that screams, "I'm my own person and no one is going to tell me what to wear to church!" The new fad that really bothers my family is when boys wear baseball caps inside the house. Men and boys should remove their hats upon entering a home. (We are so used to seeing men wear their baseball caps everywhere, including while eating, during an invocation, or the singing of the national anthem.) Once again, you can't ask your kids to do something that you're not willing to do.

Teach your kids to be diligent and persevere until they get the job done. You require that they begin and complete jobs to the best of their ability. We started this with our kids when they were only four by taking music lessons. They were expected to practice for a half an hour daily from the very beginning. This disciplined them so that the fruits reaped spilled over into their schooling. I've never had a problem with them completing their assignments. You need to be diligent in requiring them to complete what they set out to do. Don't let them quit just because they're whining. Parents tend to give up on music lessons because the kids start to complain. Don't give in! Music is just as important as their book schooling. You never hear an adult say, "I wish my parents would have let me quit." You always hear, "If only my parents would have made me play, I would be playing now!"

A disciplined child is orderly. "Cleanliness is next to Godliness!" Teach your kids to be organized. Don't let them live like slobs. All you'll be doing is creating another adult that can't pick up after themselves! (Everytime I look at other kids I think about what kind of adults they'll grow up to be. Would I want my daughter or son marrying a person who's disorganized and untidy? I want my kids to be able to cook, clean, build, and sew so they'd make good mates for others.) Plan a schedule for each of your children. They are not guests in your home but co-inhabitants. They need to take responsibility for certain chores and a certain amount of schoolwork.  Kids should receive an allowance, as this is their way to financial independence, but I don't believe that chores should be tied up into their allowance. Chores need to be done for the family and home; an allowance is given because they are members of the family and they also need money for their expenses (more on this later).  Incentives for doing their chores could include baking cookies together, reading a book aloud, going on a special trip to a museum.  The punishment for not doing chores could be the very same one in reverse: take away a special trip, or computer time or play.

All of our disciplinary training can be quickly unraveled when we spoil our children. Don't give them everything they ask for, especially in a store.  Love cannot be equated to how much we spend on our kids.  In this day and age, the opposite is true; you show your real love by not buying them every toy ever made.  If they have everything, the child will never experience the joy of wanting something so badly and waiting and perhaps saving for it.  I make it a point never to buy the kids anything they ask for while we're shopping, because the next time they'll expect more of the same. (If you want to buy them a treat, **you** initiate it, not them.)  This is what also leads to that horrible behavior in supermarkets where the kids are screaming their heads off in the line demanding gum or candy.  Mom becomes so flustered and embarrassed that she usually gives in.  If their behavior is so bad, leave the grocery cart on the side and take them to the car to be disciplined.  Don't **ever** let them get away with bad behavior, or they'll make it a habit. You need to be consistent and this takes lots of parent patience.

Ensure that all your hard work doesn't go to naught by having your kids get plenty of sleep.  An infant up to about five-years of age needs at least twelve hours of sleep.  After age five, my children sleep for about eleven hours. At the age of thirteen, my daughter still needs ten hours of sleep to feel refreshed and ready to go. If my kids go to bed later than normal, the next morning they are usually very cranky.  Sleep and a proper diet are very important to growing kids.

Lastly, discipline training requires a lifestyle free of too many outside activities.  A special activity once in awhile is a treat, but too much activity is a stimulant that tires both the child and you, and doesn't allow the time to focus on discipline.  Turn your hearts toward home.  In Karey Swan's book, **Hearth & Home**, she points out that most families never get beyond organizing and cleaning their homes.  They're never home long enough to enjoy the comforts of home: baking bread, creating crafts, entertaining and ministering to family and friends.  Our goal should be to learn to stay and thrive in the homes that we so painstakingly create. If we're out everyday running around and buying this and that, our children will grow up thinking this is what they must do.  We're going to raise children who will run out of the house at the very first opportunity.  Where will they be going? The answer is malls, bars, and places where there's excitement and stimulation. They will seek others, offering them the love that they couldn't find at home.  Children will not be content at home if their parents are not content at home. Parents and children need time together at home to be able to develop mutually loving relationships.

Undoubtedly, the hardest lesson to instill in a child is to obey the first time. Discipline requires one to obey immediately. You must relentlessly strive by constantly correcting. If you succeed in training them to obey the first time, your life (and theirs) is going to be immeasurably easier. Everything else will fall into place. If you manage to achieve this goal, guard it like a hawk by being 100% consistent. If you see your children starting to slip, catch them immediately and re-train. It will be well worth the effort.

More importantly, teach your children to obey with a cheerful and willing heart. This may take years to achieve, but keep working at it. Make them realize that our ultimate goal is heaven. Hard work, diligence, and even suffering, are part of the Christian walk. We were not put here to lay around and languish. Work is part of life. No one is ever going to run away from work completely. I think that our generation was spoiled because we were the first to be raised with every sort of technological comfort. Life became very easy: washing machines and dryers, dishwashers, microwaves, and more. We grew up expecting leisure time. In reality, life is all about working and earning our leisure. We must all, including parents, learn to work with a cheerful and willing heart. In fact, if you achieve this state in your own life, homeschooling your children will no longer be a task that needs to be endured; it will become a joy in your life, especially when you reap the fruits.*

As important as discipline training is, holding your child's heart is paramount. You can train a child to obey but unless he does it with a willing, cheerful heart you really haven't gained anything. Your desire is to have a child do something because he really wants to please you (and thereby please our Lord). How do you accomplish this?

First and foremost, you need to always keep the lines of communication open. On a daily basis, talk to each of your children and ask how things are going. Are there any problems, is he angry with anyone, or has anyone offended him (it may even have been you who has offended him!)? Many times the disruptive behavior we see is a physical expression of the hurt a child is feeling inside over some situation. By taking the time to talk, we may find that we can very simply resolve the problem. There should never be a time when you don't know what your child is feeling or experiencing. You want ties between the two of you. Once these ties are severed, you have no way of knowing what's in your child's heart, what he's feeling and thinking. (Many of today's violent acts committed by kids are attributed to parents not knowing what their child was feeling or doing, or with whom he was keeping company. Make it a habit to be aware of your child's moods, activities, and actions.)

Secondly, you should encourage your children to participate in family activities. Don't let them isolate themselves. Home is where the heart is, so keep your children's hearts there. The farther they stray from home into foreign territory, the less you'll be able to keep a watchful eye. Don't let them fall under the influence of other kids, commonly referred to as "peer pressure." We seem to think it's natural for our older children to alienate themselves from us in their teen years. This is exactly the time that they should be near us. We don't want outsiders to have more influence on them than their parents. This concept of the "teenage years" or "teen attitude" is a late 20th Century phenomenon and is closely related to us gaining affluence. Society brain washes teenagers to think adults (especially their parents) don't understand them any longer; they need to dress and act differently and must hate the so-called "establishment." Well, we as homeschooling parents, can nip that in the bud by not telling them that there's such a "phenomenon." Ignore it and go right on with your life! (Don't assume that homeschool and church youth groups are free of bad influences. Remember, these are merely large groups of kids with usually only one or two adults supervising. You have no idea what these kids believe in and how they may influence your children. Always err on the side of caution before you let your child become involved in a group activity.)

Thirdly, remind your children that the reason we discipline is because we love them and God loves them. We are their first and foremost teachers, and everything we do is for their own good. Explain this to them; don't say, "That's the way it is and you better like it!" If we keep the lines of communication open, they should be willing to hear our explanations and consider them.

How do you win a new friend over? The answer is being nice to them, respecting them, caring for their needs, appreciating their good qualities and telling them so. Always remember to laugh together. They're young only once; you have them in your home for such a short time. Treat your children better than a friend. Do all that, and love them with all your heart! If you show them your heart, I believe that eventually you'll have theirs.


## TO SUMMARIZE:

1. Teach your children to obey the first time.

2. Decide on a form of punishment.

3. Be consistent.

4. Be a good role model!

5. Praise frequently; punish immediately.

6. Require respect.

7. Teach diligence.

8. Teach them to be orderly.

9. Don't spoil your child.

10. Make sure you **all** get enough sleep and nourishment.

11. Don't clutter your lives with too many activities – be selective.

12. Work on holding their hearts and giving them yours!

13. Communicate.

14. Encourage family participation.

15. Always tell them you love them.

16. Always remember to laugh – they're young for such a short time!

**FURTHER READING:**
**To Train Up A Child** by Michael and Debi Pearl (Pleasantville,TN: 1994)
**No Greater Joy**, Vol. I by Michael and Debi Pearl (Pleasantville,TN: 1997)
**Doorposts**, 5840 SW Old Hwy 47, Gaston, OR 97119.  Send a SASE for their
    free catalog of discipline & character training material.
**Hearth & Home** by Karey Swan (CO: Singing Springs Productions, 1996)

*"...It is the simple things of life that make living worthwhile, the
sweet fundamental things such as love and duty, work and rest..."*
*(pg.17 Little House in the Ozarks,*
*by Laura Ingalls Wilder)*

\* I believe that most of society's problems today are the direct result of our affluence and our abundance of "free time." We have every gadget possible to make living easier and chores quicker. Think back to life a hundred years ago. One reason people had fewer clothes was because they needed to sew everything (underwear included) themselves, and the same clothes needed to be washed by hand, dried outside (think about winter!), and pressed with an iron that was heated on a stove. All their bread and baked goods were made at home; they hunted for their food, slaughtered it themselves, and then had to preserve it. Quilts and pillows were made at home and kept for a lifetime. For cooking, you needed firewood. Diapers and feminine products were homemade and washed by hand. If you didn't have a successful garden, you didn't have vegetables that winter. Many activities, such as quilting, canning, and barn raising, were community affairs. Our ancestors had no time to develop self-induced neuroses. They were extremely busy people and probably more content and happy than the majority of today's population.

# SAMPLE OBEDIENCE CHART

| CHILD: | Viktorija | | | | | | | Giedre | | | | | | | Gintaras | | | | | | | Linas | | | | | | |
|---|---|---|---|---|---|---|---|---|---|---|---|---|---|---|---|---|---|---|---|---|---|---|---|---|---|---|---|---|
| OBEDIENCE CHART | S | M | T | W | T | F | S | S | M | T | W | T | F | S | S | M | T | W | T | F | S | S | M | T | W | T | F | S |
| OBEYED THE FIRST TIME | 3 | 3 | 2 | 3 | 3 | 3 | 3 | 3 | 3 | 3 | 2 | 3 | 3 | 3 | 3 | 3 | 3 | 3 | 3 | 3 | 3 | 3 | 3 | 3 | 2 | 2 | 3 | 3 |
| POLITE | | | | | | | | | | | | | | | | | | | | | | | | | | | | |
| ATTITUDE WAS GREAT: | | | | | | | | | | | | | | | | | | | | | | | | | | | | |
| Cheerful | | | | | | | | | | | | | | | | | | | | | | | | | | | | |
| Helpful to siblings | | | | | | | | | | | | | | | | | | | | | | | | | | | | |
| PICKED UP HIS TOYS | | | | | | | | | | | | | | | | | | | | | | | | | | | | |
| DIDN'T RAISE HIS VOICE | | | | | | | | | | | | | | | | | | | | | | | | | | | | |
| ASKED PERMISSION | | | | | | | | | | | | | | | | | | | | | | | | | | | | |
| DID ALL HIS SCHOOLWORK | | | | | | | | | | | | | | | | | | | | | | | | | | | | |
| DID HIS CHORES WILLINGLY | | | | | | | | | | | | | | | | | | | | | | | | | | | | |

I have listed various areas that can be worked on. I personally would work on only one area at a time, perhaps for a few weeks. You'll get more accomplished if you concentrate, rather than try to do it all. After you feel that you've made headway in that area, move on to another.

SCORE: 3 (GREAT), 2 ( DECENT), 1 (ROOM FOR IMPROVEMENT) IF THEY GET LESS THAN 14 POINTS PER WEEK, IN ONE AREA OF DISCIPLINE, A PRIVILEGE IS TAKEN AWAY. IF THEY GET A PERFECT 21 POINTS THEY'RE REWARDED.

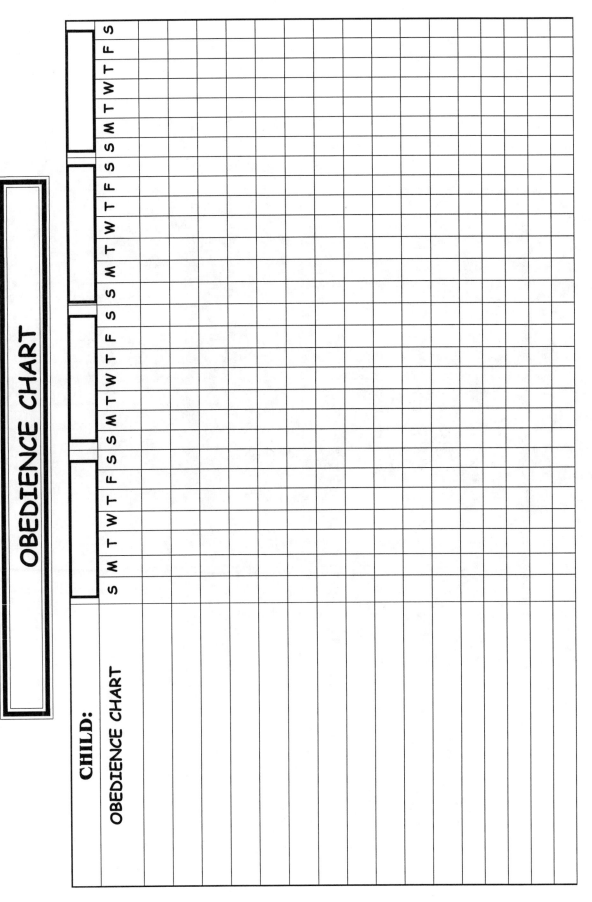

**OBEDIENCE CHART**

CHILD:

OBEDIENCE CHART

| | S | M | T | W | T | F | S | S | M | T | W | T | F | S | S | M | T | W | T | F | S | S | M | T | W | T | F | S |
|---|---|---|---|---|---|---|---|---|---|---|---|---|---|---|---|---|---|---|---|---|---|---|---|---|---|---|---|---|
| | | | | | | | | | | | | | | | | | | | | | | | | | | | | |
| | | | | | | | | | | | | | | | | | | | | | | | | | | | | |
| | | | | | | | | | | | | | | | | | | | | | | | | | | | | |
| | | | | | | | | | | | | | | | | | | | | | | | | | | | | |
| | | | | | | | | | | | | | | | | | | | | | | | | | | | | |
| | | | | | | | | | | | | | | | | | | | | | | | | | | | | |
| | | | | | | | | | | | | | | | | | | | | | | | | | | | | |
| | | | | | | | | | | | | | | | | | | | | | | | | | | | | |
| | | | | | | | | | | | | | | | | | | | | | | | | | | | | |
| | | | | | | | | | | | | | | | | | | | | | | | | | | | | |
| | | | | | | | | | | | | | | | | | | | | | | | | | | | | |
| | | | | | | | | | | | | | | | | | | | | | | | | | | | | |
| | | | | | | | | | | | | | | | | | | | | | | | | | | | | |
| | | | | | | | | | | | | | | | | | | | | | | | | | | | | |
| | | | | | | | | | | | | | | | | | | | | | | | | | | | | |
| | | | | | | | | | | | | | | | | | | | | | | | | | | | | |
| | | | | | | | | | | | | | | | | | | | | | | | | | | | | |

# CHAPTER
## ♥ 10 ♥

## ORGANIZATION

**Organize:** **to form an orderly, functional, structured whole. To arrange; systematize. (The American Heritage Dictionary, 1973)**

**Organize:** **to find a suitable place to house or store all your earthly possessions. (author)**

After you set your goals, the next step is to organize your life. (You can be doing this while you teach your kids to obey!) This usually means whipping the house into shape.  Now the best advice I can offer you is to stop school - at least your part of school. If your kids are old enough to work on some subjects on their own, such as math, then let them go ahead.  If they play a musical instrument, have them practice daily.  Otherwise stop school.  You need their help on this matter.  Log it in as home economics!  It's much too hard to try to organize your household and keep on schooling.

We are going to clean, simplify, and organize every tangible area of your life: every closet, bedroom, the schoolroom, your library, your curriculum, your menus, and more. This will take a lot of energy.  Eat well and go to sleep extra early.  Don't forget to take your vitamins! (If you're like me and always forget, assign the job of handing out the vitamins to one of the older kids. They're great at remembering!) You want to be full of vigor to undertake this mission.  Moms fail to realize just how much physical and emotional energy it takes to reorganize anything.  When you're tired, you just can't do it.  Your body won't move and your brain will go into extra slow motion.

You may even want to consider having a friend assist you in simplifying (help each other by trading work). Sometimes you need an objective observer, someone who's not emotionally attached to your things, to help you decide what to throw out and what to keep. If you consider yourself a packrat, it would really help to find a friend that is not a packrat. Look at her house. Is it organized? Would you like yours to look like hers? Perhaps you can trade jobs or goods with her.  Maybe you're a more organized cook than she is and can help her in that area, while she helps you simplify your household.

After we're done giving you and your household a complete make-over, you're going to sit down and put together some schedules to keep your household and school just buzzing along. You're going to make out a daily/weekly/monthly/and perhaps yearly schedule. You're are going to try to stick to it as religiously as possible until you have everything running smoothly.

Once you have all these steps in place, the major work is done. You can then put your brain on auto-pilot. Everything will be laid out for you so that you don't have to stop and think and worry over every little thing. Your life and home should then run efficiently. Life will become a breeze!

Let's start simplifying!

## DE-CLUTTERING GUIDELINES

1. **Always remember that clutter hurts the eyes!** The less clutter, the more clean and appealing the room will look, and thereby much more easy to keep clean! Pretend you're a guest and just walking into your home for the very first time. As you walk through the house, locate all the clutter areas – the places that just scream out to you as being total confusion.

2. Throw away anything that you haven't used in a year. If this really pains you, then do the following:

   A) Put it in a box with other items that you find difficult to throw away. Label the box "My Cherished Treasures" and put it in your closet, attic, or basement. If you haven't looked in the box for six months, take out all the items and either throw them away, give all of it to charity, or have a garage sale!

3. Throw away anything that is broken or is in bad need of repair.

4. Items that you no longer need can be placed in a separate pile to be sold in a garage sale or given away to charity or friends. (If you've never had a garage sale, seriously consider it.) First, evaluate if people will come. In our neighborhood, garage sales are so popular that before my husband can come back home from putting up the garage sale sign at the corner we already have three or four cars zooming in. We usually start around 7:30AM and are done by 10:30AM. If it hasn't sold by then, it probably won't. We've made as much as $700 when we had furniture to sell, and the last time I de-cluttered with only a few bigger ticket items we made $350. If you live at the end of an isolated dirt road, and your nearest neighbor or major road is miles away, a garage sale may not work. It's worth it only if you know people will come.

5.  Put all your charity/garage sale items in a spare room or corner out of sight.  You don't want to keep staring at it for a few reasons:

    A)  You may decide that you need to take back some items.

    B)  All the clutter may upset you and make you anxious.

6.  Ask a friend who's organized and emotionally unattached to help you simplify your home.

7.  De-clutter an area once and then come back when you're done with the entire house.  The second time around you are usually much more brazen about getting rid of needless clutter!

### I Like Housecleaning

It's fun to clean house.
The food isn't much,
And the paint's all about
That we mustn't touch;
But strange stored-away things,
Not like everyday things,
Make marvelous playthings
From attics and such.

The boxes come out
From closets and chests,
With odd sorts of clothes
Like old hats and vests,
And photographed faces,
And ribbons and laces,
And postcards of places,
And cards left by guests.

Then Mother says, "Throw
The whole lot away!"
And Father says, "Wait-
I'll need this someday."
But either way's meaning
A chance to go gleaning
Among the housecleaning
For new things to play.

By Dorothy Brown Thompson

# THE BATHROOM

I would start in an area of the house that has the least emotional attachments for you, such as the bathroom. It's amazing how much clutter can accumulate there.

## MEDICINE CABINET

1. Throw away any medicine that's expired or that you do not need anymore (like antibiotics).

2. Get rid of everything that doesn't belong there, like soap or makeup (unless there is no where else to keep it).

3. While you're at it, clean the shelves and dust the cabinet.

## DRAWERS

1. Empty every drawer and clean it.

2. Set a garbage can beneath you. Go through everything and throw away items that you never (or rarely) use, such as that ugly bright purple nail polish.

3. Organize your hair ornaments in a little box.

4. Put your combs/brushes in a box.

5. Keep your makeup together. Throw away all makeup that's old or rarely used. Just because it's new, doesn't mean you have to keep it! Give new make-up away to charity, sell it at a garage sale, or let your kids play with it.

6. Put all your toilet paper together. Keep all "lady articles" together.

7. If you have a surplus of items – my husband collects toothpaste, brushes, shampoo, and soap on sale – store it in one place.

## SHOWER STALL/BATHTUB

1. Get rid of all the clutter that accumulates in there. Keep only shampoo and conditioner - just the bare minimum.

2. It's nice to have a spray bottle of bleach / water mix handy to occasionally spray on the shower walls and floor to eliminate mildew. Also, a very large squegee (available commercially) is a great tool to wipe down the walls after a shower. Ensure that everyone does it after a shower to prevent soap scum and mildew.

## TOWEL RACK

1. Keep only one bath towel and one face towel per person. You definitely need to find a space for each person's towels or else the bathroom will always look cluttered. We bought a wooden coat rack that you attach on the wall to hang about six towels.

## MISCELLANEOUS

1. If you have clutter on your counters, take a good hard look and decide if it **really** needs to be there. **Remember - clutter hurts the eyes!** I presently have a tray that contains perfume and cologne, next to which I have a few purely decorative glasses. By my sinks, the only items are soap and cleansing cream. If the kids use this bathroom, it's nice to have a toothbrush holder so that each toothbrush can be put away. Also, small throw-a-way cups are great (more expensive, but much more sanitary), as well as a soap dish. Keep a sponge handy so that the counter and spills can be wiped cleanly and quickly.

2. If you have decorations on the wall, determine if they need to be there. They may be just gathering dust. Get rid of them and there's one less item to clean! Check your rugs to determine if they're in good condition. You may need to replace them, or decide that they are not needed after all.

3. Check whether your bathtub, shower, or sink needs re-caulking.

4. Clean out the sink/shower/bathtub drains by removing the "plugs" or metal screening. You'll be amazed how the dirt accumulates there!

5. Do your shower doors needs to be removed and thoroughly cleaned? Do your shower curtains need to be washed? (You can throw the plastic liner in the wash with some bleach to clean away the mildew, or you can buy a new liner for about $2.75.)

## KEEP ON TRUCKIN'

Once you're done with your bathrooms, you should start feeling a little better about this whole experience. You've acquired confidence. Perhaps you see the great results and say to yourself, "That wasn't too bad. I can get into this." By now your garbage can should be filling up, so it may be wise to scrounge up some super-sized big boxes to throw away the excess. Also, don't become too upset with the mess that you're making in the temporary storage room. Remember you're filling the boxes or bags for charity or a garage sale. Everything will soon be gone. (If you don't have the extra space, stash the filled bags or boxes under your beds.)

The next place should be your linen closet. Now, if you're like me, married for some twenty years, you probably have a lot of collected sheets, towels, etc. Some of them you bought, others you inherited, while others are in tatters. So…

## THE LINEN CLOSET

### TOWELS

1. Take everything out.

2. Clean the shelves and cover them with contact paper.

3. Separate the hand towels, bath towels, and face towels.

4. Discard any towels that you would be ashamed to showcase in front of a guest. These towels could be sent to the garage for car duty or to the pet supply closet to wash the pets. They also make great rags that can be used to clean up spills.

5. Take out any towels that you don't like or that don't dry very well. (Some have a polyester nap that doesn't absorb water.)

6. Check and see if you have too many towels. The most you should have is two bath / face / hand towels per person and perhaps one set of "fancy" towels for special occasions or guests. Any extra towels means that you're just stockpiling.

7. My kids are always after me to make up color combinations for them; each child has their own special colored towel. (I'm waiting for my towels to disintegrate and a great sale!) You may choose to monogram the towels with their names or initials.

8. Stack the towels with the fold facing you. This makes neat piles. Also, try to stack by size.

## SHEETS & PILLOWCASES

1. Divide them by sets: pillowcases, flat sheet, and fitted sheet that will make up one bed.

2. Now get rid of the ones that you could do without or are in bad shape. (When I had my garage sale the sheets and towels were the first to go.)

3. In front of you, there should be lots of piles; each pile makes up one bed. You shouldn't have more than two sets per bed (unless you have a large linen closet or there are only two of you).  One set of sheets is on the bed, whereas the other set is in the closet. If I were just starting out, I'd buy only one set per bed. What better way to save time then to wash that set and put it back on the bed. *

4. Put the sheets you chose back in the closet. Keep them together as a set. Thus, when you need to change the bed, you can grab the complete set and not have go hunt for pieces. Now doesn't that look good?

5. If you keep extra blankets in the linen closet (I keep mine in the bedroom closets), then do the same. Keep only the blankets you need per bed; additional blankets should also be kept for guests. Another good place to store spare blankets is between the mattresses.

6. A neat way to keep extra pillows is by making decorative pillow cases or shams, sticking the pillow in it, and then tossing it on your family room couch. The kids love it, and so does dad when he wants to snooze.

This should take care of the linen closet unless you keep items in there that aren't linens.  By the time you're done, you should be able to see everything you have, and have lots of room, and the sheets should be so well organized that when you need one you can just grab it.

**Hint**: If you're into saving money, buy a double flat sheet instead of the pillowcases and you'll be able to make 3-4 pillowcases! All you need to do is cut, sew up the sides, and hem.  There's also an advantage to having white sheets (in lieu of colored sheets):  they can be bleached.

# THE BEDROOMS

## DRESSERS

1. You know the drill now. First go through the dressers and take everything out. Throw away all the clothes that are stained or torn, or set them aside for painting in. Then put the ones that you can't stand anymore, but that are in decent shape, in the charity or garage sale pile. If I had a basement, I'd store painting/work clothes down there.

2. Clean the drawers before you put everything back in.

3. Think about how many changes of clothes your kids need. A lot of us get hand-me-downs or great bargains and end up with too many clothes and no where to put them. Or else you stick them in the dresser and there are so many things that by the end of the day the drawer is in shambles. A child does not need more than three or four changes of everyday clothes. Especially if you homeschool. How many socks and underpants do you have to have? Enough to make it to the next washday which you probably do at least twice a week, if not more often. In our home, washday is almost every other day. (That reminds me, kids do not need to throw out their clothes every day especially if they didn't play hard or they're not dirty. By not washing the clothes every time you wear them you're saving on wear and tear and electricity and water. The same with towels. They can be used at least three or four times before being washed. I guarantee you that seventy years ago our grandmas didn't wash clothes more than once a week.) So seriously consider how many changes they need and get rid of the excess. The same goes with Sunday clothes – perhaps two or three dresses, and one or two dress pants. And if you want to make sure that you'll get those Sunday shirts clean, buy white. Bleach does wonders!

## CLOSETS

1. Next – heaven help you – open the closet door. If everything doesn't fall out on you then you're blessed! Take everything out and clean out all the corners. Now go to it. If something's been in there for six months and no one has worn it, played with it, or even looked at it, then I consider it a prime candidate to be chucked. Closets are notorious places to collect things that you just can't part with. Well, part with it! If you have puzzles that have already been done, consider selling them. How many times do you want to put together the same 500 piece puzzle? And you can always buy another very cheaply at a garage sale or thrift store. Or better yet, trade with friends!

If you keep blankets and pillows in the closet, make sure you stick them in large plastic bags (label the bags) so they don't get dirty or dusty. Then you don't have to wash them before using them.

2.  Keep off-season clothing, or outgrown clothes, in a big plastic box marked with the gender, age, and size. If you don't have plastic bins, keep them in plastic bags. If bugs aren't a problem, put them in cardboard boxes and store in the attic or basement by size.

3.  It's nice to have a couple of shelves above your rod, and shoe shelves on the bottom of the closet. This adds a lot of space. If possible, keep sneakers in the mudroom for ready wear outdoors.

4.  Keep toys and books in marked boxes.

5.  Once again get rid of dirty, smelly shoes and consider how many pair a child needs. I find that shoes are almost impossible for me to hand down in my family. None of them wear the same type of shoe: one has a long skinny foot, the other a short fat foot, and so on.

6.  It's great to put up a corkboard in the kids' rooms for them to hang up their calendars and other important documents. Pegboards with hooks are nice for hanging things, and a rack for baseball caps is both fun and decorative for boys.

7.  Go through the clothes and discard the bad, the ugly, and the extras.

8.  If you have more than one child sharing a closet try to split it in two down the middle. (Your halfway mark could be a sheet or tablecloth hung on a pant hangar.) This makes it much easier to search for clothes when you're in a hurry.

9.  If you have more than two sharing a closet try this idea (this works well if you color coordinate your kids). Hang all the boys' brown dress pants on one hanger, their blue dress pants on another hanger, etc. Hang all the white shirts next to each other, all the blue ones together, etc. Then when it's time to dress up, it's very easy to grab the right clothes. (This suggestion came from my friend, Cynthia, who has five boys sharing one closet.)

10.  If your closet is full of "skinny" clothes waiting for the day you'll shed those extra 20 or 30 pounds, consider whether they need to be kept hanging in the closet. That day may never come and meanwhile your closet is full. Instead, pack them away in a box, label them "skinny clothes," and store them away! (Usually, when you lose the weight you're ready for a new wardrobe anyway!)

# MORE STORAGE SPACE

1.  If your kids are into Legos and you keep them in their bedroom, I suggest trying to squeeze in a table for them to work at. Above the table put up a shelf that can hold their completed projects. Near their workspace put a light.

2.  A great place to store Legos is in a plastic four or five drawer cabinet. You can buy them at the office supply stores, Sams, or WalMart. They're about four feet high and 15 inches wide. And they can store an awful lot of Legos.

3.  If your kids collect books, and they should, they need bookshelves to place them on. Each of our children has their own six or seven foot high bookshelf. Buy the highest bookshelves you can find or afford. (Garage sales are a good place to look for shelving.) Or build your own.

4.  Put a shelf up above their dresser to place models or trophies.

5.  You can buy plastic storage boxes that fit under the bed to store winter or summer clothes, or toys.

6.  A bunk bed is a great space saver except that it's a pain in the neck to make the bed. One suggestion is to use a duvet – it's a comforter covered with a sheet that can be removed to wash. This eliminates the need for a top sheet and there's no tucking in anything.

7.  Plastic crates are an alternative for storing toys and things.

8.  On the subject of toys – how many does a child need? I don't care if you get it for free, it takes up space. My baby was given so many different types of toys. Does she play with them? Of course not. A spoon or pot or pencil and paper is much more to her liking. So out the toys went!

If you're wondering why I'm so into storage, remember we live in sunny Florida where there are no basements, therefore **NO STORAGE SPACE**. You have to be real creative here. I do have a crawl space in my attic but I would never put anything of value up there because it gets tremendously hot in the summertime. I've seen what the heat does to my clothes in the house (elastic deteriorates in a few years). I would hate to see what a Florida attic would do to them!

If you've de-cluttered your bathroom, linen closet, and bedrooms, you're in great shape. You're halfway there! Keep on truckin'!

# THE LIVING ROOM/FAMILY ROOM

Each family has different things in these rooms. I would recommend looking at the following:

1. Your walls – are they cluttered? Are there too many pictures hanging? Take down what you really don't care for.  I received a lot of hand-me-down pictures and statues from my family. Some I really cherish, but quite a few I hung up and don't like at all.  Be brave, throw it out, hide it, or give it to your sister!

2. Look at your furniture. Do you have too much? Is it only cluttering up the room? Play with it; rearrange it.  See if there's a better way to show it off.  Clear excess junk off coffee tables.  If you have a tendency to make piles everywhere (books, Bible, sewing project, etc.) buy yourself a basket to put it all in.  It will look much neater during the day and if you're going to have company you can quickly hide the basket. Some neat ideas are: large baskets that can be found cheaply at garage sales, a wicker laundry basket (they come in all sizes), a plastic crate, or a wall-papered box.  Always try to buy end tables that can double up as storage space – the kind that have drawers and doors!

3. Shoes that pile up by the door can be dropped into a large wicker laundry basket.  At least they're all in one place!

4. Keep a basket near the front door (or whichever door you use all the time) to put all the little things you need to return to friends. Then they're easy to collect whenever you're ready to go out, or they stop by.

5. If you have stairs, place a container somewhere near the stairs to collect all the goodies that need to go back up, or down.

6. If you live up North, you can make or buy a wall unit made up of crates so that each child could have his own "cubby hole" to store his hat, mittens, boots.  A wooden shelf with hooks is great for jackets and scarves.

## DINING ROOM

1. If you have a china cabinet now is the time to look inside. If you're like me, you have crystal, silver, and linen that was given to you as wedding gifts.  Do I ever use them? Should I keep them or sell them? Only your heart can decide that.

2. Check and see if your china cabinet has become the secret hiding place for all your little souvenirs. If it has, do they mean anything to you? If not, take them out! (In fact, it's all those fancy doodads that we collect or get as gifts that really clutter our homes. We're so emotionally attached to them that we keep putting them anywhere there's space. Consider getting rid of them or storing them away.)

3. Get rid of any broken pieces. Crystal or china that has a crack or chip can be dangerous.

4. Don't let your dining room table become the catch all place for anything and everything. If you have to, put a big flower arrangement in the middle with a fancy tablecloth so that everyone knows this space is off limits!

## THE KITCHEN

I've saved the best for last! Kitchen drawers and cabinets can become hiding places for all kinds of junk.

1. Empty your drawers (one at a time) and clean them.

2. Check and see how many ladles you have, wooden spoons, measuring cups. How many spoons do you really need? Get rid of the excess.

3. Store cooking instruments that you use all the time in a round turntable. Pampered Chef sells an extra large one that can house a lot of utensils. If you have the space, hang utensils on hooks underneath your cabinets or on the inside of the cabinet doors.

4. Go through your pots and pans and take out what you don't use. Sell it! (For one month monitor your pot and pan needs.)

5. Check your spices. Discard old ones or those that you never use. Buy a Lazy Susan.

6. Sell or throw away cookbooks you never look at. Check and see if you **really** need them all. (Ouch!)

7. Go through your silverware. Get rid of things that don't belong there. Clean out the drawer.

8. Check your dishes and glasses. Do you need everything in there? Make sure the shelves are nice and clean before you reshelf.

9. Clean under the sink. You may be unpleasantly surprised at what you find down there. If you have small children, do not use that space to store your poisonous cleaning products. Small children love to open cabinets and take everything out. I advise keeping as little as possible down there! Perhaps the pet food? Or your large mixer?

10. Do you need all those bowls? Do you use all those plastic products that you splurged on years ago at your friend's "plastic" party? I actually sold some of our plastics at our garage sale. I got tired of having it all fall out on me every time I reached inside the pantry. (And I never know what to do with all the lids. They won't stay put!) I've finally decided it's best to keep all the lids together, sideways, against the wall. Or put them in a cardboard box, standing on end. (Then you can remove the box to find the lid.) I nest all the round containers inside one another, all the squares together, and the oddballs get tossed in the corner. Think about how much food you would have to make in order to use every single plastic container you own. Use them to freeze your food in. (I also find that it's more cost effective to use see-through containers. That way you can salvage the leftovers before they turn moldy!)

11. If you're lucky enough to have a pantry, clean it well. Here in Florida we're prone to getting invasions of bugs: ants, ants, and more ants. And if it isn't an ant, it's probably one of those weevils that invades the macaroni. Last spring we had such an invasion. It took us a year to get rid of the weevils. What a nightmare! (And to think that I actually paid the grocery store for them and brought them into our pantry myself!) We had to throw away everything, and I mean everything, that didn't have an airtight seal. Now everything, and I mean everything, is placed in airtight containers when I come home from the store.

12. Really check the pantry and make sure that it's not being used as a catch all for things that you don't know where to store. Organize. Put the food in some sort of order. Place little objects in boxes. (Use that Tupperware!) We place our soda bottles on the floor. If you buy whole grain wheat, or other products in bulk, go to your grocery store's bakery and ask them if they have huge plastic buckets they use for frosting. My store gave them to me for free. Each container holds twenty-five pounds of whole wheat kernels.

13. Clean your refrigerator inside and out. Throw away condiments and medicines that you've been saving and never use. Throw anything away that's past its expiration date.

14. On the outside, clean up those magnets and drawings. Do you really need so many? Just for fun take everything off and see what you think of the "bare look."

15. Look on top of the fridge. Is that another storage place for the unwanted and unloved?

16. Take a good look at all your cleaning products. Do you need so many different things? One can of scouring powder, one bottle of all purpose cleaning liquid (like Pine Sol or Lysol), a rug cleaning spray and brush (especially if you have pets), some window cleaner, and perhaps some furniture polish should do it. Those products can clean everything and anything. And what they won't clean, liquid bleach will.

17. Keep one old toothbrush and one old sponge under the sink for those tough dirty jobs.

18. Try and keep the mail out of the kitchen. You know what happens: someone brings it in and dumps it on the counter and it never leaves. It's been velcroed there for life! Try going through your mail before you ever come into the house; deposit the junk in the garbage! The more you train yourself to do this, the better you'll get at it, and soon you'll be throwing away the junk mail without even opening it! As you walk in, separate into piles and give each person their pile. As for your pile, go through it immediately and throw away what you don't need. If you can't make a decision as you look at it, you probably never will. Put the rest of your mail in its proper place. (Be very careful about handing out your name and address. You don't want to be put on every mailing list in the U.S.A.)

19. Don't let anyone put the newspaper on the counter. Have a basket (I use our fireplace log bin) to throw it in until you get a chance to read it.

20. Don't collect free literature unless you really want it. You know what happens to it: it gets buried underneath a large pile of "important" stuff only to resurface months later. Usually the literature sits around for months and then one day you calmly look at it, declare it "junk," and toss it in the garbage! (This is paper pollution!)

21. Books do not belong on the counters either. I throw them on the kitchen table and they must be gone before we eat.

22. You should have a place designated for recycling. We have a garbage can in our pantry that we throw the plastics and aluminum cans into. I hung a big plastic bag low to the ground for the plastic bags we collect. We use our paper bags for the garbage so we don't need to buy plastic garbage bags. Our newspapers go out in the garage. A basement is a great place to set up a recycling center. Place three large garbage cans: one for plastics, one for glass, and one for aluminum.

23. Place a large cork bulletin board in your kitchen (about 4X3 feet). Buy a large desk calendar and hang that up. That way there's lots of room to write in on each day. On top I put important phone numbers. I mark everything on that calendar. I don't use a day planner. All my important notices get pinned up there. Once every couple of weeks throw away the old stuff. Make it a habit to pin anything important up there and you'll always know where it is.

24. I just got rid of our very large microwave/convection oven and haven't replaced it. I love having the extra counter space. Instead, I now have lovely canisters with sugar and flour and tea that I use all the time. I'm going to be putting up a four-foot shelf for all my spices and pretty glass containers. Those are great decorations for a kitchen. Some of you may be appalled that I dared to get rid of my microwave. It really isn't missed at all. We're using the oven a lot more and the food is tasting a lot better. I found that I was mostly using the microwave for re-heating. If I could have a midget one tucked away in some secret corner, I would do it just so I could reheat my coffee and tea. But until the day comes to renovate our kitchen, we're going to be microwave free. (The two things I do miss a microwave for? Making popcorn and re-heating my morning coffee!)

25. I never used a dishwasher until I got eczema on my hands. Water aggravated it, so I began to use the dishwasher. The kids were always grumbling about emptying it. They hated it. Our dishwasher did not wash very well. The dishes were always coming out dirty. So we stopped using it. I wash the breakfast dishes and put them away (I wear latex gloves to protect my hands), and the others take care of lunch and dinner. The kids actually enjoy it. It gives them a chance to work together, talk, share stories, and more. I think it was one of my better moves.

26. If your kitchen is dingy and you can't afford major renovations try painting it a nice bright color. It does wonders for the kitchen and you!

27. Compost!

## SUMMARY:

The more often you de-clutter, the easier it gets and the easier it gets to clean the house.

There is no "set way" to de-clutter. No one way is better than another. Each person needs to find their own method, time, and motivation. Just do it!

*"I also have in my mind that seemingly wealthy, but most impoverished class of all, who have accumulated dross, but know not how to use it, or get rid of it, and thus have forged their own golden or silver fetters."*

*Walden* by Henry David Thoreau

## FURTHER READING:

**Clutter's Last Stand** by Don Aslett (Ohio: Writer's Digest Books, 1984)*

**Is There Life After Housework?** by Don Aslett (OH: Writer's Digest Books,1981)

**Make Your House Do The Housework** by Don Aslett Ohio: Betterway Books, 1995)

**The Sidetracked Sisters' Happiness File** by Pam Young and Peggy Jones (NY: Warner Books, 1985)

**The Simple Living Guide** by Janet Luhrs (NY: Broadway Books, 1997)

**401 Ways To Get Your Kids To Work At Home** by Bonnie Runyan McCullough and Susan Walker Monson (NY: St.Martin's Press, 1981)

*Don Aslett sells his own product line and has a quarterly newsletter he publishes, in which he gives advice and sells.  Write to:

Don Aslett's Cleaning Center
PO Box 39
Pocatello,Idaho 83204
(800)451-2402, FAX (208)232-6286

His books can be found at the public library.

# SIMPLIFYING HELP-AID

| BATHROOM: | | DISCARD OUTGROWN | | TOO MANY COOKBOOKS? | |
|---|---|---|---|---|---|
| MEDICINE CABINET | | ENOUGH SHELVES? | | CLEAN UNDER SINK | |
| DRAWERS | | ENOUGH RODS? | | TOO MANY BOWLS? | |
| SHOWER / BATH | | BOX TOYS | | OUTDATED FOOD? | |
| TOWEL RACK | | MORE SHELVES? | | ANY BUGS IN THERE? | |
| MISC. | | TOO MANY TOYS? | | CLEAN OUTSIDE FRIDGE | |
| | | NEED CORKBOARD? | | CLEAN INSIDE FRIDGE | |
| | | NEED EXTRA STORAGE? | | TOO MANY MAGNETS? | |
| LINEN CLOSET: | | | | LOOK UNDER & BEHIND FRIDGE! | |
| TOWELS | | | | LOOK ON TOP OF FRIDGE | |
| SEPARATE | | | | LOOK UNDER & BEHIND STOVE | |
| DISCARD SHABBY | | | | LOOK UNDER & BEHIND MICRO | |
| TOO MANY? | | LIVING/FAMILY ROOM: | | TOO MANY CLEANING PRODUCTS | |
| COLOR CODED? | | CLUTTERED WALLS? | | SET SPOT FOR MAIL | |
| CONTACT PAPER | | TOO MUCH FURNITURE? | | DE-CLUTTER COUNTERS | |
| | | NEED A SHOE BASKET? | | RECYCLING SPOT? | |
| BEDDING: | | NEED A TOY BASKET? | | COMPOST SPOT? (YES!!!) | |
| MAKE SETS | | STAIR CONTAINER? | | CORK BOARD? | |
| DISCARD SHABBY | | | | CALENDAR? | |
| TOO MANY? | | | | | |
| STORE BLANKETS | | DINING ROOM: | | | |
| | | TOO MUCH CLUTTER? | | MISC: | |
| | | CLEAN CHINA CABINET | | | |
| DRESSERS: | | BROKEN CHINA? | | | |
| REMOVE EVERYTHING | | TABLE CLEAR? | | | |
| CLEAN & PAPER | | NEED A CENTERPIECE? | | | |
| DISCARD SHABBY | | | | | |
| TOO MANY? | | | | | |
| | | KITCHEN: | | | |
| | | EMPTY ALL DRAWERS | | | |
| CLOSETS: | | CONTACT PAPER? | | | |
| REMOVE EVERYTHING | | DISCARD OLD/BROKEN | | | |
| STORE PILLOWS | | OR USELESS UTENSILS | | | |
| STORE BLANKETS | | TOO MANY UTENSILS? | | | |
| DIVIDE BY SEASON | | TOO MANY POTS/PANS? | | | |
| DIVIDE BY CHILD | | DISCARD OLD SPICES | | | |

# CHAPTER
## ♥ 11 ♥

# THE SCHOOLROOM
## Or
## The Last Frontier!

The last frontier to conquer is your schoolroom. I'll begin by telling you a bit about mine. I don't have one. When I first began to homeschool and only had two children, I turned one of the spare bedrooms into a real cute schoolroom. But as my kids grew up, and my family kept growing, I found that I didn't want to be locked away on one side of the house; I wanted to work in the heart of my home – the kitchen. This way we can all be together and I can still cook, clean, and do whatever I need. From this space I can see the smaller ones playing. So we moved our huge dining room table next to our kitchen. Meanwhile, my dining room became the official home of all the school books, computer, and school paraphernalia. We decided to use every square inch of our home!

Over the years, my philosophy of home education has evolved and been refined. I now truly believe that "life is school," and therefore you can't confine school to a certain area of your home. Instead, we make every room and the great outdoors our schoolroom. This is much more natural and integrates so much more smoothly into everyday life. You no longer feel as if "now it's school" and "now it's regular home." Recently we moved all of our schoolbooks and library into the family room and we all love it. Finally the heart of our home reflects our lifestyle. All of us are crazy about books and love to be surrounded by them so we don't want to hide them away in a corner. We have four huge bookcases filled with all of our favorite reading and it looks just like a real library. My husband, who sells homeschooling books, is going to move his stock into the dining room next to the computer and file cabinets. Almost every room in our house has a bookcase. Each child has his own bookcase to house his personal collection. The children grew up knowing that books are an important and meaningful part of their lives, not something to be looked at only during school hours or while at the library. By housing our books in the heart of our home the kids are always reaching for them.

I think the best way to de-clutter your schoolroom is to realize that there just isn't any more room for another book. So either you stop buying (who'd want to do that?), or you get rid of books that just aren't needed anymore, have been outgrown, were never actually used, or will never be used. I looked and touched each and every book on my bookshelves to decide which one was going and which was staying. Each book is a dear friend, bringing back fond memories and cherished stories of where and when it was received or purchased. So you can truly believe that de-cluttering my library was not an easy task, but it was accomplished! And the best part is that now I have lots of room for additional books!

I've never purchased a lot of workbooks because they're not cost efficient with five children (they're consumables) and usually they're not that much fun. Mostly my workbooks have been for lower level math and phonics. What I purchase a lot of is novels: historical, science (yes, they do have science novels or non-fiction written in a novel format), biographies, and classics. I have a huge science and history reference section. What I don't have a lot of is textbooks (see chapter "Curriculum This, Curriculum That, Which One's The Best?"). The longer we homeschool, the further we get away from them. I purchase textbooks cheaply at garage sales or used curriculum fairs and put them in my reference library. I collect classics, art books, travel books, geography, anything that looks interesting to read. Garage sales, library sales, used bookstores, and curriculum sales are the best places to find cheap deals (in that order too!).

**Hint**: Your best bet is to wait for a used curriculum fair because you're not going to make any money on your school stuff at a garage sale. A used curriculum fair is usually organized by your local support group some time in the late spring before your state homeschooling convention; it's meant to be an opportunity to sell all those books that you're done using and hopefully buy used books that you'll need. If your support group doesn't organize such a fair, you should seriously consider organizing one yourself. You'll be doing yourself and others a great service!

## STEPS TO ORGANIZING A SCHOOLROOM / LIBRARY

1. Really look at those books and decide whether they're worthy of staying and hogging up space. If you don't use a certain textbook anymore, get rid of it. I've collected so many math books, grammars, and literature readers. I don't need all of them. Don't keep the book if you don't plan on using it as a reference or reading it.

2. Before you put the books back on the shelf, dust and clean all the bookshelves and the books.

3. Now put the books back by subject. For example:

   American History
   World History
   Biographies
   Classical Literature (putting it in alphabetical order by author really helps your search)
   Historical novels
   Science reference books and novels
   Religious texts, references, and novels
   Math books and games
   English grammar, dictionary, thesaurus
   Encyclopedia
   Geography

   You won't believe how much easier life will be when you know exactly where your books are.  Think of all the frustrated minutes or hours spent searching for a book you know you own but for the life of you can't find.   And teach your kids to put them back in the right section when they're done reading!  If you're really organized, set up a "personal library" spreadsheet in the computer.  This will help you keep track of what books you own, as well as to whom you've lent them.  You can enter them by author or title.  It's a great list to take with you to curriculum fairs so you don't buy the same book twice!  If you have older children, give them this job!

4. Periodically clean out your library. Make sure the books are still in the right sections.

5. Go through all your computer programs. Discard the ones that are never being used.  Put programs that are used infrequently out of children's reach.

6. Go through each file cabinet and throw away old, useless papers and catalogs. Remember – you can't keep it all!

7. Organize your own work area. You must have a spot where you can work. I work near the computer and have two shelves above my over-sized desk. We got this desk for free and it's great. It holds my computer, speakers, keyboard and mouse, light, and CD rack. This is also where I keep all of my important documents and books that I use frequently, such as dictionaries, grammars, and thesaurus.  All these items sit on top of my desk and I still have plenty of room to work.

8. You do not need to keep every workbook your child ever used.  All you really need is your log and your portfolio, which is a sample of their

work.  I make a portfolio for my children each year. (Older children can create their own.) When they were younger I combined them all in one three-ring binder, now they each have their own.  In their portfolios I keep souvenirs of their fieldtrips, pictures, and samples of their work in each subject from the beginning, middle, and end of the year.  Any prizes or achievements they may have received are filed in the portfolio.  Then I throw away ( **Yes! Throw away!**) their workbooks.  So all you need to keep on the shelf are non-consumables.  And you only need to keep those if you have younger children.  Don't save completed workbooks unless you live in a mansion.

9. If you collect magazines for the children, or homeschooling magazines for yourself, buy some cardboard magazine holders to store them in and place them neatly on your bookshelf. (You can also make your own magazine holders out of old cardboard cereal boxes.) Throw out, pass along, or sell any that you or your child will probably never look at again.  If you do want your kids to be constantly looking at certain magazines, then don't hide them.  Put them somewhere accessible, like in the heart of your home.

10. Look though all your school supplies, such as math manipulatives.  Do you use them; have you ever used them?  If not, out they go!  (Re-sell them at the used curriculum sale.)  You'll be amazed at how much space you'll make when you get rid of all those things you've been collecting that you think you may someday use.

11. Put all your writing paper, notebooks, notepads, three ring binders, folders, sheet protectors, etc. on one shelf.  I keep a box of old discarded computer paper under my desk for the kids to draw on.

12.  Arrange a special drawer, or drawers, for all your art supplies, from colored pencils to drawing paper to crayons.  This way your kids know where all their art supplies are located,  won't have to ask you, and will actually use them.  We had an old dresser that we were going to throw away and ended up keeping in our enclosed lanai (porch). That whole dresser holds nothing but art supplies.

13. Put all your pencils, pens, markers, erasers, and rulers in a large plastic drawer (they're sold separately with the intent that you can buy many and stack them one on top of the other).  We keep this drawer in a handy place next to the pencil sharpener.  Or place writing implements in sturdy unbreakable mugs and keep them in convenient corners throughout the house. Keep a pair of paper scissors in each mug (perhaps chaining it to the handle as scissors always have a tendency to disappear).

14. Put self-stick note paper in a drawer with other important school and office supplies. The sticky papers (the small ones that look like tabs) are great to put in books to mark special sections.

15. It's a good idea to buy yourself at least one file cabinet to store all your important documents, vendor catalogs, and information on various subjects that you've collected. (Set up files in categories like this: curriculum bills, neat field trip ideas, unit study ideas, games, math info, science info, etc.) Divide your catalogs into categories such as science, math, toys, religion, etc. It will be much easier to find it next time.

16. Designate a special bookshelf or shelves for yourself. Put all of your important books here (and books of special interest) that you may need to find in a hurry.

17. We have a personal copier at home, which may seem like an extravagance, but for a homeschooling family it's almost a necessity. We seem to be making copies all the time. If you really want one, look around for a used one. If you have friends that work in offices tell them that you're looking for a used one. (Technology is changing so rapidly that many offices upgrade their equipment frequently. They may sell their old equipment to you inexpensively, or better yet, give it to you free of charge.) That's how we got a free fax machine. The office next to my husband's was moving and didn't need it anymore (probably because it was one of the original larger models). But for our purposes (a fax about every four months), it's great.

18. Make sure you tell your kids where they can set up their work area for messy projects. Tell them where you want them to work and teach them how to clean up.

# The Library

It looks like any building
When you pass it on the street,
Made of stone and glass and marble,
Made of iron and concrete.

But once inside you can ride
A camel or a train,
Visit Rome, Siam, or Nome,
Feel a hurricane,
Meet a king, learn to sing,
How to bake a pie,
Go to sea, plant a tree,
Find how airplanes fly,
Train a horse, and of course
Have all the dogs you'd like,
See the moon, a sandy dune,
Or catch a whopping pike.
Everything that books can bring
You'll find inside those walls.
A world is there for you to share
When adventure calls.

You cannot tell its magic
By the way the building looks,
But there's wonderment within it,
The wonderment of books.

By Barbara A. Huff

# MY LIBRARY LIST

| AUTHOR | TITLE | SUBJECT | LOANED TO | RETURNED |
|--------|-------|---------|-----------|----------|
|  |  |  |  |  |
|  |  |  |  |  |
|  |  |  |  |  |
|  |  |  |  |  |
|  |  |  |  |  |
|  |  |  |  |  |
|  |  |  |  |  |
|  |  |  |  |  |
|  |  |  |  |  |
|  |  |  |  |  |
|  |  |  |  |  |
|  |  |  |  |  |
|  |  |  |  |  |
|  |  |  |  |  |
|  |  |  |  |  |
|  |  |  |  |  |
|  |  |  |  |  |
|  |  |  |  |  |
|  |  |  |  |  |
|  |  |  |  |  |
|  |  |  |  |  |

# CHAPTER
## ♥ 12 ♥

## SCHEDULES, SCHEDULES, AND MORE SCHEDULES

It seems as if our lives today are run by schedules. You can't escape them. Moms now carry handy-dandy day planners with them everywhere they go so that they don't forget a date, or can make sure they have room for another pressing engagement. Has it occurred to anyone that this is not the norm; that this is a phenomenon of the nineties? Ten years ago day planners were only for executives with busy days full of urgent appointments to keep track of. Have we all suddenly become executives? (If so, where's the salary that goes with it?)

I propose that we all throw away our planners and live by the seat of our pants. And if, by chance, we forget an appointment or two, perhaps it's the will of God. My friend stated that there is no real difference between a day planner and a kitchen wall calendar. One's just like the other, used for exactly the same purpose. After considering the matter for awhile, I beg to <u>strongly</u> disagree. A wall calendar is a fixture in our kitchen. We write things on it for the benefit of the entire family. We glance at it during the day to see if there's anything special or urgent going on in the next few days. But a day planner's sole purpose is to be carried around everywhere specifically to record any and all commitments. I believe that they encourage us to over-commit!

We've undertaken the responsibility of raising and educating our kids and we're filling up day planners with lots of extraneous appointments. I know – they're field trips and excursions and doctor's appointments and luncheons and meetings and exam dates and 4-H fairs and co-op dates. Do you get the picture? Should we be doing all of this? If we spent a little more time at home raising our kids and taking care of the hearth we wouldn't need day planners. If I can't remember to put it on my kitchen calendar, it probably isn't all that important. And if I can't remember what I'm doing next Tuesday, then I'm in a heap of trouble. I should have a set routine for Tuesdays, and if there just so happens to be a special field trip or meeting that day, it should be the exception and not the rule, so I should be able to remember it without even looking at a calendar. If I have so many functions planned that I need to check my planner before I can commit to something, then I know I'm running around too much and am over-committed.

I'll let you in on what our family does for outside activities. My children have been playing stringed instruments since they were four years old, so I know that every Monday afternoon I have group lessons, and that two other afternoons of the week they have private lessons. They also play piano, but the teacher comes to our home (and that's a blessing!). This is the first year that my eldest is playing in a youth symphony orchestra on Monday evenings, but we carpool that every three weeks so it's not a big hassle. The only other permanent activity we have is Karate, which is my husband's responsibility entirely. Our reason for having the kids take Karate is this: when I was in my early twenties someone made an attempt on my life. Since then, both my husband and I have said that we would teach our children self-defense. This commitment takes most of the family out of the home two nights a week. The rest of what we do comes and goes from month to month, season to season. Most everything we do undertake is considered part of our children's schooling. I am also blessed with having a husband who has very flexible work hours, lots of vacation, and who doesn't mind taking the kids places himself. If all the driving was up to me, then we would do a lot less. Also, all of our activities are within 10 or 15 minutes of our home. (I've noticed that I sometimes become overwhelmed in the spring. I think this is an emotional reaction to the coming of the end-of-the school year. I need to consciously make sure we don't take on too many activities then.)

I've learned over the years that if what you're doing is important to you, you'll do it; if it's not important to you, you'll be very lackadaisical about the commitment. Both my husband and I feel very strongly that the activities we choose are part of our kids' ongoing education; therefore we're going to do our utmost to live up to their commitments. Parents who take extra curricular activities seriously are going to make sure that their kids do what's expected of them. The problem with many homeschoolers is that they don't feel this obligation to the activities they take on. I don't believe that they see them as part of their kids' education. Many don't even bother to call and tell you that they won't be there, or are no longer participating. Or else the kids come totally unprepared to the meeting or class because the parents never bother to follow up and find out what's expected of the children. This is so sad. Not only are they short-changing their kids on an interesting experience, but they're also teaching them that it's not important to live up to their commitments. If you're not going to follow through, don't sign up!

Another significant issue is discipline, which goes hand-in-hand with living up to your scheduled commitments. Many people are amazed at how I get my kids to practice their music day in and day out for so many years. Their woe is that their child just won't practice. The child finds it boring; they hate it. What I tell them is this: we started our kids at music early – four years old. It's a part of their lives and ours. They know that they have to practice every day and there's no argument about it. It's the very first thing they do each and every day. The older two do everything on their own; they don't need prodding at all. I believe that anything that requires a lot of concentration needs to be taken care of first thing in the morning. So after they practice their music, they do math, which is probably their hardest subject. Then after they accomplish these things, the rest of the day is a piece of cake. It's very important to instill discipline in your children, as well as yourself. If you do anything when you first begin to homeschool, you should begin with discipline training, the ability to control a behavior; it also means learning to stick to something until it's accomplished. Both should be taught together. And I believe parents need to work at it probably as much, if not more, than their children. Discipline and scheduling go together like soup and sandwich! Parents need to be disciplined enough so that once they commit to an activity, they follow through.

Before attempting to schedule your family's life, consider how you're going to handle people who call and request that you do something for them, be it one particular activity or a whole series of meetings. If whatever they're asking you to do isn't dear to your heart, it's easy to say no. But other times you begin to feel guilty about not doing what they ask you. The cause may seem so worthwhile, something that really needs to get done and you could do it so easily and well. **You need to realize that your first obligation is to your family!** You've undertaken to raise and educate your children. You can't do that if you're running around organizing other activities that have nothing at all to do with your family or interests. You must seriously consider whether this activity fits into your goals and purpose in life. If it does, then do you have enough time and energy to do it? If you don't, say no. If the activity doesn't fit into your plan, say no. You need to concentrate your attention and energy on what is important for your family. That's your number one concern. Be prepared for those interruptions and have a ready answer; don't wait until you're asked and then be caught unprepared and sputtering to think of a quick excuse.

I've also realized that with a large family it isn't necessary to have to do things with other people. We are a group and taking field trips on our own is much more fun and constructive. When you have to deal with large groups, usually you're going to encounter discipline problems, which definitely is the downside to planned field trips or classes. Try going on field trips alone, or with only one or two other families. Co-op with one or two other families, instead of always trying to organize a large group. I think you'll discover it's much more stress free and productive.

Another point to consider is that sometimes you get more accomplished at home than you do as a group. Take, for example, sewing. My daughters belong to a sewing group with a fantastic teacher. The only problem is that there are eleven girls and even though the teacher now has another lady to help her, they just can't get around to everyone that quickly. When children are learning to sew they have lots of questions and they need them answered before they can sew another stitch. So one day we "skipped" our sewing class and accomplished in an hour and a half what the class couldn't get done in four hours. You have to consider whether the "socialization" factor is important enough to leave home. (Of course, if you can't sew, or do whatever it is you're learning as a group, then it is valuable to take classes.  But I would check around to see if you don't have a friendly neighbor or aunt who could give them private lessons.)

Back to schedules.  Keep yours simple.

## Calendars:

1. Buy a large desk type calendar and hang it on a corkboard in your kitchen, or wherever you will look at it faithfully.  It's convenient to have a telephone close by. (If you have the wall space or the back of a door handy, buy a large laminated year calendar so that you can see the whole year at a glance and mark down all those important days in advance. These calendars are available in office supply stores.)

2. Keep a pen or marker nearby and faithfully record all appointments. Mark recurring commitments with a special bright marker.

3. Keep a list of the most important and frequently called telephone numbers on the corkboard.

4.  Pin all important papers on the corkboard.

5. Make this your message center where you pin up any messages that family members receive while they're gone.

*Rejoice always, pray constantly, give thanks in all circumstances; for this is the will of God in Christ Jesus for you.*
*1 Thessalonians 5:16*

## CLEANING SCHEDULE

Everyone has their own style so you need to do what works best for you and your family.  I'm going to suggest a schedule here that for us is a "work in progress," which means it's adjusted and readjusted as seen fit.  My objective is to try and run a relatively smooth household while I provide a learning environment for my kids.  In order to do this I've compromised somewhat on my cleaning methodology, but usually not on education!  I prioritize.  Education over cleaning; medical emergencies and family crisis over education.

Please - always remember not to become a slave to your schedules. Make one out as a guide for you and your family. Then do with it as feels right to you. As you grow more comfortable in your new lifestyle you'll be adjusting and re-adjusting your schedule to fit your family's priorities. Do make schedules: they help us set goals and determine what needs to be accomplished. But never become a slave to it!

My attitude regarding cleaning has also changed over the years as I've matured. Previously, I would work myself up into a real lather days before cleaning day actually came. Once I began to clean, I was mad. I just wanted to get the job done as quickly as possible; I was upset that I had to do it at all. As I grew older, and developed a better prayer life, I realized that work is part of life. **A large part of life.** It's a means to uniting myself in Christ's suffering. I offer up my chores to our Lord. My "suffering" over cleaning does not compare to Christ's suffering by any means, but in this day and age, most people shun anything to do with the home and family. Washing dishes, doing laundry, cleaning windows, preparing meals is seen as mundane, menial labor. Most people would much rather work outside their home and hire a cleaning lady to do their chores. If I listened to the "world" I would definitely consider the role of a housewife and mother as a punishment and belittling.

I began to read a lot about the Amish and their simple way of life. They spend all their days, except the Sabbath, working their farms to put food on the table. They don't use electricity, cars, or other worldly comforts because these modern conveniences also bring the common world into their midst and with that, all its evils and temptations. Instead, they choose to live a very simple life like our ancestors did over a hundred years ago. In fact, their children only attend school through eighth grade so that they wouldn't be needlessly tempted by this present age. Instead, their children take on adult responsibilities around the house until it's time for them to marry. They dress plainly so that they don't call undue attention upon themselves. Though their uncomplicated lifestyle sounds appealing in this rushed and harried world of ours, I don't believe that I would like to give up **all** my modern conveniences and travel backwards in time. I would rather try and change my present life so that's it's simpler; I want to make my days more joyous; I want to wake up in the morning desiring to do all my daily chores with love and contentment.

We must all realize that there can be real joy in working. When we come to that understanding, then we'll clean the house with a much more pleasant attitude and teach our children with real gusto and enthusiasm. Sometimes we'll have a bad day and be grumpy. But if you take time to consider why you're like that, you'll probably realize that something, or someone, has disrupted your schedule: you're expecting company, you're rushing, you're desperately trying to make everything "perfect," or you're trying to accomplish much more than can possibly be done in a short period of time.

Our forefathers knew what they were doing when they designated certain chores for certain days: Monday - laundry day, Tuesday -ironing, Saturday - baking and bath day. They paced themselves, knowing that every chore had its time and place in their week. That's what we need to learn. We also need to **discipline ourselves** to accomplish certain household tasks everyday. So let's start scheduling!

I've included my schedules so that you can see what our family does. These schedules are not to die for; they are guides to get us through the week. My goal is to have most of the house cleaned by Friday afternoon. This, of course, depends on how much running around we do on Fridays. If we get most of the cleaning done during the week and Friday, then Saturday can be spent doing those "bigger" jobs like cleaning windows, washing the car, outdoor work, sewing, mega cooking. (I would like to get to the point where Sunday's meal is all prepared on Saturday and we can truly enjoy Sunday as the Sabbath.)

The important thing to remember about any schedule is to explain it to everyone that you wish to have follow it. The kids need to know what you expect of them, by when the chores need to be done, and what to expect if they don't do them. For example, when my sons (who are five and eight) are told to clean their room and they don't do a good job, they're grounded - they can't play with their friends. If the girls don't do something (which actually is unusual as they are very diligent) then a good punishment for them might be not to be able to read a favorite book or watch a video that they want to see. I think half the battle of schedules is setting them up and then making sure that you, the household overseer or manager, see to it that everyone completes their tasks.

For those of you who have no big kids, but only little ones, take heart. It does seem like you're completely behind the eight ball because you have no older help, but think of this:

1. Young children love to be mom's helpers. Usually we push them aside because it's so much easier and quicker to do the job ourselves. Don't! Take the extra time and patience to train them to help you. They'll grow up thinking that this is a great privilege, instead of quickly discovering that helping mom is to be avoided at all costs. Use this to your benefit! My daughter just started a compost pile and my five-year old thinks it's a privilege to take out the food to the bin. He's also the only one of all the kids who loves to feed the cats.

2. When you have three or four small children eight and younger it seems that there just aren't enough hours in the day to get everything done. They all need you so much. But remember that those little ones don't need as much time in school as the older ones. **Life is truly their school.** Every chore you do, outing you take, is a learning experience for them. Just think about how much they can learn travelling through

the supermarket. When you change **your** perspective and realize that every minute of your day together is learning time, it's going to free you from the drudgery and shackles of schoolbooks and workbooks. Bake that bread you're dying to make – teach them all about yeast and wheat. (Science! Chemical reaction, chemical change – measurement, nutrition, and health!) Take time to cut and sew an outfit – you're learning about measurement, patience, mechanical instruments (the sewing machine). Enjoy the experience no matter how "dirty" the house gets. You can always clean up later. Those experiences make memories that you will cherish forever.

3. Enjoy your children at the age they are, do the chores you need to do so that the household runs smoothly, and chalk those hours up to home economics. You can count cookies, measure pints and ounces, sort buttons. All of this is school! Don't be a perfectionist! Children are more important than having the ideal clean house. Strive for orderly and neat. There will be plenty of time for serious book learning when they are older. And then you'll have older helpers!

## Don't Forget to Keep on De-cluttering and De-garbaging:

To keep your schedule and cleaning running smoothly make sure that you keep on de-cluttering. This should become a habit . Every time you pass a corner of your house that looks like it's getting out of control, throw some stuff away. There are so many things that we needlessly hold on to assuming that we'll need them someday, or in the near or far future. So we put the article somewhere in a corner only to uncover it months later and still think that we may need it. So we keep it six months longer and we once again uncover it. Perhaps then we're ready to finally get rid of it, but usually only because we don't know where to stash it, so in the end it's easier to throw it away than to keep it.

Once you train yourself to heartlessly throw things away, you're going to notice how easy cleaning really is. You'll scream with delight when all your rooms are picked up nightly and there's no extra clutter lying all around. Make sure you train your children to put all their toys, schoolbooks, and other stuff away nightly so that you wake up to an organized home. When we de-clutter, our home is more organized and neat. When our homes are neat, we feel more cheerful and content. It's a breeze to clean when the time arrives. Don't be a gatherer of goods – be a sifter!

*A stitch in time saves nine!*

## SUMMARY:

1. Avoid becoming over-committed by being very picky about activities you participate in with your children.

2. Take your commitments seriously. If you sign up, follow through. Make sure your child completes his assignments.

3. Try going on field trips as a family, or with only one or two other families.

4. Don't over commit **yourself.** Your family is your most important responsibility. **Learn to say NO!**

5. Consider whether you really need to leave the home for classes or whether you can find someone, a friend or relative, to come to your home.

6. Create a message center in your home centered around a calendar.

7. Check your attitude regarding cleaning. Count it all joy!

8. Simplify everything.

9. Let your family in on your schedule.

10. Always encourage little ones to help you work. Take the time; you'll rejoice later.

11. Keep de-cluttering.


## FURTHER READING:

**401 Ways To Get Your Kids To Work At Home** by Bonnie R. McCullough and Susan W. Monson (NY: St.Martin's Press, 1981)

**Clutter's Last Stand** by Don Aslett (Ohio: Writer's Digest Books, 1984)*

**Is There Life After Housework?** By Don Aslett (OH: Writer's Digest Books,1981)*

**Make Your House Do The Housework** by Don Aslett (Ohio: Betterway Books. 1995)*

**The Sidetracked Sisters' Happiness File** by Pam Young and Peggy Jones (NY: Warner Books, 1985)

*See page 88.

# MASTER HOUSEHOLD CHORELIST

| CHORE | MON | TUES | WED | THUR | FRI | SAT |
|---|---|---|---|---|---|---|
| WASH DISHES | | | | | | |
| DRY DISHES/PUT AWAY | | | | | | |
| SWEEP FLOOR | | | | | | |
| WASH LAUNDRY | | | | | | |
| IRON | | | | | | |
| CLEAN BATHROOM | | | | | | |
| SCHOOLROOM | | | | | | |
| GARBAGE CANS | | | | | | |
| RESPONSIBLE FOR LIVINGROOM | | | | | | |
| RESPONSIBLE FOR FAMILYROOM | | | | | | |
| RESPONSIBLE FOR KITCHEN | | | | | | |
| PICK UP BEDROOM | | | | | | |
| | | | | | | |
| | | | | | | |
| | | | | | | |
| | | | | | | |
| | | | | | | |

THIS MASTER LIST IS HUNG SOMEWHERE PROMINENTLY. IT TELLS THE FAMILY WHO'S RESPONSIBLE FOR WHAT DURING THE WEEK. THE LISTS THAT FOLLOW EXPLAIN TO THE "WORKER" WHAT NEEDS TO BE DONE, WHEN!

## KID'S BEDROOM CHORELIST

| CHORE | MON | TUES | WED | THUR | FRI | SAT |
|---|---|---|---|---|---|---|
| MAKE BED | | | | | | |
| PUT TOYS AWAY | | | | | | |
| STRAIGHTEN BOOKSHELVES | | | | | | |
| STRAIGHTEN DRAWERS | | | | | | |
| PICK UP CLOTHES: PUT AWAY OR THROW IN LAUNDRY | | | | | | |
| STRAIGHTEN CLOSET | | | | | | |
| DUST | | | | | | |
| VACUUM | | | | | | |
| CLEAN MIRROR | | | | | | |
| | | | | | | |
| | | | | | | |
| | | | | | | |
| | | | | | | |

PLACE THIS LIST IN A VINYL SHEET PROTECTOR TO BE HUNG IN THEIR BEDROOM. CHECK OFF THOSE CHORES THAT ARE DONE DAILY, OR ONCE OR TWICE A WEEK. EACH DAY, THE KIDS COME IN AND CHECK TO SEE WHAT NEEDS TO BE CLEANED.

# BATHROOM CHORELIST

| CHORE | MON | TUES | WED | THURS | FRI | SAT |
|---|---|---|---|---|---|---|
| CLEAN COUNTER, SINK,& SOAP DISH | | | | | | |
| PUT AWAY TOOTHBRUSHES & TOOTHPASTE | | | | | | |
| STRAIGHTEN TOWELS, DISCARD DIRTY ONES | | | | | | |
| CLEAN OFF TOILET SEAT WITH ANTIBACTERIAL SPRAY | | | | | | |
| CLEAN TOILET BOWL WITH DISINFECTANT CLEANER | | | | | | |
| CLEAN TUB & TILE | | | | | | |
| CLEAN MIRROR | | | | | | |
| VACUUM & WASH FLOOR | | | | | | |
| DUST | | | | | | |
| | | | | | | |
| | | | | | | |
| | | | | | | |

PLACE THIS LIST IN A VINYL SHEET PROTECTOR TO BE HUNG IN THE BATHROOM. EACH DAY THE KIDS CHECK TO SEE WHAT CHORES NEED TO BE DONE.

# KITCHEN CHORELIST

| CHORE | MON | TUES | WED | THUR | FRI | SAT |
|---|---|---|---|---|---|---|
| CLEAN ALL COUNTERS WITH DISINFECTANT | | | | | | |
| CLEAN STOVE | | | | | | |
| CLEAN TILE WALL AROUND STOVE | | | | | | |
| CLEAN OUTSIDE OF FRIDGE | | | | | | |
| SWEEP | | | | | | |
| CLEAN SINK | | | | | | |
| WIPE DOWN CABINETS | | | | | | |
| STRAIGHTEN PANTRY | | | | | | |
| WASH FLOORS | | | | | | |
| STRAIGHTEN & CLEAN INSIDE OF FRIDGE | | | | | | |
| | | | | | | |
| | | | | | | |
| | | | | | | |
| | | | | | | |
| | | | | | | |
| | | | | | | |

PLACE THIS LIST IN A VINYL SHEET PROTECTOR TO BE HUNG IN THE KITCHEN. EACH DAY THE KIDS CHECK TO SEE WHAT CHORES NEED TO BE DONE.

# FAMILYROOM/LIVINGROOM CHORELIST

| CHORE | MON | TUES | WED | THUR | FRI | SAT |
|---|---|---|---|---|---|---|
| PICK UP & PUT AWAY | | | | | | |
| STRAIGHTEN SHELVES | | | | | | |
| DUST | | | | | | |
| CLEAN MIRRORS/ GLASS | | | | | | |
| VACUUM FURNITURE | | | | | | |
| VACUUM | | | | | | |
| CLEAN FLOOR BOARDS | | | | | | |
| CLEAN WINDOWS | | | | | | |
| | | | | | | |
| | | | | | | |
| | | | | | | |
| | | | | | | |
| | | | | | | |

PLACE THIS LIST IN A VINYL SHEET PROTECTOR TO BE HUNG IN THE FAMILYROOM OR LIVINGROOM (OUT OF SIGHT). EACH DAY CHECK TO SEE WHAT NEEDS TO BE DONE.

## SAMPLE ONE-DAY CLEANING SCHEDULE

| CHORE | DAD | MOM | VIKTORIJA | GIEDRE | GINTARAS | LINAS | KATRINA |
|---|---|---|---|---|---|---|---|
| PICK UP ROOMS | | | X | X | X | X | X |
| BEDROOMS | | | X | X | X | | |
| BATHROOMS | | | X | X | | | |
| GARBAGE | | | | | X | X | |
| BABY'S ROOM | | | | | X | | X |
| F.R. / L.R. DUST | | | | X | | | |
| LANAI: DUST | | | | | X | | |
| COMP ROOM: DUST | | | | X | | | |
| LAUNDRY: CLEAN COUNTERS | | X | | | | | |
| MOM'S BEDROOM | | X | | | | | |
| MOM'S BATH | | X | | | | | |
| VACUUM 1/2 | | | X | | | | |
| VACUUM 1/2 | | | | X | | | |
| CLEAN KITCHEN COUNTERS | | X | | | | | |
| WASH KITCHEN FLOORS | | X | | | | | |
| WASH BATHROOM FLOORS | | | X | X | | | |
| WASH LAUNDRY FLOORS | | X | | | | | |
| GARAGE PICK UP | X | | | | X | X | |
| SWEEP WALKS | | | | | X | X | |
| CLEAN YARD | X | | | | X | X | |
| MISC: | | | | | | | |
|   BATHE DOG | X | | | | | | |
| | | | | | | | |
| | | | | | | | |
| | | | | | | | |
| | | | | | | | |
| | | | | | | | |

THIS IS A SAMPLE CHORELIST FOR THE FAMILY WHO LIKES TO CLEAN THEIR ENTIRE HOUSE IN ONE DAY, INSTEAD OF DAILY.

# ONE-DAY CLEANING SCHEDULE

| CHORE | | | | | | | |
|---|---|---|---|---|---|---|---|
| PICK UP ROOMS | | | | | | | |
| CLEAN BEDROOM | | | | | | | |
| BATHROOMS | | | | | | | |
| GARBAGE | | | | | | | |
| BABY'S ROOM | | | | | | | |
| DUST FAMILY ROOM | | | | | | | |
| DUST LIVING ROOM | | | | | | | |
| MOM & DAD'S BEDROOM | | | | | | | |
| VACUUM | | | | | | | |
| KITCHEN: COUNTERS | | | | | | | |
| WASH FLOORS | | | | | | | |
| STOVE/FRIDGE | | | | | | | |
| PANTRY | | | | | | | |
| CLEAN YARD | | | | | | | |
| SWEEP | | | | | | | |
| PICK UP GARAGE | | | | | | | |
| MISC: | | | | | | | |
| | | | | | | | |
| | | | | | | | |
| | | | | | | | |
| | | | | | | | |
| | | | | | | | |
| | | | | | | | |
| | | | | | | | |

THIS CHORE SCHEDULE IS FOR YOU IF YOU LIKE TO CLEAN YOUR ENTIRE HOUSE IN ONE DAY.

# BIG JOB SCHEDULE

## (CHORES THAT ARE DONE INFREQUENTLY: MONTHLY, SEMI-ANNUALLY)

| CHORE | JAN | FEB | MAR | APR | MAY | JUN | JUL | AUG | SEP | OCT | NOV | DEC |
|---|---|---|---|---|---|---|---|---|---|---|---|---|
| WINDOWS - CLEAN | | | | | | | | | | | | |
| STOVE / OVEN CLEAN | | | | | | | | | | | | |
| FRIDGE | | | | | | | | | | | | |
| CEILING FANS | | | | | | | | | | | | |
| A/C OR HEAT RETURNS | | | | | | | | | | | | |
| BASEBOARDS | | | | | | | | | | | | |
| SHOWER DOORS OR CURTAINS | | | | | | | | | | | | |
| CLEAN & CHECK SMOKE DETECTOR | | | | | | | | | | | | |
| GARAGE | | | | | | | | | | | | |
| CLOSETS | | | | | | | | | | | | |
| DRESSERS | | | | | | | | | | | | |
| LINEN CLOSET | | | | | | | | | | | | |
| CLEAN CARPETS | | | | | | | | | | | | |
| DEFROST FREEZER | | | | | | | | | | | | |
| GARDEN VEGGIE | | | | | | | | | | | | |
| GARDEN FLOWER | | | | | | | | | | | | |
| PAINT HOUSE | | | | | | | | | | | | |
| PAINT ROOMS | | | | | | | | | | | | |
| RECAULK | | | | | | | | | | | | |
| GARAGE SALE | | | | | | | | | | | | |
| | | | | | | | | | | | | |
| | | | | | | | | | | | | |
| | | | | | | | | | | | | |
| | | | | | | | | | | | | |
| | | | | | | | | | | | | |
| | | | | | | | | | | | | |
| | | | | | | | | | | | | |
| | | | | | | | | | | | | |
| | | | | | | | | | | | | |
| | | | | | | | | | | | | |

# CHAPTER
## ♥ 13 ♥

## SCHEDULING YOUR LIFE

Now to the meat of the matter. Your day. Where do I begin? Well...I'll start by saying that I can only advise you and tell you what does and doesn't work for me. Each of you is an individual who's going to have to take what I say and mold it to your own lifestyle, or possibly throw it all aside and start from scratch. All I can say is that I'm not a stagnant person – I love, I thrive on change. So I've tried, and am willing to try, anything that sounds reasonable if it will organize my day and life any better than what it is right now.

The secret to organizing your life is simplicity. The simpler you keep it, the more smoothly it will proceed. When we try to teach or "do" ten or thirteen different subjects, life becomes difficult. If we have each of our children in different books, studying such subjects as science and history individually, we're creating extra work for ourselves and isolating our kids from one another.

Let me begin by telling you what my average, run of the mill day is like. (Please note that this is not every day! As a homeschooling mom my motto is, "Go with the flow!" If something better comes up, like a neat fieldtrip, go for it!)

### My Schedule

**6:30** Wake-up to National Broadcasting (did you ever notice that an intriguing news story can grab your attention and plummet you out of bed? The secret is setting the audio loud enough to catch your attention while you're sleeping, but not so loud as to wake up the dead!) I slowly crawl out of bed, splash some very cold water on my face, grab my clothes, put on the coffee, and walk out the door. For the next fifteen or twenty minutes I walk back and forth down my street praying for everyone and anyone and the Lord's grace to get through the day.

**7:00** Either take a shower or sit down for a quiet cup of coffee and the paper.

**7:30** Make breakfast: hot and nutritious to get everyone's engines roaring.

**7:45** Kids eat while I read to them from the Bible and books about the lives of the saints. After which we study German.

**8:15** Kids go practice their music (strings and piano) while I clean up the mess (oops, kitchen), start laundry, make my bed. Clean up a bit. Check menu and set dinner out to defrost.

**9:15** Everyone is starting to gather at the kitchen table to do their math. My oldest daughter is doing **ChalkDust Algebra** so I sit down with her to watch the video. Basically I'm re-learning everything with her and this makes doing the lessons and checking her work much easier. While we watch the video, I ask my youngest son to keep an eye on the baby. (Please note that more frequently than not we must turn off the video to reprimand the baby and remind my son that it's his job to watch her. Life is not perfect by any means!) I work on math with one of the three until almost noon. When they're done with math they write in their journal, do their English, work on a science project, or read. I haven't started to do anything specific with my five-year-old, just the basics. The two older girls are almost entirely on their own except for a few math questions. My eight-year old is about fifty percent on his own. He still needs help with math and phonics and journal. My five-year-old needs help learning his numbers, letters, and colors, but I sometimes ask my eleven-year-old daughter to work with him. And my one-year old is always underfoot and has a bad screaming habit.

**12:00** Lunch! Everyone pitches in to help. My oldest cleans up and washes the dishes. After lunch the baby goes down to sleep for (hopefully!) a two-hour nap.

**1:00** I read aloud to everyone else. They can draw, color, or build something. I usually read historical novels, or a classic.

**3:00** Quick tidy up, various lessons, computer time, outside play.

**4:00** I begin dinner so we can eat by 5:00. Usually I prefer to work on dinner alone because I want the kids to play or do their own thing. I prefer having the kitchen to myself – well almost. The one-year old is with me helping make the salad!

**5:00** Dinner.

**5:30** My second daughter and oldest son clean up the kitchen.
Evenings: They may have soccer or basketball practice, lessons, Karate. Many evenings we watch the **Waltons** together from 7:00-8:00.

**8:00**   We pick up, change, pray together, and everyone heads for their bedroom. I like the kids to be in bed by nine, but that doesn't always work out because of Karate and Symphony. Once they go to bed it's **my** time. I sew, read, or write. I have a few television programs I like, but I do best if I'm in bed by ten, perhaps reading for awhile.

Most of my week I can stay home all day because my husband gets home early enough to take the kids to their lessons. My worst day is Thursday because lessons begin early and I need to take them. When the kids were younger we tried to have a regular library day, which is a great idea because the kids look forward to knowing when they'll go. As they grew older we slipped into the habit of going when the books are due. But this is an activity that I think I'll try to re-incorporate into our schedule next year. Fridays are usually busy because we have something planned like 4-H or field trips. We try to schedule all our outside activities on Fridays. If we don't get a chance to clean the house on Friday, then Saturday is cleaning day. I can tell you that after an especially busy week no one wants to clean, but somehow it gets done. All our bigger jobs get saved for Saturday. And Sunday is the Sabbath and we really try to have a day of rest.

During the week, in between our school schedule, we sneak in the laundry, folding, ironing (we do very little of this!), some special cooking (cookies, cakes, bread, etc), and lots of tidying up. We've once again put up a clothes line, so now I try to wash a little every morning and hang it up before the heat of the day. Believe it or not I find it very relaxing to be outside with the younger ones hanging up clothes. (And not using the dryer saves a lot of money! The clothes aren't as wrinkled as they are when they come out of the dryer.) Big jobs like window cleaning, major housecleaning, car washing, and yard work get delegated to holidays (my husband has all the legal holidays off) and Saturdays. (We usually clean the bathrooms and kitchen, vacuum, and dust on Saturdays.)

### Weekend Schedule

Weekends can be calm or crazy depending on the time of year. There are Saturdays where we're running to basketball or soccer games, concerts or some other commitment. I try to be as serene about major interruptions as possible, realizing that they are just as important as cleaning our home. There are times when we only get to do major cleaning every other week. The wisest move in this situation is to make do. Clean what needs to be cleaned on a priority basis: clear the clutter, organize, and forget about it!

On "normal" Saturdays we'll wake up and have breakfast by nine in the morning or we may wake up at 7:30 and go "garage sale-ing" and pick up some bagels to bring home. I find though, that we accomplish much more if we never leave the house.   Then I have the boys pick up their room (which is a major achievement), empty all the garbage cans, pick up the family room and TV room, watch the baby, or go outside and help dad with yard work.

The girls clean their room, then they each have their own bathroom that they have to disinfect and scrub, after which they start dusting and picking up the other rooms. Meanwhile, I'll be working on my bedroom and bath and vacuuming. Saturday can become a horrible, ugly day if you haven't been keeping up with your daily pick up. But if you have kept up with the de-cluttering, and all you have to do is really clean, then it's not a major chore. And to tell you the truth, my attitude has done such a complete turn around that I miss cleaning if we don't get to it weekly. I desire a clean house and I'm starting to enjoy the process. It's a welcome diversion from other motherhood responsibilities. It makes me feel good about my home and myself! Everyone loves a clean house. The problem is that it never stays clean long enough!

I've started guarding my Saturdays… I preplan them…guard every minute so that someone doesn't run away with it. My old self would wake up on Saturday morning and think, "What should we do now? What would I like to do?" with entirely no consideration to what needed to be done in order for the household to run smoothly for the rest of the week. Now I've gotten to the point where I think ahead on Friday and plan out blocks of time. This way I know that until noon we'll all be cleaning, then perhaps dad needs to run out and coach a game. My afternoons are saved for those special projects I want to accomplish that there's no time to do during the week. (I love watching **This Old House** on PBS!) I try not to leave the house because then I end up wasting time and spending money, which is the last thing I want to do.

I do my grocery shopping on Thursday evenings, every other week, when we get paid. So Saturday all I have to do are those special errands, like clothes shopping or going to a store that's off the beaten path. But now I do even this rarely because it seems that every time I step foot into a store I spend at least a hundred dollars – remember, I have five growing kids! I try to plan a real nice meal for Saturday night since it's our one and only night to really relax as a family. A favorite meal of mine on Saturdays is crockpot cooking since I can put it in the crock in the early morning when I still have lots of energy. By the time I'm pooped and normally would say, "Let's go out to eat!" I have a wonderful meal ready to eat! (And hopefully enough food left over so that we don't have to cook on Sunday, our day of rest.) Another good meal is a laid back barbecue (hamburgers and chips)!

My attitude regarding needless running around has really changed since I've tried to budget myself. I know that the second I enter a store, I'll spend. I can always find something to buy that's a great deal, or just too irresistible to pass up. So now I even try to avoid garage sales. The best suggestion is to keep a list of things you need, or want, on or near the refrigerator. If it's really important, eventually you'll get around to buying it. If it's not that important, you'll forget it.

If it's a luxury, go and check it out to find the best buy, and then wait 30 days to see if you still want it. Always think about whether the purchase is a need (you have to have it in order to survive), a want (something that will make your life more comfortable, but not a necessity for survival), or a desire (something you just would like for the sake of having it). I know a lot of the goods I'd like to buy are merely desires – definitely not needs!

## KIDS' DAILY SCHEDULE

Usually they're all up around 7:00 AM (7:30 at the latest). My kids are truly self-motivated and I attribute that to them starting music lessons when they were so young. My thirteen-year-old daughter can basically school herself; give her the books and she's set. My eleven-year-old daughter still needs some prodding to keep her on track, but she's close to being independent. My son, who's eight, is doing great but I need to keep an eye on him to make sure that he hasn't "forgotten" or skipped something. My youngest son is just beginning his school years and we're slowly introducing him to the world of numbers and letters. My toddler keeps us hopping all the time!

I wish I knew nine years ago what I know now. I would never have worried so much about doing school with my girls when they were little. I would have been **much, much more relaxed and had more fun.** Homeschooling moms, when they're first starting out, are so nervous about messing up that they overkill – they do way too much so that they won't miss a beat. Kids are like sponges. They'll soak up anything you give them, especially if it's interesting. If your kids are all young, take the time to have lots of fun. Don't be very structured and strict about school. Make their education part of life and home. Clean a little and do a few numbers, cook and measure; exercise and sing a phonics song; garden and examine nature; relax and read. If you do this, you're going to find your kids learning and having fun and you won't be going crazy "keeping school" and "keeping home." When they're young, say eight and younger, incorporate them into **your** schedule. If you need to clean, have them clean. If you need to garden, then garden together. Think of them as little helpers, not nuisances.

If you have older children simplify your curriculum, plan your school goals together, and let them go for it. If you're like me, and like to be in the thick of things, then do science and history together with all the kids (always teaching to the oldest). What fun it is to read history novels and be taken away to different ages and adventures! What better way to make keepsake moments that will be remembered for years to come? What better way to remember history facts then by what certain characters did during that time period? If you have the wall space hang a timeline around your room and decorate it with the titles of the books you read and the years or century that they represent. Note key historical figures and events. When you go out and get dirty with the kids you're making memories that they're going to remember for years to come. Come on! Go and dissect a toad!

Now sit down, take pencil to paper, and create a spreadsheet for your week. Check out the one that I've included. Write down everything that you'd like to accomplish during your day.

1) What time would you like to wake up?

2) Do you want time for yourself in the morning to pray, exercise, do some chores?

3) What time do you want your kids up in the morning? (The first one up will rule the day – will it be you or the kids?)

4) What time are you going to have them do their more formal subjects like math?

5) What time will you eat lunch and dinner and how long do you need?

6) What big chore would you like to accomplish each day: laundry, ironing, mega cooking*, dusting, vacuuming, etc. (* When I say mega cooking I mean that you make enough for more than one meal.)

7) List your commitments for each day: what time allotment do you need for lessons outside the home or whatever else. Don't forget to include time for driving back and forth.

8) Do you need a nap or quiet time each day? Schedule it in.

9) Schedule family prayer time and/or activity time.

10) Schedule your kids' bed times and your own. Remember to consider how much sleep your family needs to be wide-eyed and bushy tailed – including you. If you want to wake up at five in the morning you better be going to bed early enough to get enough zzzzz's.

Now take a good look at your spreadsheet. Does it look realistic? Can you really get all that accomplished? Did you leave enough time to make the meals? Do you have enough time for your kids to get their formal school work done? If you think it's a workable schedule try it for a few weeks and see how it feels. Try to diligently stick to your schedule; the less you have to think about what you should be doing, the more you'll get accomplished. That's why it's so important to make it workable or do-able.  But don't be a slave to your schedule either.  If something better comes up, go for it!

Post your schedule where everyone can see it – on the refrigerator.  Make sure you talk to your family about it, as they will have to adhere to it also.  Set up a reward system for those who get their chores or school work done on time. You won't believe how kids love rewards.  Take into consideration their age.  If they're under eight years old they want immediate gratification – candy, a small car, whatever.  If they're older, they'll probably want to work for something bigger. Finish your math book by such and such a date and you'll get a Lego set or some books.  Doesn't everyone work better when there's a reward in store?  Your husband gets rewarded for putting in a good week at work with a paycheck and sometimes a bonus.  You may get rewarded for being a great wife and mom by being taken out to dinner.  So give your kids an incentive to do a good job punctually!

## SUMMARY:

1. Keep your schedule, and life, as simple as possible.

2. Give yourself plenty of sleep and wake up earlier than the kids for a "quiet time" of your own.

3. What chores do you want accomplished daily and who will do them?

4. Will you try and clean your house a little each day or all at once?

5. Make sure you schedule daily "pick up" time.

6. Figure out which day of the week you'll clean, grocery shop, run errands, etc.

7. What major chores will you do on Saturdays?

8. Plan to rest on Sunday and do absolutely nothing except enjoy your family.

9. Take into consideration how much sleep your kids need and when they should wake up and go to bed.

10. Do all of you need a daily naptime or quiet time?

# There Isn't Time

There isn't time, there isn't time
To do the things I want to do,
With all the mountain-tops to climb,
And all the woods to wander through,
And all the seas to sail upon,
And everywhere there is to go,
And all the people, every one
Who lives upon the earth, to know.
There's only time, there's only time
To know a few, and do a few,
And then sit down and make a rhyme
About the rest I want to do.
                    By Eleanor Farjeon

# SAMPLE DAILY TO-DO LIST

## MOM'S LIST

EXERCISE & PRAY
MAKE BED
DRESS & SHOWER
MAKE-UP & HAIR
MAKE BREAKFAST
WASH AM DISHES
CLEAN UP KITCHEN
DEFROST DINNER
START LAUNDRY
CHECK KIDS' CHORES
HELP W/SCHOOLWORK
MAKE LUNCH
KIDS FOLD LAUNDRY
PUT BABY TO NAP
UNIT STUDY
AFTERNOON ACTIVITIES
KIDS PICK UP
TAKE A BREAK
START DINNER

## VIKTORIJA'S LIST

MAKE BED
WASH UP & DRESS
PICK UP BEDROOM
FEED CAT
MUSIC
SCHOOLWORK
CLEAN KITCHEN AFTER LUNCH
AFTERNOON ACTIVITIES
COMPLETED CHORES
HELP MAKE DINNER
*     *     *     *     *     *

MON 4:30 VIOLIN GROUP LESSON
MON EVENING: SYMPHONY
TUES 3:00 TEACHES VIOLIN
TUES 4:00 - 5:15 VIOLIN LESSON
WED 9:30AM PIANO
TUES / WED EVENING: KARATE

## GINTARAS' LIST

WASH UP & DRESS
CLEAN ROOM & MAKE BED
FEED OUTSIDE CATS
MUSIC
SCHOOLWORK
WALK DOG NOON
COMPLETE CHORES
CLEAN KITCHEN PM
*     *     *     *

TUES / WED EVE KARATE
WED 10:30AM PIANO LESSON
THURS 2:30 CELLO LESSON

## GIEDRE'S LIST

MAKE BED
WASH UP & DRESS
PICK UP BEDROOM
FEED DOG / EMPTY KITTY LITTER
PRACTICE MUSIC
SCHOOL WORK
PICK UP HOUSE
FOLD LAUNDRY
COMPLETED CHORES
HELP WITH DINNER
CLEAN KITCHEN AFTER DINNER
WALK DOG
#     #     #     #     #

MON 4:30 VIOLIN GROUP LESSON
MON 6:30 SYMPHONY
TUES 4:00-5:15 VIOLIN LESSON
TUES / WED EVENING KARATE
WED 10:00 PIANO LESSON
THURS 4:00 - 5:30 DANCE

## LINAS' LIST

WASH UP & DRESS
CLEAN BEDROOM & MAKE BED
CLEAN OUTDOOR CAT BOWLS
HELP WITH BREAKFAST DISHES
SCHOOLWORK
PLAY WITH SISTER
FOLD LAUNDRY
PICK UP HOUSE

## COOKING

MON: VIKT
TUES: GIED
WED: MOM
THURS: BOYS
FRI: VIKT
SAT: GIRLS

## TOGETHER

BIBLE
SAINTS
GERMAN
HISTORY
LITERATURE
SCIENCE

| VIKTORIJA | GIEDRE | GINTARAS | LINAS |
|-----------|--------|----------|-------|
| MATH | MATH | MATH | MATH |
| SCIENCE | SCIE | SCIENCE | READ |
| ENGLISH | ENG | ENG | MEM |
| JOURNAL | JOUR | JOUR | |
| | | READ | |

HOMESCHOOLING BY HEART © 1999

# DAILY TO-DO LIST

## MOM'S LIST

# BIRTHDAY-AT-A-GLANCE LIST
WRITE THE PERSON'S NAME ON HIS B.D. AND THE GIFT YOU HAVE STASHED AWAY FOR HIM

|    | JAN | FEB | MRCH | APR | MAY | JUNE | JULY | AUG | SEPT | OCT | NOV | DEC |
|----|-----|-----|------|-----|-----|------|------|-----|------|-----|-----|-----|
| 1  |     |     |      |     |     |      |      |     |      |     |     |     |
| 2  |     |     |      |     |     |      |      |     |      |     |     |     |
| 3  |     |     |      |     |     |      |      |     |      |     |     |     |
| 4  |     |     |      |     |     |      |      |     |      |     |     |     |
| 5  |     |     |      |     |     |      |      |     |      |     |     |     |
| 6  |     |     |      |     |     |      |      |     |      |     |     |     |
| 7  |     |     |      |     |     |      |      |     |      |     |     |     |
| 8  |     |     |      |     |     |      |      |     |      |     |     |     |
| 9  |     |     |      |     |     |      |      |     |      |     |     |     |
| 10 |     |     |      |     |     |      |      |     |      |     |     |     |
| 11 |     |     |      |     |     |      |      |     |      |     |     |     |
| 12 |     |     |      |     |     |      |      |     |      |     |     |     |
| 13 |     |     |      |     |     |      |      |     |      |     |     |     |
| 14 |     |     |      |     |     |      |      |     |      |     |     |     |
| 15 |     |     |      |     |     |      |      |     |      |     |     |     |
| 16 |     |     |      |     |     |      |      |     |      |     |     |     |
| 17 |     |     |      |     |     |      |      |     |      |     |     |     |
| 18 |     |     |      |     |     |      |      |     |      |     |     |     |
| 19 |     |     |      |     |     |      |      |     |      |     |     |     |
| 20 |     |     |      |     |     |      |      |     |      |     |     |     |
| 21 |     |     |      |     |     |      |      |     |      |     |     |     |
| 22 |     |     |      |     |     |      |      |     |      |     |     |     |
| 23 |     |     |      |     |     |      |      |     |      |     |     |     |
| 24 |     |     |      |     |     |      |      |     |      |     |     |     |
| 25 |     |     |      |     |     |      |      |     |      |     |     |     |
| 26 |     |     |      |     |     |      |      |     |      |     |     |     |
| 27 |     |     |      |     |     |      |      |     |      |     |     |     |
| 28 |     |     |      |     |     |      |      |     |      |     |     |     |
| 29 |     |     |      |     |     |      |      |     |      |     |     |     |
| 30 |     |     |      |     |     |      |      |     |      |     |     |     |
| 31 |     |     |      |     |     |      |      |     |      |     |     |     |

# CHRISTMAS PRESENT LIST

| NAME | THEIR WISH | SIZE | $ BUDGETED | ACTUALLY BOUGHT | I HID IT HERE | RUNNING TOTAL SPENT |
|------|-----------|------|-----------|-----------------|---------------|---------------------|
|  |  |  |  |  |  |  |
|  |  |  |  |  |  |  |
|  |  |  |  |  |  |  |
|  |  |  |  |  |  |  |
|  |  |  |  |  |  |  |
|  |  |  |  |  |  |  |
|  |  |  |  |  |  |  |
|  |  |  |  |  |  |  |
|  |  |  |  |  |  |  |
|  |  |  |  |  |  |  |
|  |  |  |  |  |  |  |
|  |  |  |  |  |  |  |
|  |  |  |  |  |  |  |
|  |  |  |  |  |  |  |
|  |  |  |  |  |  |  |
|  |  |  |  |  |  |  |
|  |  |  |  |  |  |  |
|  |  |  |  |  |  |  |
|  |  |  |  |  |  |  |

# CHAPTER
## ♥ 14 ♥

## MENU PLANNING

Probably one of the most difficult areas of home life that I have to organize is planning my family's meals. I wasn't raised in a large family and my mom never made out a formal menu (none that I ever knew of). It was only my mom and dad and me at home, so a lot of times meals were planned at the very last minute on the way home from work. I had been operating in this very same manner for years. If I got involved in something, or time ran away from me, there was no dinner that night. And you know without a doubt that if you don't have some sort of dinner on the table when dad comes home – you'll have a grumpy dad and be on your way to the first fast-food joint in town.

Part of the problem can be alleviated by just changing your attitude about meals. My feeling had always been, "I worked hard all day, I'm hungry and tired, I can't deal with this. Let's go out!" Now, I have a pretty laid back husband, so he usually says, "Sure, let's go out for pizza." Once a week isn't too bad, but when your restaurant bill gets to be bigger than your food bill, then you're in way over your head! First you've got to realize that you need help: your family can not keep going out because it's too expensive, it's too time consuming, and it's not healthy!

We all know that fast food is expensive and unhealthy, but do you realize that it's also a big waste of time? You're a lot better off eating peanut butter and jelly sandwiches or scrambled eggs than going out; think of all the energy needed to drag the entire family out of the house, then waiting for the food, and finally dragging everyone back home again. Well, you say, what about the energy and time needed to wash the dishes and clean the kitchen? If that's all that's bothering you, use throwaway plates. It's still cheaper to buy paper dishes than to pay for eating out.

With each child that we had I swore that we would no longer go out to eat during the week. But I'd be so tired by 5:00PM. I wasn't organized enough to pre-plan dinner. So out we'd go! It took the birth of our fifth child for me to realize (I'm pretty thick-headed) that it was more tiring to go out than to eat anything on hand at home. Finally I was forced to think ahead about dinner!

Once I realized that my family was being harmed by constantly eating out, I decided that it was worth the extra minutes to plan ahead our meals each day. If you're like me, and always looking for an easy way out of cooking, you'll realize that it's cheaper and healthier to buy the more expensive cuts of meat than to go out. There are seven of us. When we go out for fast-food it costs us between $15 to $20 (and that's only because our kids are still relatively small eaters). That's for some greasy, grilled hamburgers or chicken pieces. (That chicken that's compressed and you don't even know what's in it. That's also the cost if all of us split two large sodas, one or two extra large servings of fries, and three of the kids splitting a box of 20-piece chicken.) We're drinking soda (lots of sugar) and nibbling on French fries. Each of us is consuming a minimum of a thousand calories (probably closer to two thousand) and half (if not more) of those calories are made up of fat!

Now, for under $10 I can make a London broil, salad, baked potatoes, and broccoli. The London broil can be thrown under the broiler or on the grill, the potatoes can be cooked in the microwave in seven to ten minutes (this depends on how many potatoes and how big) or boiled in twenty, the salad takes about ten to fifteen minutes, and the broccoli a mere minute to clean and about five to steam. (I know this is true because we did this last night!) The meal, from beginning to end, takes half an hour! (If you have a gas grill and, of course, depending on how thick the meat is and how well done you want it!) The problem is that most of us would consider this type of food a luxury and wouldn't prepare it during the week. We'd say it's too much to spend. But yet, we can afford to throw fifteen bucks out at our friendly corner burger joint and not wink an eye! When you realize the foolishness of this type of behavior maybe you'll be more prone to buy the steak! Consider how much the restaurant food costs to serve at home. You can buy a liter of soda (on sale) for the cost of a medium drink; a 20-piece chicken box (compressed) could buy two fresh chickens or one barbecued supermarket chicken; for the cost of an extra large box of fries you can buy five pounds of potatoes (on sale); and one Big Mac can buy enough ground beef to make four hamburgers!

Another, much more important point to consider about dinner time is that this is probably the only time of the day that the majority of families can eat together. In this day and age we're all so busy shuffling our kids around from one activity to another that the traditional family dinner hour has been cast aside and replaced by fast food or grabbing something on the way out the door. (Remember, mom used to always say it's not healthy to eat standing up!) As families, we must make a conscious decision to eat dinner all together at the family table.

Think about where people always congregate when you have a party – in the kitchen. Subconsciously, we all think of the kitchen as the most nurturing room in the house, as it well should be. That's why I've always dreamt of someday having a big country kitchen, where the kitchen table would be smack dab in the center of all the activity.  When I was little we had a kitchen like that and I still remember that every major decision, every important event took place around that table: betrothals were announced, deaths mourned, births celebrated.  What better or more natural place to share your daily bread together then at the kitchen table!  And consider all the wonderful discussions and conversations that you're missing if you don't eat together with your family.  Consider each family dinner a banquet. Set the table royally and festively. Sit down, pray over your food, and share your day with one another. If you don't know how to start the ball rolling have the kids rehash their day for dad and have dad ask each child what they learned.  Discuss important news issues. Family dinner time is possibly the most important time of your day. Don't miss it for the *world*!

Once you decide that going out costs too much, and you're going to create a food budget and stick to it, then you need to determine how you are going to organize your meals.  Here are three different ways in which to create meal plans for your family:

1) Make a monthly schedule and write down what you would like to have for dinner every day of the month.  (This really intimidates me. Sometimes I can't decide what to eat the very same day, let alone a week from now!)  This is especially helpful if you'd like to do once-a-month shopping and/ or cooking.

-or-

2) Decide today that you want to start planning your meals and every time you serve something that your family likes, jot the entire menu on a 3 X 5 index card.  After a week you should have seven cards and seven meals.  Put them in a small box and the next time you're getting ready to go shopping for the week pull out seven meals. Wa La! You have a menu! If you really want to be organized, jot down the recipe name on the card and then the ingredients so you have a ready made shopping list.  And if you really, really want to be organized and a wonderful teacher and mom, write down the instructions on the back so that your husband or kids can cook it if you're not home or are sick!

-or-

3) You go shopping and buy at least seven days worth of meat / food and each day you go to the freezer and pick something that you'd like to make that night.  This is the least efficient and most costly plan, but at least you have the food on hand and you won't go out to eat or starve!

My favorite plan is number two, the one with the index cards. It allows for creativity, but yet you have some idea of what you'll be eating during the week **and** you have a shopping list readily available. This really cuts down on stress and too much pre-planning.

Always have a paper and pad handy in your kitchen to jot down items that you've run out of and need to restock . (Never wait until you need an item in a recipe and discover that you're all out.) I have a pad about 5 X 8 that I've stuck a magnetic strip to and keep on my fridge. (The next time you receive a free magnet advertising pizza, glue it to the back of a pad of paper.) I know that anything I really need to buy gets put on this pad. This saves wear and tear on the brain while at the store. There are much better uses for the mind. (But don't forget to take your list with you!) Or use the grocery list that I've included to jot down items that need to be purchased. If you don't like grocery lists, then keep an inventory list in your pantry and check off items as you use them, or as you need them. While I'm on this topic, if you have a freezer, or extra refrigerator, it's nice to keep an inventory list on the door. This way you know how many chickens or casseroles are left and you won't be stuck with frost bitten ground beef!

I think my biggest problem is that when I shop I always think, "Oh that's too expensive!" Well it's much more expensive to go out, so buy a ready made pizza or steak or cold cuts. Buy it, enjoy, and don't feel guilty! If you really want to save money and time, then the next time you cook from scratch make double or triple portions to freeze for those days that you're too pooped to even make a steak. But remember that those frozen casseroles take a long time to cook if they're frozen solid like a rock, so either thaw them for a day or two in the fridge, or stick them in the oven nice and early.

Other conveniences to consider:

**Lunch or quick dinners:**
1. Pre-made pizza dough (vacuum packed and looks like a flat round slab of bread ) that you only need to add sauce, cheese, and toppings. Takes about 15-20 minutes from start to eating. The cheapest price for these is found at the warehouse stores where they come packed three to a package.

2. Pizza bites (you can find large bags of these at the warehouse stores). **(Expensive)**

3. Cold cuts (try making an Italian sub with dressing, onions, tomatoes, and lettuce). **(Expensive)**

4. Soup – Oriental Ramen noodle is a big hit at our house for quickie meals.

5. Bagels with sauce and cheese.

6. Macaroni and cheese.

7. Cottage cheese, macaroni, mozarella, and butter (or tomato sauce).

8. Grilled cheese sandwiches made in a toaster oven.

9. Leftover French toast or pancakes.

10. Yogurt, crackers, and cheese.

11. Fruit – fresh or canned (also great with yogurt or cottage cheese). **(Can be expensive.)**

12. Tuna or egg salad (kids love them stuffed in pita bread).

13. Salad with bread.

14. Leftovers from last night's dinner. (You can always make more with the intention of serving it for lunch the next day. Grilled chicken or roast beef is great as a sandwich filler.)

15. Peanut butter and jelly. (Or honey!)

16. Cold cereal is not a big hit for either breakfast or lunch. Why? Because you're hungry an hour later. When you're working hard you need brain food!

**Dinners:**

1. Spaghetti and any type of meat (chicken, meatballs, meatloaf), sauce (tomato or brown), salad (lettuce, celery, cucumbers, tomatoes, red onion, green pepper, carrot, scallions, red cabbage, radishes – the more the better!), vegetable.

2. Chinese Stir Fry – sauté chicken pieces in a wok with broccoli, Chinese cabbage, onions, mushrooms, baby corn, pea pods, etc. Add ginger and some soy sauce; rice.

3. Cheap pork roast (the kind you can buy for $1.59 per pound on sale. It's delicious!) - bake covered in oven with carrots, celery, potatoes, etc. Uncover for the last half hour to brown. (Leftover meat is delicious fried up in a pan with leftover boiled potato slices. It melts in your mouth!)

4.  Baked chicken pieces with rice, vegetable, salad.

5.  Tuna casserole (with noodles) and a salad.

6.  Pancakes with fruit.

7.  Waffles (homemade) with fruit.

8.  Cheese ravioli with a salad.

9.  Cheap cut of beef in a crock with lots of veggies, potatoes.

10. Homemade soup and bread. (Homemade soup is so easy to make and has no chemical additives or preservatives.)

11. Catfish lightly fried with onions, potatoes, salad.

12. Lasagna and salad.

13. Brisket with cabbage, onions, carrots, and potatoes made in a crockpot.

14. Hamburgers, rolls, frozen fries, chips or hash browns, beans.

15. Chili and rice (make with ground turkey).

The secret is that whatever you make, try making enough for at least two or three days. That way you can relax the next day or stick the extra in the freezer for a "rainy" day. (I need to make an aside here. This year for Lent our whole family gave up sweets and meat. Now it wasn't such a sacrifice, the going was not that tough. **BUT** the going was pretty boring! We are not bean eaters so that really cut down on potential vegetarian recipes. We ate a lot of pasta and rice with vegetables. We all felt healthier, but definitely a lot hungrier. And what I really missed was the wonderful smells that fill the house when I'm baking and cooking. Our six weeks of vegetarianism taught us all that we don't want to give up meat, but that we could if we had to.)

**Which leads us backward to breakfast**. I'm a strong proponent of a nutritious, hot breakfast. Now I've either spoiled my children or I'm right, because on the days that they're forced to eat cereal (mom's too tired or too busy to make something) they're all starving by about 10AM. (By the way, I realize that cold packaged cereal is not cheap. But we have never bought sugar cereal and we hardly ever buy a name brand. The store brands are usually half the cost of name brands. My husband used to love to coupon shop (he doesn't have the time anymore) but he would always buy cereal practically for free because of all his coupon deals. And since he eats cereal every morning with a banana we have cereal in the house.) So better to be safe than sorry, and prepare something big and powerful for breakfast.  Here are some suggestions:

1. Pancakes made with apples, milk on the side, and a half of a grapefruit or other fruit. (Recipe in the appendix.)

2. Pancake cake, fruit, milk. (Recipe in the appendix.)

3. French toast, fruit, milk. (Recipe in the appendix.)

4. Hot oatbran / oatmeal / farina with applesauce and cinnamon sugar and milk.

5. Scrambled or fried eggs with bread and milk.

6. Waffles (frozen or homemade) with fruit and milk.

When you prepare a big, nutritious hot breakfast it may take a bit more time, but the benefit is that your kids should be able to easily survive until noon, if not a bit later.  Then they eat a good-sized lunch and you're ready to roll until five with perhaps a fruit snack in between.  At five o'clock you'll have a sit down family dinner that everyone can enjoy.  Be sure to stress the fruits and vegetables, instead of the meat, and you'll be in great shape. (All the nutrition books state that meat should be served as a condiment and not the main entrée. We need more carbohydrates and fiber than protein.)

Please remember that if you aren't a big eater, or you're a bad eater (forgetting to eat till you nearly pass out), don't let your kids get into this habit. Children are constantly growing and developing and they need a good source of energy. If you're worried about them gaining weight, let them eat and make them exercise.  But make sure that they eat a well-balanced diet that starts each and every day with a nutritious breakfast!  To quote the Seventh Day Adventists, who are said to be the healthiest people in America, "Eat breakfast like a king, lunch like a queen, and dinner like a pauper!"  If you're in doubt read some books on diet.

### SUMMARY:

1. Decide that you're going to consciously save money and time by not going out to eat as frequently.

2. Set a food budget and stick to it!

3. Make it your goal to provide the most nutritious meals possible to your growing family on the amount of money you've set aside.

4. Sometimes spending more on quick food, such as chicken breasts or steak, is actually cheaper because it will stop you from giving up and going out to eat when time is short. Each time you're tempted to go to a fast food joint start calculating how much food you could buy at the grocery store for the money you'll spend (for ex. Medium soda buys a liter of brand name soda).

5. The cheapest meals are what I call "peasant" food. These are foods that require little meat and a lot of filler like potato pancakes, stuffed cabbage, pierogi, etc. Lasagna, in my opinion, is not a cheap meal because it requires at least two cheeses and usually meat. Of course the cheapest meal would be anything requiring beans as the major ingredient.

6. Learn to make meal plans for at least a week at a time, if not longer.

7. Always go shopping with a list and never go when you're hungry!

8. Take a few hours to look through your cookbooks for appropriate meals or else jot down your family's favorite recipes on index cards so that anyone in your family can prepare the meal or go shopping. Half the battle is organizing everything. After that, it's easy for the others to take over because you've done all the hard preliminary work!

9. If you want to save money and time, plan to make extra meals and freeze them. Casseroles made with ground beef or chicken can be inexpensive.

10. Make meal planning, shopping, cooking, and freezing a family project.

*Go to the ant, O sluggard;*
*Consider her ways, and be wise:*
*Without having any chief,*
*Officer or ruler,*
*She prepares her food in the summer,*
*And gathers her sustenance in harvest.*
*(Proverbs 6:6-8)*

*A cheerful heart is a good medicine,*
*But a downcast spirit dries up the bones.*
*(Proverbs 17:22)*

# RECIPES

## CROCKPOT BEEF
CHEAP CUT OF BEEF (USUALLY BETWEEN $1.59 TO 2.00)
ONIONS, MEDIUM, SLICED ANY WAY YOU PREFER
CELERY, 3-4 STALKS SLICED ANY WAY (SMALL OR LARGE PIECES)
CARROTS, 3-4 SLICED ANY WAY YOU WANT
ANY OTHER VEGGIE YOU ENJOY: MUSHROOMS, BOK CHOY,
     PEPPERS,TOMATOES, PEAS,ETC.
2 BEEF BOUILLION CUBES WITH 2 CUPS WATER OR A CAN OF BEEF
     BOUILLION
2 OR 3 CLOVES GARLIC
ANY SPICES YOUR FAMILY ENJOYS, PERHAPS WORCHESTERSHIRE
     SAUCE

Trim any visible fat off the beef and place in crockpot. Add the bouillon, onions, garlic, celery, and spices. If you are going to slow cook for 8 hours then add the rest of the veggies about 3 hours before serving. If you're going to cook on the highest temperature, which means it will be done in about 4-5 hours, you can add the vegetables right away.

## PANCAKES
5 EGGS SEPARATED
2 TSPN VANILLA
1 TBLSPN BAKING POWDER
FLOUR, UNBLEACHED, ABOUT 3 CUPS
MILK, ABOUT 3 CUPS (I USE DRY MILK)
1 LARGE OR 2 MEDIUM APPLES PEELED AND GRATED
OIL

Separate the eggs. Place the whites in a small bowl and whip them till they are stiff. Place the yolks in a large bowl, add vanilla and baking powder and half of your milk. Now add the flour and stir, continue adding milk till the consistency is of thick pea soup. Add the grated apples and slowly stir in the egg whites till they are just mixed (the egg whites make the pancakes puff up instead of staying flat as a pancake.) Drop into a hot oiled pan by the ladle spoon (our pancakes are about 2 inches in diameter, 6 per pan). We fry ours in a very hot pan till they are no longer gooey inside. (To test, press with spatula and if the batter doesn't come oozing out they're done.)  For an added treat take half the batter and add a good cup of cottage cheese, mix, and fry. Mmmm…delicious with applesauce and maple syrup!  Makes enough to serve about 7-8 people.

## OAT BRAN
OAT BRAN, ABOUT 2 CUPS
1 QT MILK, USE DRY POWDERED MILK MIXED WITH WATER
If you have a microwave then put the ingredients in a large bowl, mix, and place on high for about 5 minutes. After that you need to check every 2 minutes, or so, till the consistency is of thick pea soup. We serve with applesauce and cinnamon sugar.
Or you can prepare on the stove over medium high heat stirring constantly.
Serves about 5-6.

## FRENCH TOAST (FOR 7)
7 PIECES BREAD, PREFERABLY STALE (FRENCH BREAD IS GREAT)
@ 4 EGGS WELL BEATEN
1 TBSPN VANILLA
1 CUP MILK

Mix eggs, vanilla, and eggs together. Heat up large skillet with oil. Submerge bread piece by piece in egg mixture and place in pan. When one side is brown flip over. Inside should not be soggy when done.

## PANCAKE CAKE (FOR ABOUT 7)
½ CUP BROWN SUGAR
1/3 CUP BUTTER
½ CUP MAPLE SYRUP
1 ½ CUPS FLOUR
1 TSPN BAKING POWDER
1 TSPN VANILLA
1 CUP MILK
3 EGGS, SEPARATED

Heat oven to 350. In a saucepan heat brown sugar, butter, and maple syrup stirring over low heat until melted. Pour into ungreased 13x9x2 in pan. Whip the egg whites until they form peaks. Beat the remaining ingredients until blended and slowly mix in the egg whites. Pour batter into the pan on top of syrup mixture. Bake in oven for 30-35 minutes or until top springs back when touched in center. Serve with maple syrup and/or fresh fruit.

## HOMEMADE CHICKEN SOUP
WATER (TO FILL A LARGE STOCK POT ABOUT ¾ FULL)
(1) 4 TO 5 POUND CHICKEN OR CHICKEN PIECES (OR TURKEY). I USUALLY SAVE THE CARCASS OF A DEBONED CHICKEN FOR SOUP. OR YOU CAN BOIL AN ENTIRE CHICKEN AND THEN REMOVE THE MEAT FOR CHINESE FOOD OR CASSEROLE.
4 OR 5 BLACK PEPPERS
2 BAY LEAVES
4 CARROTS, SLICED INTO SMALL PIECES
4 CELERY STALKS, SLICED INTO SMALL PIECES
2 MEDIUM ONIONS, DICED
2 OR 3 CLOVES OF GARLIC, MINCED
SALT TO TASTE
FROZEN OR FRESH VEGETABLES IF YOU SO DESIRE   (I like to add a head of cauliflower about  20  minutes before serving.)
CHICKEN BOUILLON TO TASTE (ABOUT 5-6 CUBES FOR A LARGE STOCK POT)
FINELY CHOPPED, FRESH PARSLEY
PASTA

Fill  stock pot ¾ full of cold water. Wash chicken  (or turkey) and place in cold water with whole black peppers and bay leaves. Bring to boil and skim froth off top as it forms. Cover and lower heat to a simmer. Let simmer for about 1 ½ hours.  When the chicken is done (the meat falls off the bones) remove it from the pot and remove the bay leaves and peppers. One of the easiest ways to do this is to pour the soup through a sieve into a clean stock pot.  Add carrots, celery, onions, and garlic.  When soup starts boiling add bouillon cubes and salt to taste. Lower heat to a simmer and cover till you're ready to serve.  Add frozen or fresh vegetables about 15-20 minutes before serving. Prepare pasta separately and add to soup bowl before dishing out soup. (If you put the pasta into the soup it will absorb all the liquid and you'll have a very thick soup.) Before serving, drop some fresh parsley in each soup bowl. Bon Appetite!

## FURTHER READING:

**Ball Blue Book, The Guide To Home Canning and Freezing** (Indiana: Ball Corporation, 1977) The authoritative guide to canning and freezing!

**Barron's Cooking Wizardry for Kids** by Margaret Kenda and Phyllis S. Williams (NY: Barron's Educational Series, 1990) A cookbook and science book all rolled into one for kids.

**Dinner's in the Freezer** by Jill Bond (Florida: Reed Bond Books, 1993) A home management system book written by a homeschooling mom. Great ideas for freezing in large quantities.

**Hearth & Home** by Karey Swan (Colorado: Singing Springs Productions, 1996) Written by a homeschooling mom who has a true heart for simplicity and relationships.

**The Little House Cookbook** by Barbara M. Walker (NY: HarperTrophy, 1979) Another great kids' cookbook based on the Little House on the Prairie Series. Lots of commentary on how the Ingalls lived as well as excerpts from her books.

**Miriam's Cookbook** by Carrie Bender (Ontario: Herald Press, 1998) Written by the author of the Amish series Miriam's Journal. A lovely book of authentic Amish recipes and sprinkled with excerpts from her books.

**More-With-Less-Cookbook** by Doris Janzen Longacre (Ontario: Herald Press, 1976) This is a compilation of recipes from the Mennonite community. This book arose from the community's frustration over the plight of the world's hungry and our need to learn to make do with using less. The book addresses the question of how to do this.

**Once-A-Month Cooking** by Mimi Wilson and MaryBeth Lagerborg (CO: Focus on the Family Publishing, 1992)

**Rodale's Basic Natural Foods Cookbook** edited by Charles Gerras (NY: A Fireside Book, 1984) A wonderful book for learning to cook. Covers Everything from A to Z. Only downside is there are no pictures.

**The 15 Minute Meal Planner** by Emilie Barnes & Sue Gregg (OR: Harvest House Publishers,1994) A must read. A realistic approach to a healthy lifestyle from a Biblical perspective.

## NUTRITION:

**The Green Pharmacy** by James A. Duke, Ph.D. (PA: Rodale Press, 1997) Thousands of natural remedies for common ailments. A good book for your medical research library.

**Prescription for Nutritional Healing** by James F. Balch,M.D. and Phyllis A. Balch  (NY: Avery Publishing Group Inc., 1990) Covers all sorts of illnesses, what their symptoms are, and how to treat naturally. A must for your medical research library!

# SAMPLE MENU CALENDAR

## APRIL

### 1999

| Sun | Mon | Tue | Wed | Thu | Fri | Sat |
|---|---|---|---|---|---|---|
| | | | | **1** PASTA, CHEESE, SAUCE, SALAD | **2** GOOD FRIDAY FRIED FISH-OUT | **3** RAVIOLI & SALAD |
| **4 EASTER** RESTAURANT WITH GRANDMA | **5** LONDON BROIL POTATOES SALAD BROCCOLI | **6** CHICKEN POT PIE & SALAD CAKE | **7** HOT DOGS, PANFRIED POTATOES & SALAD | **8** PAYDAY OUT TO EAT! | **9** RAVIOLI JELLO | **10** POT ROAST W/VEGGIES AND POTATOES FRUIT SALAD |
| **11** SANDWICHES COLD PASTA FRUIT | **12** PASTA/SAUCE KOTLETAI BROCCOLI JELLO | **13** FROZEN CASSEROLE & SALAD | **14** LEFTOVER CASSEROLE FRUIT | **15** DAD'S BIRTHDAY STEAK, SALAD, POTATO, CAKE | **16** PIZZA & SALAD | **17** GIEDRE'S BIRTHDAY CAMPOUT |
| **18** SANDWICHES WATERMELON | **19** ITALIAN SAUSAGE, RICE, VEGGIES | **20** PASTA & LEFTOVER SAUSAGE | **21** POTATO PANCAKES & APPLESAUCE | **22** HAMBURGERS ON GRILL, FRUIT SALAD | **23** WAFFLES & FRUIT | **24** SLOPPY JOES & PASTA |
| **25** BARBECUE CHICKEN & COLD PASTA | **26** VIKTORIJA'S BIRTHDAY CHIX PARM/ RICE/VEGGY | **27** LEFTOVER CHICKEN & VEGGIES | **28** CROCKPOT BEEF & VEGGIES W/ POTATOES | **29** PIZZA & SALAD | **30** TUNA CASSEROLE | |

| Sun | Mon | Tue | Wed | Thu | Fri | Sat |
|-----|-----|-----|-----|-----|-----|-----|
|     |     |     |     |     |     |     |
|     |     |     |     |     |     |     |
|     |     |     |     |     |     |     |
|     |     |     |     |     |     |     |

# RECIPE CARDS

## RECIPE NAME:

*From the Kitchen of* _____

SHOPPING    LIST:

INGREDIENTS:

RECIPE:

**HOMESCHOOLING BY HEART © 1999**

## RECIPE NAME:

*From the Kitchen of* _____

SHOPPING    LIST:

INGREDIENTS:

RECIPE:

**HOMESCHOOLING BY HEART © 1999**

## RECIPE NAME:

*From the Kitchen of* _____

SHOPPING    LIST:

INGREDIENTS:

RECIPE:

**HOMESCHOOLING BY HEART © 1999**

## RECIPE NAME:

*From the Kitchen of* _____

SHOPPING    LIST:

INGREDIENTS:

RECIPE:

**HOMESCHOOLING BY HEART © 1999**

# FREEZER INVENTORY

| ITEM/FOOD | DATE PUT IN FREEZER | STACKED WHERE | ITEM/FOOD | DATE PUT IN FREEZER | STACKED WHERE |
|---|---|---|---|---|---|
| | | | | | |
| | | | | | |
| | | | | | |
| | | | | | |
| | | | | | |
| | | | | | |
| | | | | | |
| | | | | | |
| | | | | | |
| | | | | | |
| | | | | | |
| | | | | | |
| | | | | | |
| | | | | | |
| | | | | | |
| | | | | | |
| | | | | | |
| | | | | | |
| | | | | | |
| | | | | | |
| | | | | | |

# GROCERY LIST

| ITEM | COST | QTY | STORE | ITEM | COST | QTY | STORE | ITEM | COST | QTY | STORE |
|---|---|---|---|---|---|---|---|---|---|---|---|
| COLD CUTS: | | | | TUNA | | | | DETERGENT | | | |
| | | | | RICE | | | | | | | |
| | | | | JELLO | | | | CLEANERS | | | |
| BAKERY: | | | | FLOUR | | | | | | | |
| | | | | SUGAR | | | | SPONGES / BRILLO | | | |
| | | | | SPICES | | | | BREAD | | | |
| MEAT: | | | | OIL | | | | SODA | | | |
| | | | | COOKIES | | | | SNACK FOODS | | | |
| | | | | COFFEE / TEA | | | | VEGGIES | | | |
| | | | | POWDERED DRINKS | | | | | | | |
| | | | | CRACKERS | | | | | | | |
| WATER | | | | OATMEAL / FARINA | | | | FRUIT | | | |
| SELTZER | | | | CEREAL | | | | | | | |
| JUICE | | | | | | | | | | | |
| SODA | | | | DIAPERS / WIPES | | | | | | | |
| | | | | BABY FOOD | | | | | | | |
| CANNED GOODS | | | | ICE CREAM | | | | EGGS | | | |
| | | | | FROZEN FOODS | | | | FRESH JUICE | | | |
| | | | | | | | | MILK | | | |
| APPLE SAUCE | | | | FROZEN VEGGIES | | | | HALF & HALF | | | |
| TOMATO SAUCE / PASTE | | | | FROZEN DRINKS | | | | YOGURT | | | |
| MUSHROOMS | | | | PIZZA | | | | BUTTER/MARGARINE | | | |
| CANNED FRUIT | | | | WAFFLES | | | | CHEESE | | | |
| PASTA | | | | PET FOOD | | | | SOUR CREAM | | | |
| | | | | | | | | TACOS | | | |
| | | | | PAPER TOWELS | | | | PICKLES | | | |
| CANNED SOUP | | | | KLEENEX | | | | CREAM CHEESE | | | |
| DRY SOUP | | | | TOILET PAPER | | | | COTTAGE CHEESE | | | |
| BOULLION | | | | NAPKINS | | | | MISC | | | |
| MEXICAN | | | | ALUMINUM | | | | | | | |
| ORIENTAL | | | | PLASTIC WRAP | | | | | | | |

HOMESCHOOLING BY HEART © 1999

140

# GROCERY LIST

| ITEM | COST | QTY | STORE | ITEM | COST | QTY | STORE | ITEM | COST | QTY | STORE |
|------|------|-----|-------|------|------|-----|-------|------|------|-----|-------|
|      |      |     |       |      |      |     |       |      |      |     |       |
|      |      |     |       |      |      |     |       |      |      |     |       |
|      |      |     |       |      |      |     |       |      |      |     |       |
|      |      |     |       |      |      |     |       |      |      |     |       |
|      |      |     |       |      |      |     |       |      |      |     |       |
|      |      |     |       |      |      |     |       |      |      |     |       |
|      |      |     |       |      |      |     |       |      |      |     |       |
|      |      |     |       |      |      |     |       |      |      |     |       |
|      |      |     |       |      |      |     |       |      |      |     |       |
|      |      |     |       |      |      |     |       |      |      |     |       |
|      |      |     |       |      |      |     |       |      |      |     |       |
|      |      |     |       |      |      |     |       |      |      |     |       |
|      |      |     |       |      |      |     |       |      |      |     |       |
|      |      |     |       |      |      |     |       |      |      |     |       |
|      |      |     |       |      |      |     |       |      |      |     |       |

# CRAZY ESTIMATION OF DAILY FOOD CONSUMPTION (BY A WACKY FAMILY OF SEVEN)

One night I was wondering why I never seem to have enough money in my food budget. We allocate $225.00 every 2 weeks for a family of seven. Most of my kids are not big eaters yet. I became frustrated because I felt $225.00 should be more than enough money to cover our food, diapers, pet supplies, and paper goods for 2 weeks. I got my trusty paper and pencil and started computing. The following is what I discovered, and it blew my mind. The prices are approximate and the food selected is relatively "inexpensive" (the only item that's cheaper is beans, but we all "dislike" them). Take a look at my list and try to calculate your own menu and budget. I realize now that you need to keep careful track of what you spend for at least 1 month. You buy a coke here, a treat there, or some cosmetics, and you've completely blown your food budget.

## BREAKFAST
EGGS & BREAD OR
HOT CEREAL MADE W/MILK
OR HOMEMADE PANCAKES
OR HOMEMADE WAFFLES
**TOTAL COST: @ $1.50**

## DRINKS(8oz)
MILK ($3/gal) .19
ORANGE JUICE ($2.70/gal) .17
POWDERED LEMONADE .01
WATER (5 GALLON BOTTLE) .07
COFFEE .03
HERBAL TEA .05

## LUNCH
PEANUT BUTTER & JELLY ($1.20)
MACARONI & CHEESE ($1.62)
SOUP & BREAD ($2.28)
LEFTOVERS (@$1.50)
**TOTAL COST: @ $1.20-2.28**

SANDWICHES MADE WITH
COLD CUTS @ **$3.25**

## DINNER
POTATOES OR PASTA (@ .60)
AND
STIR FRY BEEF OR CHICKEN
OR
GROUND TURKEY OR BEEF
OR
TURKEY
(COST OF 1.5 LBS MEAT
@ 3.00)
AND
SALAD $2.22
AND
BROCCOLI $1.20
AND
JELLO $.33
**TOTAL COST: @ $7.35**
(LONDON BROIL AT 2.89/LB.BUY
2 LBS. TOTAL COST $10.13 PER
MEAL)

## COST PER MEAL BASED ON FAMILY OF 7

### SALAD
ICEBERG LETTUCE (.95/HEAD)
RED ONION (.45)
RADISHES (1.25)
GREEN PEPPERS ($1.00)
CUCUMBER(3/$1)
TOMATOE ($1.00)
CELERY ($1.00)
**TOTAL COST FOR ONE MEAL:
$6.65/3(MEALS)=$2.22**

## PAPER GOODS
TOILET @      3.00  TOWELS @ 2.80    NAPKINS   @   .40
DIAPERS @ 15.00  WIPES   @  2.00   CLEANERS @ $2.50
PET FOOD @ 2.00 VITAMINS @ 10.50 TOILETRIES $5.00
**TOTAL FOR 2 WEEKS: @ $43.20**

Now do your addition & multiplication: (Use the higher costs. Always err against yourself! That way there's room to negotiate.)
1.50 Breakfast
2.28 Lunch
7.35 Dinner
4.00 Drinks (average for 7)
**TOTAL:$15.13 X 14 Days =@211.82**
And that's just for "inexpensive" food. What if you want to occasionally splurge for better? Now add in your paper products, diapers, vitamins, toiletries,etc.
**$211.82 + 43.20 = $255.02**

HOMESCHOOLING BY HEART © 1999

# CHAPTER
## ♥ 15 ♥

## BUDGETING - A NINE LETTER NO-NO!

Funny as it may seem, budgeting is an integral part of your homeschooling lifestyle. If you can't budget and end up in difficult straits, sooner or later someone will suggest that you give up homeschooling and find a paying job.

Each married couple should have a budget that they compose together. If only one spouse does it, the other may never adhere to it because she or he was never included in the planning, and therefore never felt committed to making it work. It isn't hard to put one together, though emotionally it may hurt! You need to calculate how much you bring home in cash every month (net income), subtract your fixed expenses, and what you have left is yours to do with however you please (more on that later!).

What you need to do is make a copy of the budget plan that I've included, pull out your checkbook and monthly bills, and start writing in totals. If you are paid monthly, put that amount in for the net. If you are paid every 2 weeks, multiply that by 26 (paychecks) and divide by 12 (months). If you have your own business and never know how much you'll be making, use last year's net income as your average for this year and divide by 12 to obtain an average monthly total. For our purposes, this is a simple budget to help you start off in the right direction.

**Here we go.....**

1) **Net Income:** Write down how much you bring home per month (including any additional income from rentals, interest, etc.)

2) **Tithe:** If you tithe automatically, subtract the percentage you donate.

3) **Group A:** These are all your set monthly household expenditures. To ensure that it has been done properly, take the yearly total and divide by 12, or average your expenses.

4) **Group B:** This is where you write down your insurance payments and estimated medical expenditures. If you have a yearly deductible, make sure that it is averaged out per month.

5) **Group C:** Auto expenses (estimated): insurance, gas, repairs, new parts, AAA, etc.

6) **Group D:** Food budget, entertainment, educational expenses, and clothing allowance. (It is difficult to tell others how much to budget for food. Our family budgets $225.00 every 2 weeks for seven people. Of course, three of those people are not yet big eaters. Our food budget also includes paper goods, detergents, vitamins, and diapers.)

7) **Group E:** Savings. This is a category that I don't even have on our budget. My husband automatically has money deducted from his paycheck for our retirement, plus we've already put away quite a bit for our future in IRA's. Some money is put in a Mutual Fund that we use for big-ticket items, and we have rentals for our kids' futures. I consider these "forced savings" which were begun before we even had kids. (I remember telling my husband not to have an automatic deduction taken from his paycheck for a retirement fund. Boy, am I glad he didn't listen to me! At that time, it seemed like so much to lose when we needed the money for our living expenses. Years have passed, and we don't even think about that automatic deduction. It's like we never had it - but we'll see it in the future, a future that's quickly coming to pass!) We don't save every month because there is nothing left to save when we're done. If you don't have money put aside already or automatically, it's a necessity that you save even a little per month. The rule of thumb is that you should have 3 months of your salary in savings in case of an emergency. That doesn't even take retirement into consideration.

8) **Group F:** Everything else that comes up monthly such as a gift budget, kids' allowances, subscriptions, pool maintenance, Internet fee, cable TV, pest control, etc. These are fixed expenditures, yet they are also expenditures that could be eliminated if necessary.

9) **Total Expenditures**: When you're done, add all your expenditures and subtract from your remaining net (minus the tithe). This is your **remaining balance**. If you have any money left over, you're in good shape.

Keep in mind that if you have monthly charge bills that need to be paid, they should be part of your monthly expenditures. Your goal should be to live debt free. In today's society that's a tall order, but I know many people who have done it. Be persistent, be stubborn, be cheap! Get those bills paid and don't get into debt again. Make it a goal to live frugally so that you can take that much needed vacation, or perhaps retire early.

**Here are some budgeting strategies:**

**Don't buy anything you don't really need.** If I want to save money, I better stay away from office supply stores. I'll always find something there that I absolutely need: pen, marker, new plastic folder, some neat boxes (you get the picture). When I bring these supplies home, they end up in a corner, waiting (sometimes years) to be used. My other downfall – bookstores. I cannot leave without a book. There's always one that I must have or that I can't live without. The same goes for fabric stores – that sale fabric is too good of a deal to pass up. One of the best pieces of advice I received was: "If you want to buy something, wait a month." If you still want it, then go for it. You deserve it. The only exception we make to this rule is if we find a super good deal, a sale that can't be passed by. Hopefully you'll have money put aside for those times.

**Always use cash to make your purchases.** If you don't have the cash, don't buy it. You'll be surprised by how little you're able to purchase if you stick to the "cash only" rule. Use charge cards for emergencies only. I know that many people, my husband included, are using their credit card exclusively to rack up points that can be used toward purchases or trips. If you feel that you are one of those rare people who can do this without digging themselves into a huge financial hole, go for it. However, if you're anything like me, a person that can be easily tempted to buy nonessentials or spend beyond their budget, don't. Also, don't use ATM machines just to have extra cash. It's so easy to spend all your savings that way.

**Don't use checks like cash.** Recently I ran out of checks and had to wait about 10 days for new ones. I had already trained myself not to use the charge card unless it's a dire emergency or to buy gas. I basically had to live on cash. You know, it's not easy. We're so used to relying on checks and credit cards that, when it comes to paying for everything with cash, we're lost! One day the piano teacher was giving a lesson and instead of paying her by check I gave her cash. (It actually felt funny handing her $27.50!) She was stunned that I was giving her cash, and also amused that she would have cash on her for once. I think that it's too easy to rely on your checkbook in a pinch, not realizing that eventually you'll have to make a deposit or start bouncing checks.

If you decide to give up your checking account, don't revert back to using your charge card. (We each had our own checking account. A few months ago the bank charged me $29.00 for a check that bounced by mistake. I was so angry that I decided I'd never use mine again.)  It's so easy to rely on credit cards when you're in a pinch. If possible, don't carry one on you. It takes much self-control to stick to a budget and rely 100% on cash for your purchases. It seems so easy theoretically, but when you try to do it, it's tough. I'm a very practical person and not overly extravagant (unless it comes to books!), but I had just become accustomed to reaching for a check or credit card when I wanted something and didn't have the cash.  The root of the problem: our need to have things we don't yet have and the feeling that we deserve to own it. **Stick to cash – it's real!**

Keep in mind that America is a materialistic consumer society, and most of us are this society's prodigy.  We need to re-program ourselves not to buy and own everything we see.  We can desire things, but we don't need to have them all.  Most of us feel that if we want them, we should have them. I think this goes back to growing up in an age where money was much more available than it had ever been before, and there was so much to buy.  Even if you can afford the items, you shouldn't allow yourself to have everything your heart desires.  Just like we don't want to spoil our children and don't buy them everything they ask for, we need to treat ourselves in the same manner.  We recently read about Poland's Saint Hedwig who was a duchess.  Saint Hedwig had everything: beautiful clothes, jewels, servants, food, money.  Instead of lavishing in all of it, she would intentionally abstain from all the world's goods.  She would wear rough, simple clothing unless she was at an official function.  She would fast often or otherwise eat simply.  By abstaining from worldly temptations, Saint Hedwig was attempting to bring herself closer to our Lord.

**Also, keep in mind that all the extra stuff you're accumulating adds to the overall pollution of the world.**  One day you'll be throwing it out.  The less we buy, the less is made, and the less is thrown away.  I recently came to this realization, and it's given me a much deeper respect for garage sale items. If I can find an item in good condition at a garage sale, why not buy it for a mere fraction of the cost that I would have paid for it new?  Eventually, if I no longer desire the item, I can sell it at my own garage sale.  This is especially true of children's Sunday outfits.  How many times have you spent a small fortune on a Christmas outfit only to have your child outgrow it in the next month or two?  Why not sell it, make a few bucks, and let some other little one enjoy it?

**It seems that most of the fun is in the getting and not the having.** I find more times than not, that when I actually do own the item that I've desired so desperately, I wonder what drove me crazy to have it in the first place. This has to be true of most people since our society lives well above its income level. No matter how much you make, you'll always spend more than you make.  You never have enough money.  This is because there's always one more item we

**must have.** We need to learn to curb our desires (discipline ourselves); we'll then be ahead of the game and well on our way to living within our family's budget.

**SUMMARY:**

1. Pennies saved are pennies earned.

2. The less you buy, the less you need to earn (ergo work).

3. Always pay yourself first from your salary by putting something, no matter how little, into savings.

4. Use cash and lose the credit cards! Don't use checks or the ATM for extra cash.

5. Learn about the different investment opportunities available and determine which one is the best one for investing your savings (weigh possible interest earnings against potential risk).

6. Track your spending for 1 month and make a decision to reduce your spending, if necessary.

7. Check out garage sales and thrift stores for such goods as mason jars, cooking utensils, pots and pans, children's clothing, etc. Sometimes you can find brand new items.

8. Use coupons. My husband used to walk out of the grocery store with three or four bags of groceries for $5-10. (This was pre-children when he had time on his hands.) He waited for sales and bought with coupons. If you still have grocery stores that double your coupons, you can make out like a bandit. It does take time and organization. This may be a good job to give to your older child (perhaps giving him/her a percentage of the savings). Please realize that warehouse stores are not cheaper across the board. They reduce some goods tremendously to entice you into the store. However, I have found that I can beat most of the food prices by buying on sale at my grocery store. Once again it's a matter of time. If you don't have time to search for sale items, buy in large quantities at the warehouse store.

9. If you're fortunate to have a local farmers' market, go at the end of the day and bargain with the vendors. More times than not, they will reduce the price of the vegetables rather than take them back home. Be brave! Think of the possible savings in your pocket!

10. Many times you can get a reduction in price if you pay certain set bills for the entire year: Internet carriers, exterminators, etc. Check your bills to see if anything is said about a discount for prepayment.

11. If you are struggling, get rid of the cable TV (Yeah!!!), exterminator, water man, house security system, and the newspaper. Some of us take these things for granted, not realizing that they're not a necessity. Don't wash your laundry as often; make sure you fill the washing machine. Dry your clothes outside on a line. (The dryer eats a lot of electricity!)

12. **Learn to live on less.** This is definitely a lifestyle choice. You need to examine whether it's necessary to indulge in extravagances or to be content with simplicity and inner peace that comes from knowing you're not in debt.

**PS** Some of you are probably saying to yourselves, "What is she talking about! We've got five kids and just barely make ends meet. We have no extra!" No matter what our salaries are, most people spend everything they earn and then more. That's human nature. There are always ways to cut back somewhere. All of us need to re-evaluate our financial values and spending plans.

*Not that I complain of want; for I have learned, in whatever state I am, to be content.*
*Philippians 4:11*

**FURTHER READING:**
**The Simple Living Guide** by Janet Luhrs (NY: Broadway Books, 1997)
**Using Your Money Wisely** by Larry Burkett (IL: Moody Press, 1985)
> Larry Burkett is founder and president of Christian Financial Concepts, Inc., a ministry dedicated to teaching and counseling on God's principles of finance. He's author of: **How To Manage Your Money, Your Finances in Changing Times, The Financial Planning Workbook,** and **Debt-Free Living.**

# FAMILY BUDGET

| | | MONTHLY | BI-WEEKLY | YEARLY | NOTES |
|---|---|---|---|---|---|
| | NET INCOME (+): | | | | |
| | TITHE (-): | | | | |
| | REMAINING NET: | | | | |
| | | | | | |
| A | MORTGAGE / RENT | | | | |
| | ELECTRIC/GAS | | | | |
| | PHONE | | | | |
| | WATER | | | | |
| | TRASH | | | | |
| | REAL ESTATE TAXES | | | | |
| | HOME INSURANCE | | | | |
| | | | | | |
| B | LIFE INSURANCE | | | | |
| | MEDICAL INSURANCE | | | | |
| | MEDICAL DEDUCTIBLE | | | | |
| | | | | | |
| C | AUTO INSURANCE | | | | |
| | AUTO PAYMENT | | | | |
| | AUTO MAINTENANCE / GAS | | | | |
| | | | | | |
| D | FOOD | | | | |
| | ENTERTAINMENT | | | | |
| | EDUCATIONAL | | | | |
| | CLOTHING | | | | |
| | | | | | |
| E | SAVINGS | | | | |
| | | | | | |
| F | KIDS' ALLOWANCES | | | | |
| | GIFT BUDGET | | | | |
| | INTERNET / CABLE | | | | |
| | SUBSCRIPTIONS | | | | |
| | | | | | |
| | | | | | |
| | | | | | |
| | | | | | |
| | | | | | |
| | TOTAL EXPENDITURES: | | | | |
| | REMAINING BALANCE: | | | | |

# CHAPTER

## ♥ 16 ♥

## KIDS' ALLOWANCES

Allowances are ideal to teach kids financial responsibility. It's never too early to give them an allowance and very carefully direct their spending, so they are adequately prepared to budget themselves when they leave home. Consider how many children go off to college and make a total mess of their finances – or their parents' – because they were never taught to budget!

A few years ago, we decided to give each child an allowance based on his age. My ten-year old received $10, my eight-year old received $8, and my five-year old received $6, every two weeks. I put $4 away for each of the younger ones. (Periodically we put their money in the bank.) No, we don't increase their allowance by a dollar each year. It has stayed this way for the past few years. We also give $10 each to the two oldest children every two weeks for clothing. It's up to them to budget their money, and have enough to buy clothes when needed. They are also responsible for their own gift giving.

We have found that the girls tend to be very tight with their money and never spend it needlessly. My son, on the other hand, did go through a few months when he wanted to spend, spend, spend. However, he soon learned that this led to poverty and an empty wallet when he needed to buy a gift for someone. His attitude now is much more laid back. He doesn't worry about money at all. None of the three are compulsive buyers, who want everything in sight. The best way to squelch thoughts of extravagant buying is saying, "Pay for it yourself!" These words quickly cool their heels!

By giving kids an allowance you're showing them that you think they're responsible. They, in turn, learn responsibility, generosity, budgeting, and tithing. It should be a priority among parents to educate their children financially. Years ago a child always had the farm to turn to for his food and living, but today most of us are at the mercy of corporate institutions. We never know if we'll have a job tomorrow and then how are we going to eat and live without a paycheck each week? It's our responsibility to teach our children to save, and how to save. I've included two interesting charts, that show how much can be earned if you put away $25.00 or $100.00 per month. If your kids do this from the first day they start working, the money will not even be missed.  Soon they'll have quite a nest egg for their future.

## SUMMARY:

1.  Give your kids an allowance, if possible.

2.  Teach them to create a spending plan of their own: tithe, save, and spend.

3.  Teach them the difference between needing something and wanting something.

4.  Teach them to make spending lists and prioritizing their purchases.

5.  Teach them to consumer shop rather than purchasing by impulse. Have them check out the same type of item in three different stores and compare the quality and price.

6.  Set buying standards: Teach them what is too expensive a purchase.

7.  If possible, when they're old enough, give them a clothing allowance so that they are responsible for making their own purchases.

8.  Give them as much financial responsibility and freedom as you are able.

9.  When they are old enough, teach them to use a checkbook and make their own saving's deposits and withdrawals and calculate taxes.

10. Teach them about the horrors of debt.  Strongly discourage borrowing from friends. Tell them that, "A penny saved is a penny earned.  A penny spent is a penny gone.  A penny borrowed is penny that will need to be earned and given away!"

11. Teach them how to invest their money.  They need to know about the difference in interest earnings found within the various financial institutions and the risks involved. A general Rule of Thumb is: Take 72 and divide by your interest rate. This will equal how many years it will take for your money to double!

12. Encourage them to always save a portion of their salary so that they have a nest egg as soon as they begin earning.

13. Remember – always be a good example!

## FURTHER READING:

**Dr. Tightwad's Money-Smart Kids** by Janet Bodnar (Washington,DC: Kiplinger Books, 1997)

**Money Matters for Parents & Their Kids** by Ron and Judy Blue (Christian) (TN: Oliver Nelson, 1988)

**A Penny Saved** by Neal S. Godfrey (NY: Simon & Schuster, 1995)

**Simple Ways to Help Your Kids Become Dollar-$mart** by Elizabeth Lewin,C.F.P. and Bernard Ryan, Jr. (NY: Walker and Co., 1994)

Keep your life free from love of money, and be content with what you have; for He has said, "I will never fail you nor forsake you." Hence we can confidently say,

"The Lord is my helper,
I will not be afraid;
What can man do to me?"

Hebrews 13:5-6

# COMPOUND INTEREST CHART FOR $25 PER MONTH

| YEAR | DEPOSIT PER/MO | 5% | 7 1/2% | 10% |
|------|------|------|------|------|
| 1 | $25.00 | 333.25 | 337.47 | 341.76 |
| 2 | | 657.27 | 674.20 | 691.68 |
| 3 | | 997.87 | 1037.07 | 1078.25 |
| 4 | | 1355.89 | 1428.11 | 1505.30 |
| 5 | | 1732.24 | 1849.51 | 1977.06 |
| 6 | | 2127.83 | 2303.62 | 2498.22 |
| 7 | | 2543.67 | 2792.99 | 3073.96 |
| 8 | | 2980.78 | 3320.35 | 3709.98 |
| 9 | | 3440.25 | 3888.64 | 4412.60 |
| 10 | | 3923.23 | 4501.06 | 5188.80 |
| 11 | | 4430.92 | 5161.02 | 6046.27 |
| 12 | | 4964.59 | 5872.21 | 6993.54 |
| 13 | | 5525.56 | 6638.62 | 8039.99 |
| 14 | | 6115.23 | 7464.52 | 9196.02 |
| 15 | | 6735.07 | 8354.54 | 10473.11 |
| 16 | | 7386.62 | 9313.66 | 11883.92 |
| 17 | | 8071.50 | 10347.23 | 13442.46 |
| 18 | | 8791.43 | 11461.05 | 15164.20 |
| 19 | | 9548.18 | 12661.33 | 17066.23 |
| 20 | | 10343.66 | 13954.79 | 19167.42 |
| 21 | | 11179.83 | 15348.67 | 21488.64 |
| 22 | | 12058.78 | 16850.75 | 24052.92 |
| 23 | | 12982.70 | 18469.45 | 26885.72 |
| 24 | | 13953.90 | 20213.81 | 30015.14 |
| 25 | | 14974.77 | 22093.59 | 33472.26 |
| 26 | | 16047.88 | 24119.31 | 37291.38 |
| 27 | | 17175.90 | 26302.28 | 41510.41 |
| 28 | | 18361.62 | 28654.73 | 46171.24 |
| 29 | | 19608.01 | 31189.80 | 51320.11 |
| 30 | | 20918.16 | 33921.67 | 57008.13 |

## COMPOUND INTEREST CHART FOR $100 PER MONTH

| YEAR | DEPOSIT PER / MO | 5% | 7 1/2% | 10% |
|------|------------------|----|--------|-----|
| 1 | $100.00 | 1333.00 | 1349.88 | 1367.03 |
| 2 | | 2629.09 | 2696.80 | 2766.73 |
| 3 | | 3991.48 | 4148.28 | 4313.00 |
| 4 | | 5423.58 | 5712.45 | 6021.18 |
| 5 | | 6928.94 | 7398.04 | 7908.24 |
| 6 | | 8511.33 | 9214.49 | 9992.89 |
| 7 | | 10174.67 | 11171.96 | 12295.83 |
| 8 | | 11923.11 | 13281.39 | 14839.93 |
| 9 | | 13761.00 | 15554.58 | 17650.42 |
| 10 | | 15692.93 | 18004.24 | 20755.20 |
| 11 | | 17723.69 | 20644.08 | 24185.10 |
| 12 | | 19858.36 | 23488.85 | 27974.15 |
| 13 | | 22102.23 | 26554.48 | 32159.97 |
| 14 | | 24460.91 | 29858.09 | 36784.09 |
| 15 | | 26940.26 | 33418.17 | 41892.43 |
| 16 | | 29546.47 | 37254.63 | 47535.67 |
| 17 | | 32286.00 | 41388.93 | 53769.83 |
| 18 | | 35165.70 | 45844.18 | 60656.79 |
| 19 | | 38192.73 | 50645.31 | 68264.91 |
| 20 | | 41374.63 | 55819.51 | 76669.69 |
| 21 | | 44719.32 | 61394.66 | 85954.57 |
| 22 | | 48235.13 | 67403.01 | 96211.69 |
| 23 | | 51930.82 | 73877.80 | 107542.87 |
| 24 | | 55815.58 | 80855.25 | 120060.57 |
| 25 | | 59899.10 | 88374.38 | 133889.03 |
| 26 | | 64191.54 | 96477.23 | 149165.52 |
| 27 | | 68703.58 | 105209.13 | 166041.66 |
| 28 | | 73446.47 | 114618.91 | 184684.95 |
| 29 | | 78432.02 | 124759.19 | 205280.43 |
| 30 | | 83672.64 | 135686.7 | 228032.53 |

# PART THREE

## THE HOMESCHOOL HIGHWAY

## OR

## "EMBARKING ON THE JOURNEY"

# CHAPTER
## ♥ 17 ♥

## THE WISDOM OF KING SOLOMON

*"Blessed are those who hunger and thirst for righteousness, for they shall be satisfied.*                                  *Matthew 5:6*

*To him the gatekeeper opens (to the shepherd); the sheep hear his voice, and he calls his own sheep by name and leads them out. When he has brought out all his own, he goes before them, and the sheep follow him, for they know his voice.*          *John 10:3-4*

Undoubtedly, the most troublesome aspect of homeschooling is the actual homeschooling. If you've taken my suggestions to heart, then you're in the process of simplifying your life; do this **before** you even consider tackling your children's future course of study. Once you're armed with a set of life goals for your family and each child, and you've begun training your children to obey, go ahead with this chapter. Before I begin, let me explain how I feel about setting a course of study, or curriculum planning.

I truly, truly believe that the education of our children takes place every minute of every day of their lives. There is no one set time or place or curriculum that can teach our children everything that they need to know. Our most important job as their parents is to instill wisdom, the type King Solomon had when the two women came to him, each claiming to be the mother of the child they brought before him.

*And all Israel heard of the judgement which the king had rendered; and they stood in awe of the king, because they perceived that the wisdom of God was in him, to render justice.*          *I Kings 3:28*

That type of wisdom cannot be learned from books, only as a gift from the Lord. **Noah Webster's 1828 American Dictionary of the English Language** states that *"If wisdom is to be considered as a faculty of the mind, it is the faculty of discerning or judging what is most just, proper, and useful, and if it is to be considered as an acquirement, it is the knowledge and use of what is best, most just, most proper, most conducive to prosperity or happiness."* Put plainly: Wisdom is knowing how to make the best possible choices in everyday life.

The question is, "What's the best choice?" Each individual's vision of best is different. I would like to qualify that with, "the best moral choices in life." I don't want my children to separate morality from secular life (exactly what is occurring in schools). They're both tied together hand in hand. One example is Disney – we don't do Disney. Why? Because the Disney Corporation has made some pretty bad moral decisions by supporting anti-Christian values. For the past 3 or 4 years, we've avoided spending money on anything to do with Disney. (I'll let you in on a secret: Boycotting Disney is not at all difficult for kids as long as you explain the "whys." Children like to be told what's black and white, right and wrong. Once you tell them, they'll stick to it and make sure you do also. It's extremely difficult for the parents though, because we are under the assumption that we're somehow depriving our children. It's the parents that have emotional ties to Disney, not the kids.) We'd love to boycott goods made in China because of their disregard for human life. We tried that, but boy is that a difficult one. It seems like almost everything in the stores (that's affordable) comes from China.

The point I'm trying to make is that as parents, it's our responsibility to develop our children's character, to teach them what's morally right and wrong, and to learn to live by these truths in the real world, not just theoretically. I believe if we're able to successfully train our children's character, then homeschooling has served its purpose. This can be referred to as character training, and I believe that this should **always** take precedence over academia.

**Did you homeschool for purely academic reasons or were there other reasons besides the academics?**

_____
_____
_____
_____
_____
_____
_____
_____

CHARACTER: *By way of eminence. Distinguished or good qualities; those which are esteemed and respected; and those which are ascribed to a person in common estimation.* (Noah Webster's 1828 American Dictionary of the English Language)

Training: *To coach in or accustom to some mode of behavior or performance.* (The American Heritage Dictionary, 1973)

**Do you believe that instilling character qualities such as thoughtfulness, thoroughness, diligence, truthfulness, and respect, should prevail over scholastic book learning? If you do believe this, then to what extent are you willing to change your curriculum expectations to meet these goals?**

_____
_____
_____
_____
_____
_____
_____
_____

May I suggest that you take a break right now and think long and hard about this. Don't just say, "Of course I want my child to know right from wrong, but I can just add that along with the book learning." Nope. It doesn't work like that. What usually happens is that character problems arise (usually in more than one child simultaneously), and we're so busy (undisciplined) that we don't take the time to correct, teach, and punish (if necessary). Instead, we scream, threaten, and go on with whatever we are doing when we were so rudely interrupted. Just like everything else in life, character training needs to be taught with patience, love, and diligence.

Let me give you an example. Let's say that one of your children occasionally lies – not too often (that you know of), but the lies that you catch are big enough to warrant further investigation into his character. The child also never willingly confesses. This happens once, twice. You deal with it at the time, but otherwise ignore it. The child then tells a whopper, and you sternly discipline with a spanking and punishment. You also warn him that he no longer has your trust. You also warn him that if he lies to you again, stronger measures will be taken. A week later he lies again, and you barely get a confession out of him (you're 99.9% sure that he's lying). What do you do now? Yell? Spank? Punish by withholding something he cares about?

First, when you're dealing with a morality issue, a spanking is always due. Calmly do this. Tell the child why you're disappointed – you can't trust him any longer. Tell him he has sinned in God's eyes. Punish by withholding something: no computer for a week, no friends, whatever. You may even want the child to read some Scripture and memorize it. All this has taken time, probably at least a good hour of your day. Book work is at a standstill for the child. Real, honest to goodness learning is taking place that day. Now it's your job to stay on top of things and make sure you discipline if he lies again. The key is to praise good character. Also, always be a good role model and consistently emphasize it!

There are ideal ways in which to do this. One way is with unit studies, like **Konos**, that are centered entirely around character traits. While you are teaching your child science, history, or geography, the theme may be patience. Bill Gotthard's **ATIA** program bases its entire curriculum, which is a unit study approach, on the Gospel of Matthew and the Beatitudes. You spend years studying these character traits. You can make up your own study by reading **The Book of Virtues,** by William J.Bennett, and discussing the character traits. Talk about how important good character is and how we can try to make ours as free of sinful blemishes as possible. Another excellent book for younger children is **Wisdom and the Millers.**

If you are willing to make your homeschooling journey a lifestyle, you need to make a decision about which direction is more important to you: character or academia. After you've made your choice, the rest will fall in place.

I've included some character trait goal charts. One chart includes the character traits that I want my children to eventually have. The other chart is a weekly one where you choose a trait to work on for the week. The entire family works on the same trait. At the end of the day, the child comes to either mom or dad and rates himself. Of course, you get to confer on the score the child says he deserves. You give the child points, anywhere from 0 to 5, which you record on this chart. You decide on the reward and how many points are needed.

## SUMMARY:

1. Decide how you're going to work on character training.

2. Use a goal chart and reward your kids for good character.

3. Always be a good example yourself!

*"Character is more caught than taught!"*
*Sheriff Ray Nash*

**FURTHER READING:**
**The Book of Virtues** by William J. Bennett (NY: Simon & Schuster, 1993)
**Prudence and the Millers** by Mildred A. Martin (OH: Green Pastures Press, 1993)
**Konos, (Vol I-III)** by Jessica Hulcy and Carole Thaxton, 1984
**Storytime With The Millers** by Mildred A. Martin (OH: Green Pastures Press, 1992)
**Wisdom and the Millers** by Mildred A. Martin (OH: Green Pastures Press, 1989)
**Character Booklets** from Character Institute, 520 West Main, Oklahoma City, OK 73102.
**Character Development Materials** for families, schools, and businesses from Character Pitch, 1437 Davis Drive, Ft. Myers, FL 33919.

> But I say, walk by the Spirit, and do not gratify the desires of the flesh. For the desires of the flesh are against the Spirit, and the desires of the Spirit are against the flesh; for these are opposed to each other, to prevent you from doing what you would. But if you are led by the Spirit you are not under the law. Now the works of the flesh are plain: immorality, impurity, licentiousness, idolatry, sorcery, enmity, strife, jealousy, anger, selfishness, dissension, party spirit, envy, drunkenness, carousing, and the like. I warn you, as I warned you before, that those who do such things shall not inherit the kingdom of God. But the fruit of the Spirit is love, joy, peace, patience, kindness, goodness, faithfulness, gentleness, self-control; against such there is no law. And those who belong to Christ Jesus have crucified the flesh with its passions and desire.
>
> If we live by the Spirit, let us also walk by the Spirit. Let us have no self-conceit, no provoking of one another, no envy of one another.
>
> Galatians 5:16-25

# CHARACTER GOALS

| CHARACTER TRAIT | DATE | | | | | |
|---|---|---|---|---|---|---|
| OBEDIENCE: TO LISTEN AND DO AS REQUESTED | | | | | | |
| DILIGENCE: PERSISTENCE, ATTENTIVE- NESS, AND ENERGETIC DESIRE | | | | | | |
| ENTHUSIASM: TO APPLY ONESELF CHEEFULLY AND WILLINGLY | | | | | | |
| ORDERLINESS: TO BE SYSTEMATIC | | | | | | |
| HUMILITY: TO BE RESPECTFUL AND NOT PROUD | | | | | | |
| RESPECT: TO HONOR | | | | | | |
| COMPASSION: TO PITY OR SYMPATHIZE | | | | | | |
| | | | | | | |

# WEEKLY CHARACTER GOAL CHART

| WEEK | CHARACTER TRAIT | M | T | W | T | F | S | S | M | T | W | T | F | S | S | M | T | W | T | F | S | S | M | T | W | T | F | S | S |
|------|-----------------|---|---|---|---|---|---|---|---|---|---|---|---|---|---|---|---|---|---|---|---|---|---|---|---|---|---|---|---|
| | | | | | | | | | | | | | | | | | | | | | | | | | | | | | |
| | | | | | | | | | | | | | | | | | | | | | | | | | | | | | |
| | | | | | | | | | | | | | | | | | | | | | | | | | | | | | |
| | | | | | | | | | | | | | | | | | | | | | | | | | | | | | |
| | | | | | | | | | | | | | | | | | | | | | | | | | | | | | |
| | | | | | | | | | | | | | | | | | | | | | | | | | | | | | |
| | | | | | | | | | | | | | | | | | | | | | | | | | | | | | |
| | | | | | | | | | | | | | | | | | | | | | | | | | | | | | |
| | | | | | | | | | | | | | | | | | | | | | | | | | | | | | |
| | | | | | | | | | | | | | | | | | | | | | | | | | | | | | |
| | | | | | | | | | | | | | | | | | | | | | | | | | | | | | |
| | | | | | | | | | | | | | | | | | | | | | | | | | | | | | |

UNDER WEEK, PUT THE DATE. UNDER CHARACTER TRAIT, WRITE DOWN THE TRAIT THAT YOU WANT YOUR KIDS TO WORK ON. IT CAN TAKE UP TO 1 MONTH TO WORK ON 1 TRAIT. YOU DON'T WANT TO CHANGE EVERY WEEK.

SCALE: 0-5    5   EXCELLENT, TRIED THEIR VERY BEST          300 POINTS: GET TO GO OUT FOR
              3   TRIED, BUT DIDN'T ALWAYS SUCCEED                        SPECIAL LUNCH

HOMESCHOOLING BY HEART © 1999

# CHAPTER
## ♥ 18 ♥

## CURRICULUM PLANNING
## Or
## Planning Your Child's Course of Study

The second most important value that I want to instill in my kids after wisdom is the love of learning.  I want them to love learning…really, honest to goodness, love it.  I want them to want to look up the answers in an encyclopedia because they have to know the answer, not because mom told them to do it "or else."  I want to raise children who will grow up being self-motivated learners. That's real education, isn't it?  This is what we, as adults, do in the real world, isn't it?  How much algebra and biology and French do you remember from your school days?  I bet you remember much of what you study now – whether it's about gardening or plumbing or the study of herbs - and that's because you want to learn about it, you need to know the answer, and you know exactly where to find the answer.

Along with instilling a love for learning, you need to add another very, very important ingredient to your school plan – fun. Yes, fun.  We're not trying to duplicate the public school system. We know that doesn't work; we've seen and heard all the gruesome statistics. We want to have fun at home with our kids and enjoy education; otherwise why do it? **Education should be a thrill, an adventure!  It should be exciting!** It shouldn't be drudgery and boring and tedious. You, their mama, should be having just as much fun learning as the kids. If either you or the kids dislike it, there's a problem, a real problem.  Something needs to change. Your two most important educational goals should be: Instilling a love for learning and always having fun!

You know what? I can tell you how to do it!  Yes I can! Let me tell you something else – I bet you're thinking there's no way I can teach you!  Think that if you must, but I'm still willing to tell you.  Here it goes…are you ready?

The secret to instilling the love of learning in your kids is **by loving to learn yourself!** The secret to having fun learning is **to make sure all of you are always having fun!** Yup…that's it, and that's all there is to it. I can prove it to you! Well…I could, if I had your kids.

Folks, there's nothing mystical about the love of learning, and having fun doing it. A child that's ready and wants to learn, will always learn. If he wants to learn, it means that the child is having fun. Of course, the reverse is also true. If your child's not ready to learn and doesn't want to learn, you are going to have one horrible time forcing the issue. (Read the Moore's books. See Further Reading.) Yes…you can force him (just like you can potty train a one-year old), but who's the one doing all the learning? You are! The child eventually will learn, but it will take so much longer. In the course of this "learning" the child will come to hate anything to do with education! On top of having a kid who hates school, you'll probably have one who's a discipline problem with an attitude to boot! Do you remember the kids that used to be labeled the "trouble makers" in your class? Year after year they'd have the same label and sit in the corner of the room ostracized. They were great at disrupting the entire class with their jokes, rude noises, or stupid questions. They probably began this behavior because they didn't want to learn: They couldn't sit still for two minutes, but the teacher made them do it. Instead of cooperating, they became the class troublemakers. Today they'd probably label them ADD, or some such tag, give them medication, or stick them in a special learning class. This is one way of eliminating the worst discipline problems from a very full classroom. **Avoid pushing your children to learn; when they're ready, they'll learn. Always have fun!**

So what do you do? How do you begin this crazy love affair? You begin by shutting off the TV (perhaps throwing it out the window along with the dishwasher!), getting a great book, and sitting down to read silently to yourself. After a few puzzled looks from the peanut gallery, some pushes, shoves, and snickers, one may dare come up to you and ask you what you're doing. "Reading, my dear," you'll reply. After another few minutes, they'll slide right up to you, hang over your arm, and sneak a peak at what you're reading (OK, perhaps it will take you one or two days to get this far, but remember, the TV's off; they're inside with nothing to do!). At this point, you can casually put the book down and quietly say, "Would you like me to read to you?" (You do this no matter what the age – 6 months or 16 years old.)

Hook them on books! Come on, you can do it. Be sly…be sneaky…get a great picture book or mystery novel. Hook 'em and reel them in!!! Remember, you're setting the example…keep reading yourself. They need to see that reading is important to you and that you love to read! If you are successful in producing good readers who love to read, they will be able to learn anything, anytime, anyplace. **Reading is the key that opens every door in life!**

Now at this point, I need to make another aside. I love to read. There's nothing I'd rather do. When I was younger, I'd read till 3:00AM to finish a good book. (I've even been known to read by the light of a flashlight till 5:00AM when I was a kid!) Soon I realized that this just wouldn't work raising kids; now I read a lot of nonfiction so that I can put it down and go to bed at a decent hour. However, give me a good novel, and you've lost me till I'm done! What about those of you who aren't good readers or hate to read? Well, let me put it this way. I have a real fear of teaching upper grade math. I did fine until Algebra and lost it after that. Guess what? My daughter doesn't like math; she'll do it because she knows she has to do it, but I can sense there's no love. I'm still working on this problem, but I've come to realize that in order for her attitude to change, I need to change mine. We learn by example, don't we?

Another interesting area is science. I like science, but I'm not thrilled with it. I'd rather read any day then do experiments. Biology is the only area that I can really get into. Now, I've known this from the first day we started homeschooling, so I've made it a priority to fill my house with science related books. My two oldest are girls and they bear through it, but would always rather reach for a history book. But it's interesting that my son is reaching for these science related books. My ruse is working! In fact, at the age of eight, he's reading the newspaper every day and telling us about the headlines and major events. He's totally different from the girls, much more interested in nonfiction and science. Thus, there's hope yet. Also, my older daughter was part of a biology dissection co-op this year. I made her go (she felt that she didn't have enough time), and she discovered that she's fascinated with cutting up dead critters. (They dissected a rat as their last experiment. They actually removed all the skin so that they could see the muscles. Now I think that's both gross and interesting!) The point is that no matter whether you're good at something, or don't like a certain subject area, you have to learn to love it for the kids' sake. You can't expect them to be fascinated by subjects you aren't even willing to discuss. There's an old saying, "The apple doesn't fall far from the tree..."

If you feel that you're not a good enough reader, or that you aren't smart enough to set a good example, think again. Almost every homeschooling parent I've ever known has said that they learn or re-learn along with their kids. Many parents don't remember ever having learned the information in school and now they're intrigued with learning alongside their children. If you're not a reader, it's probably because no one took the time to teach you properly or you never were given any interesting material to read. Go to the library and ask the children's librarian to help you. (I've included a short list of read-a-loud books that we've enjoyed over the years. If you don't want to ask the librarian, try these.) Tell her you're not the greatest reader, but you'd like to read aloud to your kids and could she please help you find some interesting books that all of you would like. If you feel you're not smart enough – that you barely passed in school – then now is your chance! You don't have to tell a soul what you're doing, just do it. Do unit studies with your kids and learn right along with them. Pick subjects that are interesting to you and make the learning contagious. Chances are you'll be the best and brightest student because you want to learn! Don't be afraid. Think of this as your opportunity to get the education of a lifetime. Remember...if you truly love your children, they'll learn. **Love makes everything possible!**

I hear a lot about kids and their reading problems. A few years ago, I taught at a nationally known reading learning center as a tutor. Parents spend well over $100 a month to send their kids there for remedial reading work. The center tests the child to see what level he's at, and he usually comes twice a week for one hour. During this time, the child is given short reading selections along with comprehension questions. The children do this for about 40 minutes and then play trivia games. The ratio is one tutor to three children. As an incentive, the students are given play money as a reward for answering questions, and after their session they can spend it at the school store or save up for a bigger prize. There are no secret recipes, no extra-special books. Each child is placed at a comfortable reading level and then slowly progresses forward, rewarded all along the way.

Can't you do that? **The key here is patience.** You had the patience to do everything else when your child was young. So-called educational experts now have led you to believe that you're not capable of teaching your own child to read. There are no secret codes, no special texts. You don't even need a reading program to teach reading. All you need is a book that the child wants to read, and much patience, time, and love. Has anyone told you that children **have** to learn to read by a certain age or grade? The fact is that whether one child begins reading at three-years old and another at ten-years old, the second will catch up with the first. If you've been reading aloud to your child since he was an infant, the child will "know" everything that the three-year old reader will have read on his own. In fact, your child will probably know more because you will have been reading above his reading level (you should always read aloud to the child's comprehension or maturity level).

I believe that there are children with special reading problems, but I don't believe that the percentage is as high as the reading experts want us to believe. (For serious reading problems, see Further Reading for **Learning Connection Visual Training** information.) My opinion is that many of these kids are pushed into reading much too early; they're not physically and/or mentally ready to take on the reading challenge. Also, they haven't been given the time needed to develop their reading proficiency. They are given material that's too hard for them and probably too boring. To top it off, we make them answer a zillion comprehension questions when all we have to do is ask, "So, what was the story about?" or "What did you like about the story?" **Learning to read should always be set at the child's pace.** You can't push the child to go faster. **He** sets the pace!

When my first child, Viktorija, was born, my dad, God rest his soul, said, "The two of you (my husband and I) better speak only in Lithuanian at home if you want her to speak the language. Even a baby recognizes sounds and will eventually begin imitating them." (Richie and I were both born in the U.S.A. to Lithuanian parents and so our first language was Lithuanian. However, we felt more comfortable talking to each other in English.) We started to speak

Lithuanian at home all the time (that was quite an adjustment for us!). Viktorija was never "taught" a word of English. We never purposely conversed with her in English. She'd hear English on the radio and walk around the house reciting commercials. She'd hear English from the few friends we had (we had just moved to Florida). She never spoke in English, but we knew she would learn it as well as us. When she was about 4 ½ years old, she decided to speak English – in complete sentences and with a Lithuanian accent! (It was adorable!) The little turkey didn't want to talk until she could talk well enough to be understood and carry on a conversation! We had complete trust in her abilities and desire to learn, and she proved us right.

When I began teaching Viktorija, I taught her everything in Lithuanian. I taught her the Lithuanian alphabet so that I could teach her to read. My theory was that if I taught her to read Lithuanian first, she'd never forget it. If she learned to read English first, she'd never want to learn to read in Lithuanian because there weren't any interesting books available. Every evening before bedtime I'd read stories to her, always in Lithuanian (I translated as I read). When she was about 5, we began to read novels in English, like **Heidi**. Toward the end of first grade, I began to teach her to read English. She was an auditory learner and basically taught herself from phonics tapes. However, she didn't want to read books. I think her fear was that if she began to read on her own, I'd stop reading aloud. (Ha! Reading aloud is my homeschooling joy!) Eventually, near the end of second grade, she started reading books. Today she can read a book a day and never leaves home without one. (The biggest joke in our house when we travel on vacation is deciding which books are going long before anything else is packed!) All my other children - Giedre, Gintaras, and Linas - have taught themselves to speak English, but they had a lot of help from their older brother and sisters, and from all their friends. They've also followed in Viktorija's reading footsteps – though I did have to teach them to read. Perhaps I was pushing too much; perhaps I should have waited longer…

In conclusion, this is what I feel should be the basis of our curriculum – the development of wisdom, the love of learning, and having lots of fun together. These should take precedence over everything else you do. If you see your child fighting over a moral dilemma – stop everything and focus on it. If you see character flaws, work on correcting them immediately. If your child is dying to find the answer to a question that has absolutely nothing to do with their studies, drop everything and go to the library. If you're not happy with a particular book, chuck it. If you see that your children are struggling and becoming frustrated, drop it. There is much more to education than curriculum. Books, especially texts and workbooks, should be tools that are used at your discretion. Never depend on them entirely. You're raising a child, not a computer. You want that child to be prepared to live in the world outside your front door. You need to teach him right from wrong, and how to survive in the real world. Provide the child with real tools first, such as cooking, cleaning, carpentry, canning, sewing, medicine, and more. Teach him about the world around you. Don't rely on pages in a text book. Use those pages only to supplement the learning process. You're educating a living, breathing person, not sculpting a statue.

### SUMMARY:

1. Concentrate on instilling the love of learning by setting a good example yourself. Remember, reading is the key that opens every door!

2. You should always have fun learning. If you or the kids aren't having fun, stop and re-assess.

3. Never push a child to learn to read or write or do math. Wait for signs that tell you the child is ready to learn to read.

4. **When teaching to read, set your pace to the child's.**

5. Read aloud daily from a book that's interesting to all of you. Remember, if the book is too difficult, slow, boring, etc., the chances are your kids will feel the same way.

6. Always read aloud to the oldest child's maturity level. If there's a large age span between the kids (I read to my 13 year old and the youngest is 5 years old), then occasionally read a book that's "less mature" for the younger child's benefit. You'll probably be surprised that even the older one may enjoy it. Sometimes we become so intent on the older ones that we forget about the youngest. Give them some reading time of their own, with either you or one of the other kids reading aloud to them. This sharpens the reader's narrative voice. It enables them to put some life into their reading. Never stop reading aloud to your children. A child is **never** too old or young to listen to a good story. Reading together brings the family closer together. Let the kids draw, color, sew, knit, or build with their blocks or Legos during this time (unless their activity starts disrupting your reading).

7. Be patient! Remember patience is a characteristic of love. If you love someone, you are always patient. **A child does not have to know how to read by a certain age.** If you take your time, eventually he will learn and love it, especially if you set a good example by reading yourself. Try not to be impatient. If it's important to you, soon it will be important to him. Children learn when their "season" arrives.

## FURTHER READING:

**Better Later Than Early** by Raymond and Dorothy Moore (NY: Reader's Digest Press, 1975)

**Beyond Survival, A Guide to Abundant-Life Homeschooling** by Diana Waring ( WA: Emerald Books, 1996)

**Charlotte Mason Companion** by Karen Andreola (USA: Charlotte Mason Research & Supply, 1998)

**Home Grown Kids** by Raymond and Dorothy Moore (TX: Word Publishing, 1981)

**Homeschooling For Excellence** by David and Micki Colfax (NY: Warner Books, 1988)

**School Can Wait** by Raymond and Dorothy Moore

**The Simplicity of Homeschooling** by Vicki Goodchild (FL: HIS Publishing, 1997)

**Wisdom's Way of Learning** by  Marilyn Howshall (WA: Howshall Home Publications, 1994)

## For Serious Reading Problems contact:

**Learning Connection Visual Training,**

> The Learning Connection
> 12510 Kaibab Court, Colorado Springs, CO 80908
> http://www.thelearningconnection.com  (1-800-299-7323)

# When Mother Reads Aloud

When Mother reads aloud, the past
Seems real as every day;
I hear the tramp of armies vast,
I see the spears and lances cast,
I join the trilling fray;
Brave knights and ladies fair and proud
I meet when Mother reads aloud.

When Mother reads aloud, far lands
Seem very near and true;
I cross the desert's gleaming sands,
Or hunt the jungle's prowling bands,
Or sail the ocean blue.
Far heights, whose peaks the cold mists shroud,
I scale, when Mother reads aloud.

When Mother reads aloud, I long
For noble deeds to do-
To help the right, redress the wrong;
It seems so easy to be strong,
So simple to be true.
Oh, thick and fast the visions crowd
My eyes, when Mother reads aloud.

Author unknown

## GREAT READ ALOUD BOOKS FOR THE ENTIRE FAMILY

### BOOKS TO READ WITH CHILDREN 8 YEARS OR YOUNGER

*Lighter Reading:*

Box Car Kids Series by Gertrude Chandler Warner
Happy Hollisters by Jerry West
Three Cousins Detective Club Series by Elspeth Campbell Murphy
The Cul-de-Sac Kids by Beverly Lewis
Adventures in Odyssey Series by Paul McCusker
Cam Jansen Mysteries by David A. Adler
The Bobbsey Twins Series by Laura Lee Hope
Wishbone Classics by Mary Wollstonecraft Shelley
The Ballet Shoes by Noel Streatfeild
The Theater Shoes by Noel Streatfeild
Dancing Shoes by Noel Streatfeild

*More Classic Literature:*

Little House On The Prarie Series by Laura Ingalls Wilder
Peter Pan by J.M. Barrie
The Mitchells by Hilda van Stockum
Little Princess by Frances Hodgson Burnett
Little Lord Fauntleroy by Frances Hodgson Burnett
The Secret Garden by Frances Hodgson Burnett
Indian Captive by Lois Lenski
Strawberry Girl by Lois Lenski
Shoo-Fly Girl by Lois Lenski
Judy's Journey by Lois Lenski
Caddie Woodlawn by Carol Ryrie Brink
Magical Melons by Carol Ryrie Brink
A Yankee Girl At Bull Run by Alice Turner Curtis
The Little Maid Historical Book Series by Alice Turner Curtis
A Bird's Christmas by Kate Douglas Wiggin

# BOOKS TO READ WITH CHILDREN 9 YEARS AND OLDER

### *Lighter Reading:*

Cooper Kids Series by Frank Peretti

Rebecca by Daphne du Maurier

The Rover Boys Mysteries by Arthur M. Winfield

Tom Swift Mysteries by Victor Appleton II

Sumerhill Secrets Mysteries by Berverly Lewis

The Heritage of Lancaster County Books by Beverly Lewis

Sugar Creek Gang Series by Paul Hutchens

### *More Classic Literature:*

Swiss Family Robinson by Johann Wyss

Cheaper By The Dozen by Frank B. Gilbreth, Jr. & Ernestine Gilbreth Carey

Belles On Their Toes by Frank B. Gilbreth, Jr. & Ernestine Gilbreth Carey

By The Great Horn Spoon by Sid Fleischman

Pollyanna by Eleanor H. Porter

My Side Of The Mountain by Jean Craighead George

Far North by Will Hobbs

Anne Of Green Gables by L. M. Montgomery

A Christmas Carol by Charles Dickens

Johnny Tremain by Esther Forbes

Madeline Takes Command by Ethel C. Brill

The Cabin Faced West by Jean Fritz

Shades Of Gray by Caroline Reeder

Streams To The River, River To The Sea by Scott O'Dell

Early Thunder by Jean Fritz

Trumpet Of The Swan by Stuart Little

The Golden Goblet by Eloise Jarvis McGraw

The Bronze Bow by Elizabeth George Speare

Augustine Came To Kent by Barbara Willard

Otto Of The Silver Hand by Homer Pyle

Adam Of The Road by Elizabeth Janet Gray

Little Women by Louisa May Alcott

Little Men by Louisa May Alcott

## BOOKS TO READ WITH CHILDREN 9 YEARS AND OLDER

An Old-Fashioned Girl by Louisa May Alcott

The Adventures of Robin Hood by Roger Lancelyn Green

The Winged Watchman by Hilda Van Stockum

Red Hugh, Prince Of Donegal by Robert T. Reilly

The Adventures of Huckleberry Finn by Mark Twain

Saint Joan by George Bernard Shaw

The Old Man And The Sea by Ernest Hemingway

Our Town by Thorton Wilder (A Play)

Canterbury Tales (Geoffrey Chaucer) Retold by Barbara Cohen

"Rip Van Winkle," by Washington Irving

"The Birthmark," by Nathaniel Hawthorne

"The Purloined Letter," by Edgar Allen Poe

The Chronicles of Brother Cadfael Mysteries by Ellis Peters

The Red Badge of Courage by Stephen Crane

"The Man Without A Country," by Edward Hale

The Hobbit by J.R.R. Tolkien

The Lord of The Rings by J.R.R. Tolkien

The Chronicles of Narnia by C.S.Lewis

Irish Red by Jim Kjelgaard

A Girl of the Limberlost by Gene Stratton Porter

Freckles by Gene Stratton Porter

Laddie by Gene Stratton Porter

The Harvester by Gene Stratton Porter

The Keeper of The Bees by Gene Stratton Porter

Julius Caesar by William Shakespeare (A Play)

Son of Charlemagne by Barbara Willard

A Wrinkle in Time by Madeline L'Engle

A Wind In the Door by Madeline L'Engle

A Swiftly Tilting Planet by Madeline L'Engle

The Tempest by William Shakespeare (A Play)

The Black Arrow by Robert Louis Stevenson

Kidnapped by Robert Louis Stevenson

# CHAPTER
## ♥ 19 ♥

## "SCHOOL"
### (OR BETTER YET)
## "YOUR WORK IN PROGRESS"

"All right," you say to yourself, "I know what *she* thinks is important regarding schooling at home, but how do I actually school them? I need to do something more than just read to them, train their character, discipline them, and organize our home. If that's all I do, they won't know anything to pass the _____ Exam (fill in with any standardized test name)!"

Think again about what you said: "If all I do is read to them, work on their character, and discipline them..." **ALL**? If you do all that, and do it well, you'll have succeeded in raising brilliant, caring, self-sufficient children! Children that will probably rule the world if given the opportunity.

What's the most important thing we can do for our children? Help them find the path to heaven! Yes? If that's **all** you accomplish, **you've done it all!** A child - who knows right from wrong, is obedient and respectful, loving, compassionate, and diligent - is worth his weight in gold. If he loves to learn and is having fun, you can't possibly ask for more. By avoiding "schoolish work," we're not hurting our children scholastically. We're creating individuals who'll have strong ideals and will want to achieve something in life, whether it's being a farmer or nuclear scientist or policeman. His future will be of his own design. Our real job is to make sure that our sons and daughters grow up to love the Lord will all their heart; secondly, that they should be caring fathers and mothers, loving spouses, or compassionate celibates. The key here is that we need to teach them to love with all their hearts and to love one another as God loves us.

We need to teach them to survive in the real world, not just learn all sorts of theoretical mumbo jumbo. Yes, there is a place for Algebra and Physics and Literary Criticism, but not at the expense of knowing how to survive in today's rather cruel and shaky world. What if our economy collapses, or a one-world government takes over and suppresses the people, or a hurricane or tornado strikes? Will your children know what to do in a medical emergency? How will they eat if all the stores have closed? Will they know that hybrid seeds won't self-produce and will they have good seed on hand? Will they be able to deliver a baby, be it human or animal? Will they know how to slaughter livestock for food? Will they be able to scour the forest for healing herbs that will ease pain and discomfort? How about building a shelter if inclement weather hits? What about preserving food or sewing their own clothes? Will they know how to purify their drinking water?

Our job is to raise responsible, self-sufficient adults who are on fire for the Lord; therefore you should expect to be constantly shifting gears. You're working with human beings and your lives are always in motion and changing. Whether you like it or not, your day is filled with intrusions and surprises. You would have to be locked up in a windowless box for it to be otherwise. I always tell parents that the first year is the hardest, especially if you're taking your children out of school. You have many adjustments to make, the first being that mom is now in charge of the kids' education. Discipline and character need to be addressed, and of course, school will no longer be typical. It's easier to start from the first day when no one has any set expectations of what school is going to be like. You just do it.

Because the first year is the toughest, don't expect too much "book" learning; expect many real life experiences. Work on your lifestyle. Each subsequent year will become a little bit easier. Don't try to do everything at once. Start with one subject area and work solely on that area. Add another until eventually you're covering everything you want.

Each year that I homeschooled (at the very beginning), I would add a subject. It took me five or six years before I was able to efficiently cover everything I wanted to during my day. You need to realize that this is not a "quick fix" but a slow process, like aging wine, that gets tastier as the years go by. You need to be relaxed and ready to change directions when you see fit. Don't buy a curriculum expecting it to suit everyone and last forever.

Your ways of teaching will, and should always, be changing. I hope and pray that you're not doing the same curriculum year after year. There's no faster way to kill the desire to learn. I've found that a lot of parents who take their kids out of school to homeschool want a "full curriculum" program. They opt for this choice because they feel unsure of themselves, and they want to make sure their kids aren't missing a beat. What they fail to realize is that all they're doing is bringing "school home." They haven't changed anything except taken away the school building and all their kids' friends. In order for homeschooling to thrive, it has to be the **best** alternative to your existing problem. The kids have to be excited about wanting to be home and learning. You have to light their fire! Chances are they will not be excited about doing the same old stuff they did back at the schoolhouse.

## SUMMARY:

1. Strive to create self-sufficient learners who will know what to do in life if ever a need arises. In other words, their knowledge needs to be practical hands-on learning, not merely theoretical.

2. Be willing to grow with your kids and be their role model.

3. Expect intrusions and delays; learn to live with them peacefully and contentedly.

4. Expect the first year to be the toughest, especially if you're bringing them home after they've attended school.

5. Go with the flow. If something doesn't work – change directions!

# In Go-Cart So Tiny

In go-cart so tiny
My sister I drew;
And I've promised to draw her
The wide world through.

We have not yet started-
I own it with sorrow-
Because our trip's always
Put off till to-morrow.

Kate Greenaway

Don't put off till tomorrow,
What you can do today!

"Sow a thought, you reap an action:
Sow an act, you reap a habit;
Sow a habit, you reap a character:
Sow a character, you reap a destiny."

Eugene P. Bertin

# CHAPTER
## ♥ 20 ♥

## CURRICULUM THIS, CURRICULUM THAT, WHICH ONE'S THE BEST?

There is no pat answer to this question. I wish there were because it would truly make life easier for every parent that begins to homeschool. However, wouldn't this be boring? All of us teaching the same way to all our kids? We wouldn't have anything to discuss or argue about! We wouldn't need curriculum fairs or catalogs!

If you feel comfortable with a complete "set" curriculum (one that provides every book for every subject including the pencils!), then go for it. The major disadvantage to learning this way is that it's just like attending school: lots of workbooks, a very set routine. The plus side is that your kids can work at their own pace, and if they're motivated they can probably zoom through grade levels.

If you're more of a do-your-own thing type of person, but want to make sure that you cover all subject areas, then you definitely need to set yearly and bi-yearly goals, put your curriculum down in writing, and set a schedule. The more responsibility you take for creating their curriculum, the more organized you'll need to be so that work actually gets accomplished. I remember moms always saying that they love to co-op because they can be sure to have a well-planned day when they teach. It seemed to me that co-op day was probably the only day that was planned for by some of us.

If you want to unschool*, then go for it. This poor word has been badly maligned in the homeschooling circles. Here's my definition of unschooling (and you're welcome to change it to fit your lifestyle): Unschooling is the idea that a person learns best when he's self-motivated. In other words, I have a keen interest in birds. I love birds. I go to the library and borrow some books to learn all about them. I may save my money and buy myself a bird or I may set up birdhouses and feeders so that I can observe my feathery friends in their natural habitat. I may take a trip to an aviary to see how birds are bred and even start breeding them myself. Soon I realize that breeding birds and hand feeding them is even more work than raising babies. I may do this for a short while and then sell my breeders, or I may do this for a lifetime and in doing so become an ornithologist, or a bird specialist. Because I'm not involved in a lot of other uninteresting subjects, I can delve into this one.  While I'm studying my birds, I'll be learning about geography (flight patterns), anatomy (the bird's), aeronautics (flight), birth and death (breeding), psychology (bird's natural instinct to build nests, care and defend their young, etc.), math (calculating my expenditures), history (how birds have been used as carrier pigeons and hunters), and much more.   If I'm busy working with a dozen different workbooks and hurrying to all sorts of activities, I'll never have the time to accomplish it all. (I did do this as a young mother of three. We set up an aviary in our lanai, and I raised birds for about six or nine months until I discovered it was much more tiring than raising children. As a result, I sold my breeders.  The sad part was that my children were too young to remember the experience.   If I have the desire and motivation to do all of this in my "old age," how much more would our kids want to do it as children?)

Unschooling is giving our kids the freedom to experience and experiment and explore.  This requires parental patience and trust.  Why trust? You need to have trust in God and yourself so that the kids can learn.  And they will! Unschooling means setting up the best possible library that you can afford and placing it in the center of your home activity, not in some obscure closet or out of the way room.  Children are just like their parents – lazy.  If they need to look something up and have to climb the stairs or go searching for the book, chances are they won't do it!  The material needs to be at hand.  There should be plenty of pencils, pens, markers, crayons, play dough, paper, art supplies, and learning games.  There should be building material, sewing material, and cooking supplies.  There should be books everywhere: in the car, laundry room, and all the bathrooms.  It creates major clutter, but it also creates readers.  In other words, your home should be "child friendly" in all ways; a place where they can freely work and discover.  Don't hide the materials or say, "Don't touch!" or "You'll get it dirty!"

Another aside: Let's go back to Viktorija not speaking a word of English and neither my husband nor I worrying or doing anything about it.  That's not entirely true; we were teaching her a lot in Lithuanian. We read aloud every day for at least an hour, she sharpened her thinking skills by memorizing poetry, we taught her to count and recite her ABC's, and more.  This scenario is roughly equivalent to the idea of unschooling where we give the child the freedom to learn and explore on his own.  We don't just ignore him. We create the learning environment and become the "enablers" by taking him to the library, buying supplies, going to interesting places and sights, and accumulating books that interest him. **We practice parental patience and trust him explicitly.** Just as Viktorija learned to speak English on her own, your child also will learn on his own.  More importantly, the self-learning will stick! (By the way, we did this with all of our children.  With each child, learning English became easier due to more contact with other homeschoolers and the constant exposure to the language.)

A careful balance is needed when you unschool. You must know when to carefully open learning doors. If done too soon with some kids, it would be like hitting a stone wall. They just won't get it because it's way too soon. Remember, let the kids set the pace; as they resist, back off. When ready, the kids will learn at the speed of lightning.

My favorite homeschooling philosophy is Dr. Arthur Robinson's (**Robinson Curriculum**). Let me warn you, this requires a lot of trust, but it doesn't need to be as formal or rigid. Dr.Robinson proposes two hours of math a day (which may be too much for a young child, but he's a mathematical person so he puts more emphasis in that area) and composing a one page paper (the child's choice of topic) that will be corrected by you and returned for a possible rewrite. The remainder of the time is spent reading anything in your personal library (the books are there because they're good, right?).

Dr.Robinson proposes the right combination for education: reading, 'riting, and 'rithmetic. The three R's! There doesn't seem to be much exploration or hands-on activity in his style, right? Ah, but that's where you're wrong, because he lives on a farm that needs to be taken care of exclusively by him and the kids (he's a widower). This also means that the kids need to cook and clean. Do you see what I see? **He covers the basics, and all the life skills are part of their real world.**

Not all of us live on farms or in the country. Some of us live in the heart of the city. We can still create this type of learning environment by allowing our children the use of their own home. Why can't they learn to can, dehydrate, and cook in your kitchen as part of home economics, along with the cleaning? Is this not school? Can't they have a corner for keeping an old sewing machine (buy it at a garage sale - I've seen old machines as cheap as $30.00) and learn to sew with their mother's patient help (don't tell me you can't sew – learn together!). How about a small workshop in the corner of the garage with a pail full of wood scraps to build boxes, birdhouses, and perhaps go-carts? Include books on the study of herbs and medicine in your library (books can be bought cheaply at garage sales, thrift stores, and library sales) for the purpose of learning first aid. Set up feeding stations by your bedroom windows for the birds and view them at your leisure. Small children will love it. My one-year-old sees blue jays and cardinals visit everyday. She knows that the seed brings the birds to the feeding stations. Create a butterfly garden in a corner somewhere. Start a garden in pots outside your front door, on a balcony, or prepare a small raised bed. Learn to fish (and clean the fish)! Make this all part of "school" with you, of course, leading the way.

When your children are small, learn math the natural way by counting M&M's and pennies. Set up a small store on your kitchen counter and let them "buy" their goods with money. Sing counting songs – there are some great tapes out there. Keep them in the car and pop them in as you do your errands. (If your car doesn't have a tape player, it's a great educational investment to buy a portable one with a power cord that can be plugged into the cigarette lighter.) Draw big numbers or letters and place them on your refrigerator door for the kids – that would be their letter or number of the week. When the kids are ready, introduce them to sets and then simple multiplication and division. I do believe that certain math facts need to be memorized to make future math work easier. Have the kids learn their addition, subtraction, and multiplication tables, but do it in a fun way, perhaps with a song. Some kids love manipulatives. Gather plenty of buttons and pennies, and have them count. Provide the kids with a ruler to measure and a measuring cup to fill. Cooking, sewing, and carpentry are great math teachers as well as dexterity builders!

Learn a Bible verse together. Write the verse on a piece of paper and display it in a prominent area of your home. Make it your family's goal to learn a verse a week. Within a one year timeframe you'll have learned 52 verses! Spend your mornings doing chores, practicing musical instruments, learning Bible verses, doing some math, perhaps writing a one-page composition (which also can be in a journal), reading, or other activity. After lunch, take a nap and then read aloud together, go on a nature hunt, sew or quilt, or whatever. **Make school your life and life your school!**

As your children grow older, test out the waters to determine when they're ready for higher level math. See if there's a desire to learn. Perhaps this is the one area where you'll decide to have them do a math book every year. Do what's most comfortable for you. However, don't push too hard, and demand too much, or else the kids will soon learn to hate math and resist. If they understand the math reasonably well, there is no need to have them solve every problem or work every page. By having fun with math, your kids (when teenagers) will be ready to tackle algebra and geometry on their own. If they need help, find someone who's willing to provide assistance. Barter for the tutor's help.

History has always been fun at our house. We pick a topic and read historical fiction or biographies. We fill in the gaps with facts. I try to give my children a sense of timeline, but I think they're still too young to grasp the enormity of time. As teenagers, you may decide to ask them to read at least one history text a year so they grasp the chronology. I'm not talking about those textbooks that are used in schools, but history books written especially for **real** people. Geography won't be a problem because you'll be constantly referring to your maps or globe. A great idea I gleaned from others was to put a world map under a vinyl tablecloth on the kitchen table for accessibility at a moment's notice.

Science should be hands-on as much as possible. There are some great unit studies available to aid you in your endeavors. Science can also be learned by reading various nonfiction books written like novels (see page 192). You may also decide to hunt for a good text with your kids - something they would enjoy studying. (We found a series that my kids enjoy called ACE [Accelerated Christian Education], which consists of twelve magazine type booklets. These series of books are less intimidating than a large textbook.) Experiments should be a natural part of your homeschooling life. If you're squeamish about dissecting, ask your husband or a friend to do it. The best dissections we've ever done were unplanned. We were at the beach one day when the kids discovered a dead nursing shark, about two feet long. We tossed it in the freezer for a later time. Eventually, a doctor friend of ours dissected the shark for us. Another time we were given a cottonmouth snake, and once again our doctor friend dissected it for about twenty kids. It was fascinating!

**There is no need to use textbooks. Buy them if they make you feel more secure, but use them as a tool. Don't be a slave to them! Let them be your servants!** Your child does not have to read the book cover to cover. When your kids are old enough, have a discussion regarding what area they'd be interested in tackling that year; for example, biology. If you feel comfortable, buy a used text and look at the table of contents. If the child wants to read the entire book, go for it. If there's resistance, set out on your own adventure and learn about biology in the world around you, going back to the text when you need a more in-depth explanation. Look at the various unit studies on the market. Think of grades Kindergarten through eight, or up through the age of 13, as their time of exploration. Give your kids a chance to discover the outside world and learn science hands-on. When they're about 14 years old, give them some books to study. At this age, your kids will be able to understand more readily and appreciate what they're learning.

The same is true for English grammar. Don't make your children do a grammar book each year. How utterly boring and useless! When they are ready, they will learn it. There is no sense in repeating sections over and over. (Each year grammar books go a little bit more in depth than the previous year, but each grade covers the same areas.) My suggestion is to wait until sixth or seventh grade and test your kids with a grammar book. If they take to it like a fish to water, do it, then put the book away. The process should take anywhere from six months to a year. If they resist, put the book aside for later. Please note that we learn to write well not from grammar rules but by the way we speak. You don't give a toddler a grammar book to teach him to talk. You talk, correctly and clearly, which is how the child learns. The same applies for writing. You learn by writing, making mistakes, and being corrected. A grammar book does teach proper usage of words and phrases, but more times than not (according to my daughter), the rules are broken by exceptions to the rules! Don't waste your child's time or your own on grammar every year. Use it sparingly as you would salt, just a dash to spice up their learning!

**Composition is nothing more than putting your thoughts in writing.** If you know how to organize your thoughts clearly and concisely, you'll be a good writer. Parents can be intimidated by writing, which in turn can affect your child's skill in learning how to write. Don't be scared! When your child begins to show an interest in reading, have him start a journal. Perhaps purchase a very special notebook because the child will be using it for some time. Have him dictate his thoughts to you. In later years, it will be such a treat to re-read the journal! Eventually have him start writing a few sentences on his own. When ready, he should be able to write a full page. My daughters never had a problem coming up with, and writing about a subject, which is not the case for my son. I try to help by throwing some ideas his way. The key is to write something, at least a sentence or two each day. Later, introduce him to creative writing, poetry, essays, and short research papers. Be comfortable with the idea, and they will feel the same way. If you feel that you do not have the complete know-how to correct their writing, find a friend who would be willing to help. Barter for their services (a loaf of homemade bread for proofing a paper and offering suggestions). Don't apply any pressure when they're young. By the time they reach their teen years, your kids should be writing relatively well because it's natural and fun. If they seem to show an interest in this area, suggest that they enter some writing contests or submit their work to a magazine. Wouldn't it be great if their article was published? I'd be thrilled! What a confidence builder!

Many of us are of the impression that writers are part of a unique pool of talent in which there is no place for us. Wrong! Writing is 10% inspiration, 85% perspiration, and 5% magic! In other words, **we can all aspire to be writers**. The secret is work: diligence, patience, perseverance (all those neat character traits!). When it's important to you and enjoyable (fun) you'll do it. Once again, I would throw a good writing handbook to the child only when they start showing a real interest in writing. (I would also like to be so bold as to suggest that you try writing in a journal yourself. The more you write, the better you'll write, and you'll have more empathy for them as they struggle to write. It will also provide great motivation and set an example for them!)

There's absolutely no need to talk about religion or Christian upbringing because this is already part of your lifestyle. I'm sure you have a set time for reading the Bible, studying your Catechism and the lives of saints, and prayer. It's all a part of your family's character training program.

I don't feel a need for a formal literature program because it should be included as part of their daily reading. Once the kids are older, you may want to hand them a list of books that they should read, (or at least look at) before they finish their education and perhaps apply for college. This can be done in one of two ways. There are books that tell you what every college bound student needs to have read, or you may want to do it by historical periods and suggest appropriate books to read. I prefer the second alternative because it blends in so nicely with the study of history. If you feel your kids need more, start a literary discussion group. Once a month have a group of kids, hopefully all the same maturity level if not the same age, come together at your home and discuss the same book. It can be as informal as picking any great classic, or you can decide on a theme or literary period for the year. Someone needs to be the leader of the group. This person must have thoroughly read the book, researched background information on the author, read critiques of the book, and must keep the discussion moving along. He can ask leading questions: What was it about the book that really grabbed you or that you disliked, and why? Questions need to be open ended. Discuss the characters and their relationships. How would you have acted if you were in the same situation? What did you learn about yourself or others? How did the author's life, or the age he was living in, affect the story? Questions like these will keep the discussion going for hours. If you're worried that the students will not have enough to talk about (which I assure you they will), then have a poem handy ready for analyzing.

A foreign language is very tricky to learn if you have no one proficient in the desired language to rely on for help. Colleges are not looking for students who can merely speak another language. They want kids to be familiar and comfortable with the grammar. Foreign language grammar is hard to teach when you aren't fluent. (It's even hard when you are fluent! Take English grammar as an example.) I have no real advice other than try to find someone who's fluent to help you.

Vocabulary learning should be lots of fun, a game. Most people tend to give their kids vocabulary building workbooks. Try this idea. Pick a word, perhaps one you just read or heard, and write it down on the big board you have in your kitchen/schoolroom/whatever. Write down its pronunciation (if needed), origin, and definition. Perhaps each child could have their own word for the week or you can work on five or six together. Keep the board out where they will see it constantly and remember to quiz one another. The kids should know the words by heart within a week. Another idea is to carry a pocket-sized dictionary with you. When you come across a "strange and foreign" word, look up its origin and definition. This will familiarize the kids with parts of words. (For example: Tele (from Greek) means distance; phone (from Greek) means sound, voice; a telephone brings distant sounds, or voices, to you. Learning words, and parts of words, in this way will definitely build their vocabulary.

You know the greatest thing about unschooling? By its very nature and the very sound of its name, unschooling blends into your new lifestyle completely. When someone asks what you do for school, say "I unschool. Life is our school!" **Amen!**

## SUMMARY:

1. Do you want to use a set curriculum, "do-your-own" thing, or unschool?

2. Do you think unschooling is more prone to encourage the love of learning and having fun learning?

3. Are you willing to become your children's "en-abler?"

* This year at our Florida Homeschool convention, I picked up a book that coins a new word that probably better describes this type of schooling: eclectic. Basically eclectic schooling means that you use whatever method best fits your child. He may use a text for math, write articles for a kids' magazine for composition credit, has a part time job at the veterinary clinic for science, plays **Where In The World Is Carmen Sandiego** for geography, reads historical fiction for history, and is learning photography for art credit. According to my **American Heritage Dictionary,** eclectic means *choosing or consisting of what appears to be the best from diverse sources* (from the Greek eklegein, to single out). What a great word to describe a wonderful schooling style!

*"For what are the classics but the noblest recorded thoughts of man? ...Books must be read as deliberately and reservedly as they were written."*
*Walden* by Henry David Thoreau

## FURTHER READING AND CURRICULA:

### THEORY:
**Beyond Survival** by Diana Waring (WA: Emerald Books, 1996)
**Charlotte Mason Companion** by Karen Andreola (USA: Charlotte Mason Research & Supply, 1998)
**Christian Educators' Curriculum Manual 1997-'98** (Grades 7-12) by Cathy Duffy (CA: Grove Publishing, 1997)
**Dr.Beechick's Homeschool Answer Book** by Ruth Beechick (CA: Arrow Press, 1998)
**Homeschooling For Excellence** by David and Micki Colfax(NY: Warner Books, 1988)
**Home-Spun Schools** by Raymond and Dorothy Moore
**Home Style Teaching A Handbook for Parents and Teachers** by Raymond and Dorothy Moore (TX: Word Publishing, 1984)
**Learning All The Time** by John Holt (MA: Addison-Wesley Publishing Co., 1989)

## PRACTICAL ELEMENTARY K-8:

**The Language Wars and Other Writings for Homeschoolers** by Ruth
Beechick (CA: Arrow Press, 1995)
The following three are packaged together:
**A Strong Start in Language** by Ruth Beechick (CA: Arrow Press, 1985/86)
**A Strong Start in Arithmetic** by Ruth Beechick
**Home Start in Reading** by Ruth Beechick
**You Can Teach Your Child Successfully** (Grades 4-8) by Ruth Beechick
(CA: Arrow Press, 1993)


## GRAMMAR:

**Daily Grams** by Wanda C. Phillips (AZ: ISHA Enterprises Inc., 1987)
A 5-10 minute daily grammar review.
**Easy Grammar Plus** by Wanda C.Phillips (AZ: ISHA Enterprises Inc., 1995)
A complete grammar book of reproducible worksheets.
**Editor In Chief, Grammar Disasters and Punctuation Faux Pas** by
Michael Baker (USA: Critical Thinking Books & Software, 1995)
**Writers Express** by Dave Kemper, Ruth Nathan, and Patrick Sebranek
(WI: Write Source Educational Publishing House, 1994)
A good handbook for young writers, thinkers, and learners. Geared for
beginning writers through about 6$^{th}$ grade.
**Writers Inc** by Patrick Sebranek, Verne Meyer, and Dave Kemper
(MA: D.C.Heath & Co., 1996)
A writer's handbook for about 7$^{th}$ grade and up.


## PHONICS:

**Teach Your Child To Read In 100 Easy Lessons** by Siegfried Engelmann,
Phyllis Haddox, and Elaine Bruner (NY:Simon & Schuster, 1983)
A wonderful and inexpensive (less than $20.00) manual to teach your
child to read. When he's done with this he should be able to start reading
the Pathway Readers.
**Pathway Readers** (IN: Pathway Publishers, 1975)
A reading book series all about the Amish farm life and community. Strong
moral values.


## LITERATURE GUIDES:

**Books Children Love** by Elizabeth Wilson (Westchester: Crossway Books,
1987)
**Honey For A Child's Heart** by Gladys Hunt (MI: Zondervan Books, 1989)
**Let the Author Speak** by Carolyn Hatcher (Joelton: Old Pinnacle Publishing,
1992)
**Robinson Self-Teaching Home-School Curriculum**, Oregon Institute of
Science and Medicine, 2251 Dick George Road, Cave Junction, OR
97523

## WRITING:

**Any Child Can Write** by Harvey S. Wiener (NY: Oxford University Press, 1990)

**Creating Books With Childern** by Valerie Bendt (FL: Bendt Family Ministries, 1993) Teaches you how to write a book and bind it.

**The Elements of Style** by William Strunk,Jr. & E.B.White (Ontario:The MacMillan Co., 1959) A must for learning to write! Should be read and re-read.

**If You're Trying To Teach Your Kids How To Write, You've Gotta Have This Book!** By Marjorie Frank (TN: Incentive Publications, 1979)

**Writer's Express** by Dave Kemper, Ruth Nathan, and Patrick Sebranek (Burlington: Write Source Educational Publishing House, 1994)

**Writing Down the Days** by Lorraine M. Dahlstrom (MN: Free Spirit Publishing Inc., 1990)


## HIGHSCHOOL COMPOSITION, LITERATURE, GRAMMAR, AND ORGANIZATION:

**The Columbia Anthology of American Poetry** by Jay Parini (NY: Columbia University Press, 1995)

**Famous Books Ancient and Medieval** by Robert B. Downs (NY: Barnes and Noble,Inc., 1964)

**Form and Style** by William Giles Campbell and Stephen Vaughan Ballou (MA: Houghton Mifflin Co.,1974)

**A Glossary of Literary Terms** by M.H.Abrams (NY: Holt, Rinehart, and Winston,Inc., 1971)

**Hodges' Harbrace College Handbook** by John C. Hodges and Mary E. Whitten (NY: Harcourt Brace Jovanovich,Inc., 1972)

**Home School, High School, and Beyond, A Guide for Teens and Their Teachers** by Beverly Adams-Gordon (WA: Castlemoyle Books, 1996)

**How To Read A Book** by Mortimer Adler and Charles Van Doren (NY: MJF Books,1972)

**Masters of Modern Drama** by Haskell M. Block and Robert G. Shedd (NY: Random House,1962)

**MLA Style Sheet** Modern Language Association of America (NY: Publications Center,1970)\

**The Norton Anthology of American Literature**, Vol. 1 & 2

**The Norton Anthology of English Literature**, Vol. 1 & 2

**The Norton Anthology of World Literature**, Vol. 1 & 2

**The Oxford Companion to Classical Literature** by Sir Paul Harvey (Oxford: Oxford University Press, 1986)

**Reading Lists For College-Bound Students** by Doug Estell, Michele L. Satchwell, and Patricia S. Wright (NY: Prentice Hall,1993)

**Reading Strands, Understanding Fiction** (Niles: National Writing Institute,1993)

**Senior High: A Home-Designed Form+U+La** by Barbara Edtl Shelton (WA: Howshall Home Publications, 1993)

**Writing Strands** (Levels 1-7) (Niles: National Writing Institute)

**LITERATURE UNIT STUDIES FOR MIDDLE SCHOOL / HIGH SCHOOL:**
**Beautiful Feet Literature Unit Studies,** 139 Main Street, Sandwich Village,
 MA 02563
**Learning Language Arts Through Literature** (Gold Level) (FL: Common
 Sense Press,1992)
**Progeny Press Study Guides** (WI: Progeny Press)
**Total Language Plus Student Study Guides, Language Arts With A
 Christian Perspective for Middle & Upper Grades** by Terry and Barbara
 Blakey


## UNIT STUDIES:


**CHARACTER:**
**The Book of Virtues** by William Bennett (NY: Simon & Schuster, 1993)
**Konos,** (Vol. I-III) by Jessica Hulcy and Carole Thaxton , (TX: Konos,1984)
**Prudence and The Millers** by Mildred A. Martin (OH: Green Pastures Press,
 1993)
**School Days and The Millers** by Mildred A. Martin (OH: Green Pastures
 Press, 1995)
**Wisdom and The Millers** by Mildred A. Martin (OH: Green Pastures Press,
 1989)


**SCIENCE UNIT STUDIES (MIXED K-12):**
**Beautiful Feet: History of Science Through Literature,** 139 Main Street,
 Sandwich Village, MA 02563
**Bird Unit Study** by Kym Wright (FL: AlWright Publishing, 1997)
**Botany Unit Study** by Kym Wright (FL: AlWright Publishing, 1997)
**Creation Anatomy: A Study Guide to the Miracles of the Body** by Felice
 Gerwitz and Jill Whitlock (FL: Media Angels, 1996)
**Creation Astronomy: A Study Guide to the Constellations!** by Felice Gerwitz
 and Jill Whitlock (FL: Media Angels, 1995)
**Creation Geology: A Study Guide to Fossils, Formations, and the Flood!** by
 Felice Gerwitz and Jill Whitlock (FL: Media Angels, 1998)
**Creation Science: Hands-On Study Guide!** by Felice Gerwitz and Jill Whitlock
 (FL: Media Angels, 1994)
**Goat Unit Study** by Kym Wright (FL:AlWright Publishing)
**Microscope Unit Study, 4th Grade and Up** by Kym Wright (FL:AlWright
Publishing,
 1997)
**Poultry Unit Study** by Kym Wright (FL: AlWright Publishing)
**Sheep Unit Study** by Kym Wright (FL: AlWright Publishing, 1997)
**Teaching Science and Having Fun!** by Felice Gerwitz (FL: Media Angels, 1999)

## SCIENCE READ ALOUD BOOKS:

**Kids Discover Magazine** (Monthly) $26.95 Kids Discover, PO Box 54205,
Boulder,CO 80328

**Handbook of Nature Study** by Anna Botsford Comstock
This wonderful reference book is a must for every home library!

**The Field Guide to Wildlife Habitats of the Eastern U.S.** by Janine M. Benyus

**Fields and Pastures New, My First Year as a Country Vet** by Dr. John
McCormick (My daughters love both his books.)

**A Friend of the Flock** by Dr. John McCormick

**The Curious Naturalist Seasons of the Wild** by Sy Montgomery

**How Does A Bee Make Honey? And Other Curious Facts** by Martin
M. Goldwyn

**Everglades Adventure** by James Ralph Johnson

**The Weather Companion** by Gary Lockhart

**Naming Nature, A Seasonal Guide for the Amateur Naturalist** by Mary
Blocksma

**The Nocturnal Naturalist, Exploring the Outdoors at Night** by Cathy Johnson

**The Edge of the Sea** by Rachel Carson

**The Birds & the Beasts Were There** by Margaret Millar

**North Carolina Nature Writing** edited by Richard Rankin

**The New Way Things Work** by David Macaulay

**The Curious Naturalist**, National Geographic Society (A beautifully
Illustrated book that I had my books read.)


## MISCELLANEOUS UNIT STUDIES:

**Beautiful Feet Book Studies,** 139 Main Street, Sandwich Village, MA 02563
These are wonderful literature based unit studies. Write for a catalog.

**Information Please!** (three levels) by Pat Wesolowski (Fl: D.P.K. Productions,
1993) These are guides that teach kids to look up information.

**Victorian Sewing & Quilting for Older Students** by Kym Wright (FL: AlWright
Publishing, 1998)


## GEOGRAPHY:

**Runkle Geography Program – Physical World of Geography,**
http://www.runklepub.com/ or call toll free at 877-geotext
I haven't seen the actual book but I have looked at their
website and it looks like a very comprehensive program.
It is expensive though.

**Mapping The World By Heart** (Grades 5-12) by David Smith (USA: Tom
Snyder Productions, 1996)

## FOREIGN LANGUAGE PROGRAMS:
**Power Glide**
**Artes Latinae**
**Learnables**


## HISTORY:
**Beautiful Feet History Unit Studies,** 139 Main Street, Sandwich Village, MA
02563
- **Early American History / Primary**
- **Early American History / Intermediate**
- **US and World History Through Literature** (from the Civil War to Vietnam) Advanced
- **Medieval History Through Literature**
- **Ancient History Through Literature**
- **History of California Through Literature**

**The Civil War** (A Unit Study) by Pat Wesolowski (FL: D.P.& K. Productions, 1996)

**The Greenleaf Famous Men Series** by Cynthia A. Shearer and Robert G. Shearer (TN: Greenleaf Press)

**The Greenleaf Guides To History** by Cynthia A. Shearer and Robert G. Shearer (TN: Greenleaf Press)
- **Guide To the Old Testament**
- **Guide To Ancient Egypt**
- **Guide To Ancient Greece**
- **Guide To Ancient Rome**
- **Guide To the Middle Ages**
- **Guide To The Renaissance and Reformation**

**A History of US** (Vol.1-10) by Joy Hakim (NY: Oxford University Press, 1995) This series is great for all ages.

**The Story of Mankind** by Hendrik Willem Van Loon (London: Liveright Publishing Corp., 1984) 6th-8th grades.

**Christ The King Lord of History** by Anne W. Carroll (IL: Tan Books and Publishers, Inc., 1994) A Catholic World History for 6th-8th grades.)

**Puritans' Progress** (5 Vols.) by Matthew Anger, Peter Chojnowski, and Rev. Kenneth Novak (MO: Angelus Press, 1996) A Catholic perspective of American History. (Highschool)


## HOMESCHOOLING CATALOGS:
There are many, many catalogs available. The only reason I include the following three is because they offer information which is not available elsewhere.

**Elijah Company,** 1053 Eldridge Loop, Crossville,Tn 38558
www.elijahco.com
The owners of Elijah Company have taken a lot of time preparing their catalog. They include explanations of the various learning

styles, teaching suggestions, and lots more. A great catalog for the novice homeschooling mom.

**Greenleaf Press Catalog,** 3761 Highway 109N, Unit D, Lebanon, TN 37087 www.greenleafpress.com (615)449-1617
This is a wonderful history book catalog.  You need to always keep one on file so that you can plan your history reading for the year. They also offer historical unit studies.

**Timberdoodle Co,** 1510 E Spencer Lk Rd., Shelton, WA 98584 (360)426-0672
This is a totally hands on type of catalog with plenty of projects to keep minds busy (including mom's!).  They sell only products that they themselves have used. Definitely a must see!

## More  homeschooling resources to check into:

**Catholic Heritage Curricula**, PO Box 125, Twain Harte, CA 95383-0125
www.chcweb.com or (800)490-7713 (Resource for Catholic books.)

**Chalk Dust Company**, 11 Sterling Court, Sugar Land, TX 77479
www.chalkdust.com or (800)588-7564 (Complete math programs with video.)

**Critical Thinking Books and Software**, PO Box 448, Pacific Grove, CA 93950-0448, www.criticalthinking.com or (800)458-4849 (A complete line of thinking skill books.)

**Home School Legal Defense Association**, PO Box 3000, Purcellville, VA 20134 (540)338-7600 (Legal services)

**Lifetime Books and Gifts**, 3900 Chalet Suzanne Dr., Lake Wales, FL 33853-7763 www.lifetimebooksandgifts.com or (800)377-0390 (Home of **The Always Incomplete Resource Guide**, a source for your every homeschooling need.)

**Love To Learn**, 741 N. State Road 198, Salem,  UT 84653-9299
www.LoveToLearn.net or (888)771-1034 (Another good catalog for homeschooling resources.)

**Media Angels Creation Science**, 16450 S. Tamiami Trail, Ste.3 PMB #116, Ft. Myers, FL 33908 www.mediaangels.com and www.virtual-field-trips.com (Creation science unit study publisher. Also offers a website for virtual fieldtrips.)

**Modern Curriculum Press**, 4350 Equity Drive, Columbus, OH 43228, (800)321-3106 (Source for good phonics workbooks)

**Pathway Books**, 2580N 250W, LaGrange, IN 46761 (Amish publisher which offers a wonderful graded reading series entitled **Pathway Readers**.)

**Solomon's Secrets**, 1264 Alhambra Drive, Ft. Myers, FL 33901
www.solomons-secrets.com, (941)332-7138  (Offers a variety of historical novels, as well as the complete series of **Usborne Books** and **Adventures in Odyssey** audio and video tapes.)

**Tobin's Lab**, PO Box 725, Culpeper, VA 22701  (800)522-4776  (Offers a wide variety of science resources.)

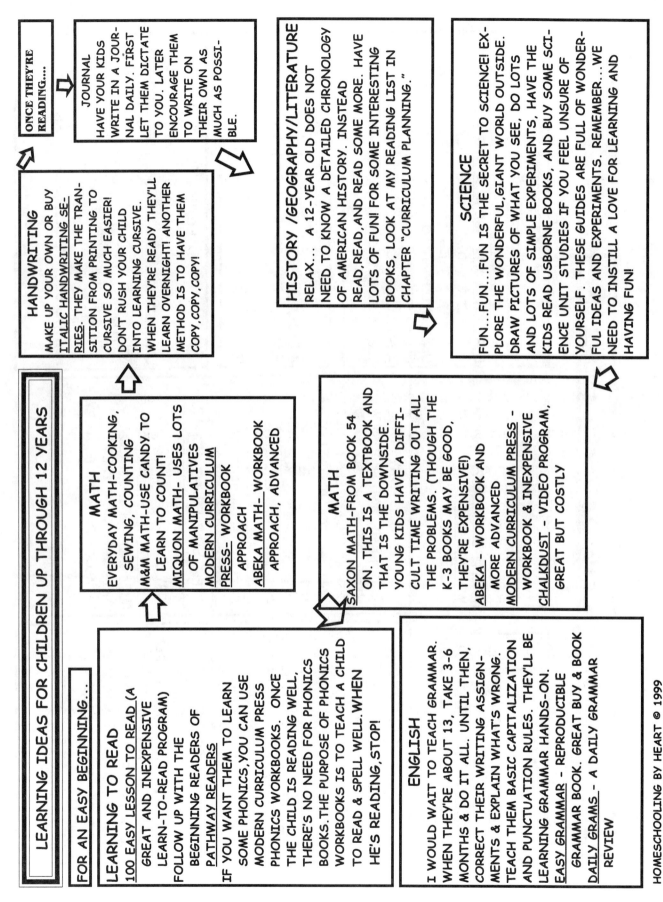

# LEARNING IDEAS FOR CHILDREN UP THROUGH 12 YEARS

## FOR AN EASY BEGINNING...

### LEARNING TO READ
100 EASY LESSON TO READ (A GREAT AND INEXPENSIVE LEARN-TO-READ PROGRAM) FOLLOW UP WITH THE BEGINNING READERS OF PATHWAY READERS

IF YOU WANT THEM TO LEARN SOME PHONICS, YOU CAN USE MODERN CURRICULUM PRESS PHONICS WORKBOOKS. ONCE THE CHILD IS READING WELL, THERE'S NO NEED FOR PHONICS BOOKS. THE PURPOSE OF PHONICS WORKBOOKS IS TO TEACH A CHILD TO READ & SPELL WELL. WHEN HE'S READING, STOP!

### ENGLISH
I WOULD WAIT TO TEACH GRAMMAR. WHEN THEY'RE ABOUT 13, TAKE 3-6 MONTHS & DO IT ALL. UNTIL THEN, CORRECT THEIR WRITING ASSIGNMENTS & EXPLAIN WHAT'S WRONG. TEACH THEM BASIC CAPITALIZATION AND PUNCTUATION RULES. THEY'LL BE LEARNING GRAMMAR HANDS-ON.
EASY GRAMMAR - REPRODUCIBLE GRAMMAR BOOK. GREAT BUY & BOOK
DAILY GRAMS - A DAILY GRAMMAR REVIEW

### MATH
EVERYDAY MATH-COOKING, SEWING, COUNTING
M&M MATH-USE CANDY TO LEARN TO COUNT!
MIQUON MATH- USES LOTS OF MANIPULATIVES
MODERN CURRICULUM PRESS- WORKBOOK APPROACH
ABEKA MATH- WORKBOOK APPROACH, ADVANCED

### MATH
SAXON MATH-FROM BOOK 54 ON. THIS IS A TEXTBOOK AND THAT IS THE DOWNSIDE. YOUNG KIDS HAVE A DIFFICULT TIME WRITING OUT ALL THE PROBLEMS. (THOUGH THE K-3 BOOKS MAY BE GOOD, THEY'RE EXPENSIVE!)
ABEKA - WORKBOOK AND MORE ADVANCED
MODERN CURRICULUM PRESS - WORKBOOK & INEXPENSIVE
CHALKDUST - VIDEO PROGRAM, GREAT BUT COSTLY

### HANDWRITING
MAKE UP YOUR OWN OR BUY ITALIC HANDWRITING SERIES. THEY MAKE THE TRANSITION FROM PRINTING TO CURSIVE SO MUCH EASIER! DON'T RUSH YOUR CHILD INTO LEARNING CURSIVE. WHEN THEY'RE READY THEY'LL LEARN OVERNIGHT! ANOTHER METHOD IS TO HAVE THEM COPY, COPY, COPY!

### ONCE THEY'RE READING....

### JOURNAL
HAVE YOUR KIDS WRITE IN A JOURNAL DAILY. FIRST LET THEM DICTATE TO YOU. LATER ENCOURAGE THEM TO WRITE ON THEIR OWN AS MUCH AS POSSIBLE.

### HISTORY /GEOGRAPHY/LITERATURE
RELAX... A 12-YEAR OLD DOES NOT NEED TO KNOW A DETAILED CHRONOLOGY OF AMERICAN HISTORY. INSTEAD READ, READ, AND READ SOME MORE. HAVE LOTS OF FUN! FOR SOME INTERESTING BOOKS, LOOK AT MY READING LIST IN CHAPTER "CURRICULUM PLANNING."

### SCIENCE
FUN...FUN...FUN IS THE SECRET TO SCIENCE! EXPLORE THE WONDERFUL, GIANT WORLD OUTSIDE. DRAW PICTURES OF WHAT YOU SEE. DO LOTS AND LOTS OF SIMPLE EXPERIMENTS. HAVE THE KIDS READ USBORNE BOOKS. AND BUY SOME SCIENCE UNIT STUDIES IF YOU FEEL UNSURE OF YOURSELF. THESE GUIDES ARE FULL OF WONDERFUL IDEAS AND EXPERIMENTS. REMEMBER...WE NEED TO INSTILL A LOVE FOR LEARNING AND HAVING FUN!

# LEARNING IDEAS FOR KIDS 13-YEARS AND OLDER

## MATH
SAXON
ABEKA (VIDEO AVAILABLE)
CHALKDUST VIDEO
HAROLD JACOBS MATH

## ENGLISH
EASY GRAMMAR
DAILY GRAMS
EDITOR-IN-CHIEF
WRITERS INC

## LITERATURE
READING LISTS FOR COLLEGE BOUND
STUDENTS
LEARNING LANGUAGE ARTS THROUGH
LITERATURE - GOLD BOOK
UNIT STUDY-HISTORICAL SETTING
UNIT STUDY-BY COUNTRY
UNIT STUDY-BY GENRE OR THEME
A GOOD DISCUSSION GROUP
KEEP A SIMPLE READING JOURNAL

## COMPOSITION
WRITE, WRITE, AND WRITE!
IF YOU FEEL UNCOMFORTABLE
CRITIQUING YOUR CHILD'S
WORK FIND A MENTOR THAT
BOTH OF YOU TRUST.
NEED WRITING IDEAS?
CHECK THIS CHAPTER UNDER
"FURTHER READING AND
CURRICULA"

## HISTORY
READ, READ, AND READ SOME
MORE! THERE ARE SO MANY
HISTORICAL NOVELS (WHICH
ALSO CAN COUNT FOR LITERA-
TURE STUDY).
LOOK IN LET THE AUTHOR
SPEAK. IN THIS BOOK, THE
NOVELS ARE CATEGORIZED BY
CENTURY AND A BRIEF DE-
SCRIPTION OF THE BOOK IS
GIVEN. SUPPLEMENT WITH
SOME GOOD NONFICTION HIS-
TORY SUCH AS:
A HISTORY OF US (SERIES)
THE STORY OF MANKIND
CHECK GREENLEAF PRESS
CATALOG FOR MORE HISTORY
BOOKS.

## FOREIGN LANGUAGE
ARTES LATINAE
POWER GLIDE: SPANISH, FRENCH, GERMAN,
ETC.
LEARNABLES

## GEOGRAPHY
THE BEST APPROACH IS BY
PLACING A MAP OF THE WORLD
UNDER A CLEAR VINYL TABLE-
CLOTH ON YOUR KITCHEN
TABLE. EVERYDAY, AS YOU EAT,
CHECK OUT A NEW SPOT!
MAPPING THE WORLD BY HEART
RUNKLE GEOGRAPHY

## SCIENCE
UNIT STUDY APPROACH: SEE LIST IN CHAP-
TER
"CURRICULUM THIS, CURRICLUM THAT,
WHICH ONE'S THE BEST?"

ALWAYS USE THE SCIENTIFIC METHOD!

HOMESCHOOLING BY HEART © 1999

# PLANNING A LITERATURE DISCUSSION GROUP
## A LEADER'S GUIDE

- SCHEDULE THE LITERATURE DISCUSSION ONCE A MONTH.
- PLAN YOUR MEETING DATES IN ADVANCE, AND HAND OUT A CALENDAR AT THE FIRST MEETING.
- IT'S EASIER IF YOU SELECT THE BOOKS TO BE READ. PICK A THEME, HISTORICAL PERIOD, OR COUNTRY. TEENS SHOULD BE ABLE TO READ ONE NOVEL PER MONTH. PRE-PLAN YOUR READING LIST AND HAND IT OUT AT THE FIRST MEETING. THIS WAY THE KIDS CAN ACTUALLY READ AHEAD IF THEY WANT. SOMETIMES IT'S DIFFICULT TO FIND A BOOK, SO GIVE THEM AS MUCH ADVANCE NOTICE AS POSSIBLE. IF THE BOOK IS A TRANSLATION CHECK TO SEE WHICH TRANSLATION YOU WANT THE KIDS TO READ. ALSO, SOME LONG AND COMPLEX NOVELS HAVE ABRIDGED VERSIONS THAT ARE SLIGHTLY EASIER TO COMPREHEND.
- MAKE SURE YOUR READING CHOICES ARE VARIED: NOVELS, POETRY, PLAYS, TRAGEDY, COMEDY. DON'T COMPRISE YOUR READING LIST OF ALL "HEAVY LITERATURE," OR THE KIDS WILL BECOME DISCOURAGED.
- DEPENDING ON THE SIZE OF THE GROUP, CONSIDER HOSTING AT YOUR HOME (IF IT'S MORE CONVENIENT FOR YOU). LIBRARIES USUALLY HAVE MEETING ROOMS.
- SET THE TIME IN ADVANCE. A PERIOD OF 90 MINUTES IS SUFFICIENT TO ALLOW FOR DISCUSSION.
- AT THE FIRST MEETING, HAND OUT A LIST OF LITERATURE TERMS TO THE KIDS. USE THE TERMINOLOGY FREQUENTLY IN YOUR DISCUSSIONS SO THAT THEY BECOME COMFORTABLE WITH THE TERMS.
- YOU SHOULD BE FAMILIAR WITH THE CONTENTS OF THE BOOK, HAVE IMPORTANT PASSAGES EARMARKED, AND HAVE READ ABOUT THE AUTHOR'S LIFE AND OTHER PEOPLE'S CRITICISM OF HIS WORK. ALSO, HAVE AN IDEA OF WHERE THE AUTHOR AND HIS WORK FIT INTO A HISTORY AND LITERATURE TIMELINE.
- USE THE INTERNET AND THE LIBRARY TO FIND LITERARY CRITICISM.
- PREPARE (IN WRITING) QUESTIONS (AND ANSWERS) AND BIOGRAPHICAL INFORMATION. KEEP IT TOGETHER IN A BINDER.BEGIN THE DISCUSSION WITH PREPARED QUESTIONS, BUT IF THE KIDS KEEP THE BALL ROLLING WITH THEIR OWN QUESTIONS AND COMMENTS, LET IT ROLL.

## ABOVE ALL - HAVE FUN!

## READING JOURNAL #1

TITLE:_____

AUTHOR:_____

DATE WRITTEN:_____NATIONALITY:_____

FICTION_____DRAMA_____OTHER:_____
POETRY_____NONFICTION_____BIOGRAPHY_____

### CHOOSE A FEW OF THESE QUESTIONS TO ANSWER IN YOUR READING JOURNAL

Did you enjoy this work and why or why not?

Describe the protagonist and the antagonist.

Name the conflict and how it was significant.

What's the theme and how is it significant to today's reader?

Did the author use any special writing style in his work?

Did the setting play an important role in developing the plot?

Was this author influenced by any style of writing or age?

Would you recommend this book to someone else and why?

# READING JOURNAL #2

TITLE:_____

AUTHOR:_____

DATE WRITTEN:_____NATIONALITY:_____

FICTION:_____DRAMA:_____POETRY:_____

NON-FICTION:_____BIOGRAPHY:_____OTHER:_____

## ANSWER AT LEAST TWO OF THE FOLLOWING QUESTIONS

PICK A CHARACTER IN THE BOOK AND EXAMINE HIS MORAL VALUES.

DO ANY OF THE CHARACTERS REMIND YOU OF REAL PEOPLE? EXPLAIN THEIR SIMILARITIES.

CHOOSE A PASSAGE IN THE BOOK THAT MOVED YOU AND EXPLAIN WHY.

WHAT INSIGHTS HAVE YOU GAINED BY READING THIS WORK?

PICK A THEME AND EXPOUND ON IT.

PICK A THEME FOUND IN THE WORK, AND COMPARE OR CONTRAST IT TO A THEME IN ANOTHER WORK YOU'VE READ.

WAS THERE ANYTHING DIFFERENT ABOUT THE STYLE OR SETTING IN WHICH THIS WORK WAS WRITTEN? EXPLAIN.

GIVE YOUR OWN INTERPRETATION OF THE THEME.

IF YOU COULD CHANGE THE BOOK, WHAT WOULD YOU CHANGE AND WHY?

# JOURNAL AND COMPOSITION IDEAS

When your child is writing comfortably in his journal, encourage branching out into other writing arenas. He needs to be exposed to the following: poetry, editorials, news articles, research material, letter writing, short stories (creative writing), plays, book reports, and more. The more he reads, the better writer he'll be. Simultaneously, he needs to be writing as much as possible in order to develop his writing skills and his narrative voice. Reading and writing go hand-in-hand.

# LITERARY TERMS

Every student of literature should be acquainted with the following terms and be able to identify the various elements.

**PLOT:**

**BEGINNING (EXPOSITION):** Introduces the action and the characters.

**MIDDLE (RISING ACTION):** Develops the conflict or problem and leads up to the climax.

**CLIMAX:** The turning point in the action.

**FALLING ACTION:** Follows the climax; the "untying"of the plot (denouement).

**ENDING (RESOLUTION):** The end. All problems are resolved.

**CONFLICT:** The story's "problem." There are five basic types:

**Man vs Man**          **Man vs Nature**

**Man vs Society**      **Man vs Destiny or Fate**

**Man vs Himself**

**SETTING:** The story's location in time or place.

**THEME:** The idea or the message that the author is trying to convey to his readers.

**STYLE (TONE):** The author's choice of language and the mood that is conveyed to the readers.

**POINT OF VIEW:** From whose perspective the story is being told. It can be written in the First Person "I" or the Third Person "he, she, it, they."

"I slowly crept across the wet grass as gun shots sprayed the air like hail."

*or*

"As the child tottered along the sidewalk, a car came careening down the road and she began to cry."

# LITERARY FORMS OR GENRES

BALLAD: A song that tells a story.

COMEDY: A funny story.

DRAMA: A form of literature, a play. (Dramatic means emotional, exaggerated.)

EPIC: A long narrative poem that relates a people's heroic tradition.

ESSAY: A composition expressing the writer's point of view.

FABLE: A fictitious story that teaches a lesson or moral and often uses animals as characters.

FICTION: An imagined story.

FOLKLORE: Oral stories handed down from generation to generation.

MELODRAMA: The characters are one dimensional; the good guys are the very best, and the bad guys are super evil. Lots of exaggerated action; often times violent.

MYTH: A primitive story that explains nature's mysteries.

NON-FICTION: Factual material.

NOVEL: A full length story.

ODE: A lyric poem. (A lyric poem has a songlike quality.)

ROMANCE: The author writes a story about how he imagines life should be like. A romance can be an adventure, love story, mystery, etc.

SATIRE: Makes use of ridicule or irony to reveal someone's wickedness or faults.

SYMBOLISM: Anything which signifies something else. (For example: Uncle Sam or the bald eagle symbolize the USA and patriotism.)

TRAGEDY: A story about a hero who has a character flaw that he needs to overcome. This flaw results in unhappiness. The flaw can be jealousy, greed,...

# CHAPTER
♥ 21 ♥

## LEARNING GOALS

If you set up goals for your family, make them general enough so that you feel free to add or subtract from them. Set up learning goals very much like the ones you created for yourself and your family. Start with the furthest objectives; what you wish your child would accomplish by the end of the year. When you're setting goals, consider which character traits you'd like to work on with each child.

**For example**:
### Gintaras: End of the year goals

- Work on orderliness both in setting goals and meeting them, as well as keeping an orderly room
- Work on truthfulness, and discerning between right and wrong and why it's important
- Learn to listen carefully
- Memorize multiplication tables through the 12's
- Practice neatness in writing, and experiment with cursive writing
- Read a book each week
- Do a short research paper
- Keep a daily journal

### By January:

- Have the Ten Commandments memorized
- Know multiplication tables through the 8's
- Pick a topic of interest and start research paper
- Write name and address in cursive

With these goals in mind, I would then make a schedule about 1 month before the new school year begins. See the following examples:

### *Gintaras (8 years old):*

| | |
|---|---|
| **Math:** | Abeka 3rd grade |
| **Composition:** | Write in his journal daily |
| **Science:** | Encourage to read **Usborne** books and **How Things Work** on a daily basis (show him where all the science related books are kept) |
| **Reading:** | Read from 6th grade reader and read at least one book each week from our library |
| **Writing:** | Practice his writing skills by copying a passage from a classic |
| **Journal:** | Dictate to mom and copy |
| **Religion:** | **Faith and Life**: reads on his own a chapter a week |
| **Bible:** | As a family |
| **Public Speaking:** | Friday evenings at the Extension Center |
| **Research Paper:** | Has decided that he wants to learn more about soap box derbies and how to build a soap box car. Will do research and include a sketch, as well as detailed instructions on how to build a car. Paper will be at least one-page (double-spaced and type-written). If interest holds, will attempt to build a soap box. (Ask builder friend for scrap wood!) |
| **Music:** | Private piano and cello lessons |
| **Phys Ed:** | Soccer / Basketball / Karate |

### *Viktorija (13 years old):*

| | |
|---|---|
| **Math:** | **Chalk Dust Algebra I** |
| **English:** | **ACE** 9th grade (This is the last time we'll be covering grammar. She chose to do this program.) |
| **Literature:** | One book per week <br> Literature Discussion: Once per month |
| **Science:** | **ACE** 8th grade (Physical Science), group science class once per month |
| **Religion:** | **Faith and Life**, 8th grade |
| **Bible:** | As a family |
| **German:** | Aloud each morning together with mom and sister |
| **Journal:** | Each day |
| **Research Paper:** | Has decided to write about Wilderness Survival |
| **Home Ec:** | Sewing and cooking all day, two times per month (part of 4-H) |
| **Music:** | Practice piano and violin daily after breakfast |
| **Public Speaking:** | Each Friday night at the Extension Center |
| **Debate:** | Second semester, each Friday night at the Extension Center |
| **Newspaper:** | Edit and write monthly |
| **Symphony:** | Each Monday night and concerts |
| **Phys Ed:** | Karate |

When you write down everything that you plan to do during the school year, the list usually looks very impressive. It's your job to make sure that your list is workable. If you want to accomplish these objectives, ensure that the kids do a certain amount of work each day. Take for example Gintaras. He's too young to be left alone for long. You need to ask him daily if he's done his work. To help him organize himself, I would hand him a school schedule at the beginning of the year that looks like this:

| | |
|---|---|
| **Math:** | Three pages per day / five days per week |
| **Science:** | Read five pages per day (this assignment changes weekly) |
| **Reading:** | One book per week – divide book into five parts |
| **Religion:** | One chapter per week |
| **Music:** | Practice cello and piano each day first thing after breakfast |
| **Research Paper:** | Go to library by end of this week to pick out books (this assignment changes weekly) |
| **Public Speaking:** | Do weekly assignment |

I would tell Gintaras that this is the minimum that must get done during the week. If he knows that a field trip is coming up, he better double up on some work or work ahead of schedule.

The 13 year old's schedule would allow for greater flexibility and responsibility on the child's part. She has much more room to maneuver:

| | |
|---|---|
| **Math:** | Have Chapters 1-5 done before we break for Christmas. This could be accomplished by doing ½ a lesson per day and watching the video every other day. We need to correct the lesson as soon as it has been completed, go over any mistakes, and email the teacher if there are any questions. |
| **English** | Have five **ACE** books done before Christmas. This means that you need to do a minimum of five pages per day/5 days per week. |
| **Science** | Ditto |
| **Literature** | One book per week |
| **Religion** | One chapter per week |
| **German** | Together. Work on memorizing vocabulary. |
| **Journal** | Write daily. |
| **Public Speaking** | Do weekly assignment. |
| **Research Paper** | Mom will check monthly deadlines. |

As you can see, each child is treated differently depending on his/her age. Your children need to take the lead and follow through on their own. Your job is to be the encourager, the cheerleader, the instigator. Always remember to plan in breaks for Thanksgiving, Christmas, Easter, birthdays, etc. Plan your vacation time into your schedule if you want to be done with subjects by a certain time. Pre-plan those subjects that need to follow a schedule (like math). Take the time to organize your school year; the year will run more smoothly and you'll have an enjoyable time!

I find it easier not having to adhere to the public school year schedule. It alleviates stress and there is no worry that all of the work needs to be completed by June. We school year round and we just keep on truckin' along, stopping when we want to take a break. All of my kids are above "grade level" in math - the only subject that I always use a text for - because we never stop working during the summers. Thus, they may finish their math text in January, and immediately start a new one.

Never make your kids do pages in a workbook just so that you can say they completed the "whole book." Remember, workbooks were created to keep kids busy. This is not **our** intent. We want our kids to learn. If they know the material, skip the pages. The reverse can also be true. Never speed through a book so that you can get it done by a certain deadline. If the child is having major difficulty, slow down or you may even need to obtain a different book.

Mothers of large families have a unique opportunity in their homes. They can have their older kids learn patience, compassion, and diligence by teaching their younger siblings to read, write, and learn their colors (the game **Twister** is ideal for this), numbers, and ABC's. No one ever said mom had to do it all. If you need to work with one child, have another play learning games, read, or teach counting to the younger ones. (Actually games are a wonderful way to teach.) This frees you up to concentrate on just one child; and it gives the youngest kids much needed attention. Instead of lamenting that you're coming undone, use your children to assist you. Contrary to what some others believe, it's much easier to do unit studies with the whole family.

Competitiveness among siblings seems to be very common. I would definitely discourage it by stressing that it's not a character trait we want to emulate. Competitiveness has its place in certain areas of life, but it should never be cut-throat. At our home, we tell our kids, "Life is not fair. Get used to it." If I had this problem at home, I would only worry if the "winner" bragged about his accomplishments. I would not try to make things "fair" for the child who's losing. If you have a child that is naturally always finishing first, getting everything right, excelling at everything, you need to learn to live with it just like the kids. You're probably making the situation worse by empathizing with the others. Never allow the "winner" to gloat, but on the other hand if that person is truly always "winning," and it's natural, then there's nothing you can do about it.

**Always remember, go with what works for you, what makes learning a loving experience and fun!**

## Other suggestions:

1. Train your kids to wait their turn. Don't allow them all to demand your attention at once. If you're busy helping someone else, tell them to skip the problem they're having trouble with until you get a chance to come to their assistance. Make sure that they always have alternatives to work on if you're too busy to help them.

2. Don't answer the phone. Let the answering machine do it. You can always pick up if it's an emergency. Think about how much of our day is wasted on the phone needlessly gabbing, and how much of your kids' day is wasted waiting for you to get off the phone.

3. Teach your kids to help one another. The older ones can teach the younger ones to read, count, tell their colors and write. They can also help them with math work. When I was in second grade (in a very small private school), we used to teach the first graders how to read. What an extraordinary educational experience that I still remember today! Make learning a family affair. Encourage the children to help each other.

4. If your kids are working from textbooks, stress the importance of making a schedule and trying to stick to it. One of the most frequent complaints I hear in the spring is moms groaning, "We're not even half way through the book! What do we do?" If the reason for this is laziness, then get to it. However, if the reason is that there's too much busy work, skip the extra problems (if they know it, they know it!). If the book's too hard for the child, let them take an easier pace or find a different book.

5. Always try to get the most difficult subjects out of the way first. In our family that's music practice and math. When done, the rest of the day is a breeze! Always try to have them complete their hardest subjects before lunch when their energy level is at its highest.

6. Try a more relaxed approach to education. Make education part of your lifestyle. Learn from life.

7. Always have fun together! If you find it drudgery, then it's drudgery for them; reconsider what you're doing.

8. Don't overload your children with workbooks. Don't make them do every page if they already know the material. Workbooks created for the schoolroom include a lot of extraneous material. If your child fully understands the material, there is no need to continue on with the workbook. **Remember, let your books be your servants. Don't let**

**them make you their slave! They are only a tool that's used as needed.** If you teach year-round, and go right into the next math book without a break, your child can probably skip anywhere from 25 to 50 lessons because they're all basic review from the last book.

9. If time permits, take a quiet time after lunch for everyone to refresh themselves. Sometimes all you need is thirty minutes.

10. If you read aloud to your kids, do it (if possible) during the baby's nap time. This insures a peaceful and quiet reading time.

11. If you need grades and a transcript for your older kids, investigate contract writing. This is when both of you agree to certain requirements in order to receive a grade. If the child doesn't do everything as agreed upon, he doesn't receive an "A."

12. Always re-assess your school year at midterm and the end of the year. What I like to do is write each child's yearly scholastic goals in their log. At the end of the year, I write an assessment in their log. This makes a great diary of their school year.

13. Always take a small break before starting your new school year so that you can refresh and re-energize yourself. Also, write down your new school year's goals and schedule. If you school year-round and don't really have a beginning and an end, you still probably start a fresh topic in at least one subject, such as history. Make this the time to set new goals and schedules.

14. As the kids grow older, work on their goals and schedules together.

15. Keep re-reading books about homeschooling and looking for new materials to enhance your teaching. New ideas keep us vitalized!

**FURTHER READING:**
**The Simplicity of Homeschooling** by Vicki Goodchild (FL: HIS Publishing Co.,1997)
**Dr. Beechick's Homeschool Answer Book** by Ruth Beechick (CA: Arrow Press, 1998)

# A DREAM DAY

I thought it would be fun to add this chart of what a more relaxed day could be like - if we allowed ourselves to school like this. Take a look and see what you think.

6:30 MOM WAKES UP TO WALK AND PRAY

7:00 KIDS WAKE UP, DRESS, CLEAN UP THEIR ROOMS & DO SOME READING.

7:30 BREAKFAST, AFTER WHICH READ FROM THE BIBLE, SOME LITERATURE ON THE SAINTS AND CHURCH, WHATEVER YOU WANT TO DO AS A FAMILY TOGETHER FIRST THING IN THE MORNING.

8:00 KIDS GO OFF AND PRACTICE THEIR MUSIC WHILE MOM CLEANS UP THE KITCHEN WITH THE YOUNGER KIDS' HELP. THEY START THE LAUNDRY AND TAKE OUT DINNER.

8:45 MOM SITS DOWN WITH THE YOUNGER KIDS AND READS THEM A STORY, THEY PLAY SOME NUMBER GAMES AND LEARN A LETTER.

9:30 THE OLDER KIDS START DOING THEIR MATH AND MOM HELPS. MOM WATCHES ALGEBRA VIDEO WITH OLDEST DAUGHTER. MOM SEWS AS SHE WATCHES.

10:30 MOM GOES FOR A WALK WITH THE YOUNGER KIDS WHILE THE OLDER ONES FINISH UP THEIR MATH, JOURNAL, SCIENCE, AND MAKE LUNCH.

12:00 LUNCH.

12:45 BABY TAKES NAP AND EVERYONES ELSE MAKES THEMSELVES COMFORTABLE TO READ. SOME DRAW, SOME BUILD WITH LEGOS, ONE PUTS TOGETHER A PUZZLE.

2:30 WE ALL GO OUTSIDE TO WORK ON GARDEN AND COMPOST. MOM SUGGESTS THAT KIDS DRAW SOME OF THE VEGETABLES THAT HAVE SPROUTED UP IN THEIR DRAWING JOURNAL.

3:30 ALL THE KIDS GO OFF TO DO WHAT THEY WANT WHILE MOM SITS OUTSIDE WITH THE BABY AND SEWS.

4:15 MOM STARTS DINNER WITH ALL THE KIDS.

5:00 DINNER. THE KIDS SET THE TABLE AND CLEAN THE KITCHEN WHEN FINISHED WITH DINNER. AFTER DINNER, WE ALL WORK INDIVIDUALLY ON OUR OWN PROJECTS. (THERE ARE NO OUTSIDE ACTIVITIES TO RUN AROUND TO WHICH DISRUPT THE FAMILY. ABOUT 8:00PM THE FAMILY GATHERS TOGETHER TO READ AND TALK.

8:45 PRAYER AND BEDTIME.

# SAMPLE MOM'S MASTER LEARNING LIST

| SUBJECT | MON | TUES | WED | THURS | FRI |
|---|---|---|---|---|---|
| BIBLE: VIKTORIJA | X | X | X | X | X |
| GIEDRE | X | X | X | X | X |
| GINTARAS | X | X | X | X | X |
| LINAS (WITH MOM A.M.) | X | X | X | X | X |
| MUSIC: VIKTORIJA | X | X | X | X | X |
| GIEDRE | X | X | X | X | X |
| GINTARAS | X | X | X | X | X |
| MATH: VIKTORIJA | CHAP.5/#1 | #1 | #2 | #2 | QUIZ |
| GIEDRE | PG.66-69 | 70-73 | 74-77 | 78-81 | 82-85 |
| GINTARAS | PG.55-58 | 59-62 | 63-66 | 67-70 | 71-74 |
| LINAS:LEARN 11-15 | X | X | X | X | X |
| JOURNAL: VIKTORIJA | X | X | X | X | |
| GIEDRE | X | X | X | X | |
| GINTARAS | X | X | X | X | |
| SCIENCE: VIKTORIJA | 5/1-5 | 6-10 | 11-15 | 16-20 | |
| GIEDRE: | 5/16-20 | 21-25 | 26-30 | 31-35 | |
| GINTARAS: MACHINES | 5 PAGES | EACH | DAY | | |
| LITERATURE: VIKTORIJA | A MAN | FOR ALL | SEASONS | | |
| GIEDRE | STRAWBE | RRY GIRL | | | |
| GINTARAS | INDIAN | CAPTIVE | | | |
| UNIT STUDY: MEDIEVAL | ST.JOAN | OF ARC | | | |
| | | | | | |
| FRIDAY: 4H ( 9:30-2:00 )  TOASTMASTERS ( 5:00 ) | | | | | |
| | | | | | |
| | | | | | |
| | | | | | |
| | | | | | |
| | | | | | |

# MOM'S MASTER LEARNING LIST

| SUBJECT | MON | TUES | WED | THURS | FRI |
|---------|-----|------|-----|-------|-----|
|         |     |      |     |       |     |
|         |     |      |     |       |     |
|         |     |      |     |       |     |
|         |     |      |     |       |     |
|         |     |      |     |       |     |
|         |     |      |     |       |     |
|         |     |      |     |       |     |
|         |     |      |     |       |     |
|         |     |      |     |       |     |
|         |     |      |     |       |     |
|         |     |      |     |       |     |
|         |     |      |     |       |     |
|         |     |      |     |       |     |
|         |     |      |     |       |     |
|         |     |      |     |       |     |
|         |     |      |     |       |     |
|         |     |      |     |       |     |
|         |     |      |     |       |     |
|         |     |      |     |       |     |
|         |     |      |     |       |     |
|         |     |      |     |       |     |
|         |     |      |     |       |     |

NAME: _____

# KIDS' PERSONAL DAILY LESSON SCHEDULE

| SUBJECT | TIME | MON | TUES | WED | THURS | FRI | SAT/SUN |
|---------|------|-----|------|-----|-------|-----|---------|
|  |  |  |  |  |  |  |  |
|  |  |  |  |  |  |  |  |
|  |  |  |  |  |  |  |  |
|  |  |  |  |  |  |  |  |
|  |  |  |  |  |  |  |  |
|  |  |  |  |  |  |  |  |
|  |  |  |  |  |  |  |  |
|  |  |  |  |  |  |  |  |
|  |  |  |  |  |  |  |  |
|  |  |  |  |  |  |  |  |
|  |  |  |  |  |  |  |  |
|  |  |  |  |  |  |  |  |
|  |  |  |  |  |  |  |  |

HOMESCHOOLING BY HEART © 1999

# CHAPTER
## ♥ 22 ♥

## LITTLE KIDS, LITTLE PROBLEMS...

### OR

### THE TODDLERS! WHAT ABOUT THEM???

Well, yes, many of us do have a few of them running in between the chairs and around the living room, with a great big permanent marker grasped in their chubby little hand. At one time, I had a five-year old, three-year old, and a one-year old in my household. On several occasions, I wondered how I would ever make it through the day. I remember being lonely, overworked, and desperately in need of adult stimulation. My husband's favorite way to describe a mother's desperation over being home alone all day with babies is, "Dad comes home, opens the front door, and a wiggly baby is pushed into his arms as his frantic wife runs out the door screaming, 'I'll be back in awhile!' " Believe it or not, I never did do that to him, but it does accurately describe the frustration which I felt many-a-day.

The problem, as I see it, is that we weren't prepared by our culture for parenthood. I had absolutely no experience in handling or caring for a baby. One day I'm an independent working woman making important and responsible decisions and the next day I'm home alone with a screaming infant. There's nothing that can bring you to your knees faster than a "colicky" baby! Days can be quite long when you have no one to talk to and no relatives nearby to ask for help. In a nutshell, this is the beginning of a family. One day down the road we decided to homeschool. We were entirely unprepared because most of us are the product of the public school system. Unless we have a homeschooling support group to rely on, it can be a very harrowing experience – especially if you pull your kids out of school.

Homeschooling from the beginning and having other younger children in the house can be overwhelming. By putting it all in perspective, I think you'll survive and even enjoy the experience. Remember this:

1. When you were a kid, Kindergarten was meant to be a place to learn to socialize and interact. It was not meant to be first grade. Most of us went for only three hours because it was an introduction to school.

Therefore, make your Kindergarten just as delightful. Your child does not need to learn to read, write, and do arithmetic. Introduce him to his letters, colors, and numbers. If he's ready, go forward and if not, stop and re-assess.

2.  Do not compare your kids to other kids. Do not compare boys to girls. Generally, boys seem to be much slower getting the hang of this learning process than girls.

3.  Don't overdo it. Let the child set the pace. Do 10 minutes of numbers; eat some raisins; teach 5 or 10 minutes of letters; run around; have a snack; read a story to the whole crew; perhaps work another 10 minutes on having him identify beginning sounds of words (for example, mama "mmm", daddy "ddd") while the little ones are asleep; or, do all your schoolwork while the others are sleeping! All of it shouldn't take more than 45 to 60 minutes, and it can be split into 5 or 10 minute increments. Have them draw a picture while you're making lunch. Don't overdo it. Sometimes a little is better than a lot!

4.  Always put discipline and character training first – above all! Without these values, learning means absolutely nothing and is truly difficult to accomplish.

5.  While you're working with the Kindergartner have the toddlers nap, play in the yard, build a fort, or draw pictures. Better yet, they can be part of the lesson too! Frequently we try to set up these "perfect" situations where we're only working with one child at a time. Try to include all your children. The worst that can happen is that they'll become bored and leave you alone; the best, of course, is that they may actually learn! All of this learning can even be done at the picnic table or on the driveway with chalk, with the little ones drawing or coloring. Another method is to allow the little ones to play in the sandbox while you and the "learner" are tracing letters in a cardboard box using sand! It's also a good idea to have a special box of toys that the younger ones can play with only when you're doing school. If they want to do school, encourage them to have their own school supplies! Give your toddler a muffin pan and beans. Sit the child in the highchair and have him "count!" Don't get upset if the kitchen or schoolroom becomes messy – let them enjoy themselves, allowing you a few extra minutes to work with the others. When my daughters were nine and seven, I had a four-year old son and an infant. We'd all work together in one room: the girls were at the table, the four-year old played with the toys on the floor, and the infant either slept or was in a chair. It seemed so important to us at the time to have "real school" with a set block of time for studying. We all need to realize that nine and seven-year old children are too young to work for long periods. They need

time to have a break, run around, and explore. If you're doing "hands on" learning, all the children will have the opportunity to be involved (and not be bored or disruptive!).

6. Read to your toddlers everyday. If your oldest is eight-years old or younger and the others are toddlers, read to all as a group. By reading to your children daily, they become used to sitting still for long periods of time. (They need to learn attentiveness.) Instill the love of reading in them from an early age!

7. Make sure you have a weekly library day. All the children must know to be quiet in the library and to be familiar with where their favorite books are kept. A child of two years should be able to sit quietly for at least 20 minutes and look at pictures. If you have younger children that have a hard time being quiet, have your husband or older children go along with you and take turns watching the toddler(s). If you don't start them young, it will only become that much harder later. Also, by setting a weekly library day, your children will anticipate their trip to the library and borrowing new books.

8. Go to the library and find books on toddler activities. Make out an index card for each activity you like with a list of necessary items. (This is a great job for an older child.) File the cards in a small box, and keep the necessary items separate from the kids' other toys. When you need an activity to occupy the toddlers, you have everything prepared!

9. Another idea is to have "time out" for toddlers in their bedroom (each toddler needs to be in a separate room). You can start with a few minutes and continue to increase the time. Eventually the toddler should be able to stay in his own room for at least 30 minutes, if not longer. While there, the toddler has to play quietly with blocks, books, or puzzles.

10. Teach your toddlers to obey. Have them practice coming to you when calling their name. Also, have them help with chores, so as you start to teach them you won't have all the burdens of the household on your shoulders. Remember the extra effort it takes to teach a young child a chore is well worth the time in the long run. One day you'll turn around and your kids will be doing all their chores without your help or prodding.

11. When your child progresses to first grade work, don't feel that you need to sit down and do school for long hours. At that age, the child is still very young. Remember, most young children can accomplish all their schoolwork in about 1 hour. The rest of school time can be filled with lots of good stories read by mom. Those stories or novels should

be well above their reading level because they're listening. When my oldest was in Kindergarten we were reading **The Little House on the Prarie**, **Heidi,** and **The Chronicles of Narnia.** Special projects such as cooking, cleaning, music lessons, ballet, gymnastics, and field trips are all part of school.

12. **Remember that they're only young once.** Enjoy them. **Let them work hard for short periods of time; let them play equally as hard to exert their youthful energy.** The time will come soon enough to do more school! They'll be physically and emotionally ready!

13. Don't be discouraged. Many of us have been there. Look for support from someone who has children the same age as yours. Lean on each other. Co-op, take fieldtrips together, go to the playground, and have fun. Have your kids help in cleaning the house a little bit everyday. Take the time to make good, nutritious meals. Do what's most important first and save the rest for later – perhaps when the kids are older! If you don't make a big deal out of this learning business, they won't even know that they are learning. What fun!

14. Always remember to have fun and create memories!

## SUMMARY:

1. Work on raising wise children.

2. Instill the love of learning and have fun doing it.

3. Get messy!

*Have no anxiety about anything, but in everything by prayer and supplication with thanksgiving let your requests be made known to God.*

*Philippians 4-6*

## FURTHER READING:
**Creative Family Times** by Will & Lindy Wilson and Allen & Connie Hadidian (IL: Moody Press, 1989). This book includes practical activities for building character in your preschoolers.
**What Every Child Should Know Along The Way** by Gail Martin (CA: Growing Families International, 1998) Teaches practical life skills in every stage of life.

# TODDLER ACTIVITY IDEAS

- ♥ PLACE POTS AND PANS ON THE FLOOR WITH SOME WATER AND LOTS OF CONTAINERS TO FILL AND EMPTY (AFTER WHICH YOU WASH THE FLOOR!)
- ♥ GIVE THEM SOME BEADS AND MUFFIN TINS AND LET THEM "COUNT!"
- ♥ SIT THEM AT THEIR TABLE AND LET THEM STRING MACARONI
- ♥ FILL A SPECIAL BOX WITH THE FOLLOWING (THAT THEY ARE ALLOWED TO PLAY WITH ONLY WHEN YOU NEED TIME WITH AN OLDER CHILD): PUZZLES, LEGOS, SPECIAL CONSTRUCTION PAPER AND CRAYONS, BLOCKS, ETC.
- ♥ PLACE AN OLD SHOWER CURTAIN, OR PLASTIC SHEET, ON THE FLOOR AND LET THEM FINGER PAINT.
- ♥ LET THEM PAINT WITH WATER COLORS.
- ♥ PLAY DRESS UP. GET A LARGE BOX AND START COLLECTING INTERESTING CLOTHES AT GARAGE SALES OR FROM YOUR MOM.
- ♥ LET THEM CUT AND PASTE. GET A BOX AND START COLLECTING GREETING CARDS, COLORED PAPER, BEADS, TO MAKE ART PROJECTS. (LEARNING TO CUT WITH SCISSORS IS A GREAT FINE MOTOR SKILL.)
- ♥ COLLECT LACE AND RIBBON AND BUTTONS AND LET THEM GLUE TO PAPER, FELT, OR CARDBOARD.
- ♥ GIVE THEM SOME BROWN PAPER (THE TYPE USED TO WRAP PACKAGES) AND LET THEM START MAKING CHRISTMAS OR BIRTHDAY WRAPPING PAPER.
- ♥ MAKE A "BOOK" OUT OF CONSTRUCTION PAPER AND LET THEM WRITE OR DRAW IN IT. IT'S A GREAT PRESENT FOR DAD OR GRANDPARENTS!
- ♥ PUNCH SOME HOLES IN FELT AND THREAD YARN IN A SUPER SIZED PLASTIC NEEDLE AND LET THEM "SEW!"
- ♥ PLAY DOUGH: YOU CAN MAKE YOUR OWN OR BUY READY MADE. CONSIDER BUYING SOME OF THE "TOOLS." KIDS LOVE THEM (EVEN 13-YEAR-OLDS)!

WE, AS PARENTS, DON'T LIKE TO GIVE OUR KIDS ARTSY PROJECTS BECAUSE WE HATE THE MESS. THIS CAN BE AVOIDED BY SETTING UP A SPECIAL CORNER WHERE THE KIDS CAN FREELY "EXPRESS" THEMSELVES. IT'S ALWAYS GREAT TO HAVE A TODDLER-SIZED TABLE AND CHAIRS. IT REALLY MAKES THEM FEEL SPECIAL!

# ACTIVITIES FOR BEGINNER STUDENTS

SING

NATURE HIKES

NATURE DIARY: DRAW CRITTERS AND SPECIMENS.

NATURE BIOLOGY: LOOK AT YOUR SPECIMENS UNDER A MICRO-
SCOPE. KEEP CRITTERS IN A JAR TO OBSERVE.
(MAKE SURE YOU LET THEM GO ALIVE.)
DRAW THE PARTS OF YOUR SPECIMENS AND
LABEL.

STUDY SPIDERS AND DRAW WEBS.

MAKE A BOOK: CUT PICTURES OUT OF A MAGAZINE, DRAW AND LABEL.
HAVE THEM DICTATE THE TEXT TO YOU.

FINGER PAINT

BUILD CITIES WITH BLOCKS OR LEGOS.

SEW ON BUTTONS, CUT SIMPLE PATTERNS, MAKE CRAFTS,
GLUE TO EMBELLISH

MEMORIZE SCRIPTURE OR POETRY AND RECITE TO AN AUDIENCE.
(GREAT MEMORY BUILDERS.)

ART: COPY FAMOUS PICTURES.

MAKE PAPER DOLLS, AIRPLANES, FORTS.

COUNT BEADS AND MAKE NECKLACE.

COOK BY HISTORICAL THEME. (CHECK OUT THE LAURA INGALLS
WILDER COOKBOOK.)

WOODBURNING (AGES 8 AND UP)

BUILD A BIRD HOUSE OUT OF WOOD OR MAKE IT OUT OF A PLASTIC
GALLON MILK JUG.

MAKE A WEATHER CALENDAR: HAVE THEM DRAW THE WEATHER EVERY
DAY ON CALENDAR. (RAINDROPS, CLOUDS, SUN, ETC.)

KEEP A RAIN GAUGE. MEASURE AND RECORD RAINFALL.

SET UP A BIRD FEEDER TO WATCH BIRDS.

SET UP A STORE, PUT PRICES ON ITEMS, AND HAVE THEM LEARN
TO COUNT CHANGE.

TEACH SAFETY.

ROLL OUT LARGE PAPER, TRACE THEIR BODY, AND HAVE THEM DRAW THEIR
BODY PARTS AND LABEL.

BUILD A COMPOST AND HAVE THEM BE IN CHARGE OF THE FAMILY'S
DAILY ORGANIC TRASH.

# PART FOUR

ESTIMATED TIME OF ARRIVAL

OR

"ARE WE THERE YET?"

# CHAPTER
## ♥ 23 ♥

## AND THEN THEY GROW UP...

I've heard every type of story as to why it's necessary for mom and dad to put their teenaged son or daughter back in high school:

- "I've only got two kids.  If I had as many as you they wouldn't be so lonely. They need to go to school for friends."

- "I've got so many kids I can't do the oldest one justice anymore. He needs to go to school so that he learns what he needs to learn."

- "My son wants to play baseball or basketball or soccer or whatever. He needs to be in school."

- "I want my daughter to go to college. She needs to be in a good program so that she can build her resume and win a scholarship."

- "My child is mature and has enough character not to be influenced by her peers."

And so the stories go.  So sad.  Do you remember I asked you before to consider why you began to homeschool?

- Was it to ensure their moral upbringing?

- Or was it because they weren't learning anything in school?

- Was it because schools are dangerous and violent places?

- Or was it the negative peer pressure?

- Was it because of the alarming values that they pick up there?

Has that reason suddenly dissolved? How did it manage to disappear? Now that your son or daughter is in his or her teens with their hormones raging, their desire to flex their individuality and independence growing, is it time to put them in school with hundreds of other kids in exactly the same situation?  Do you really think that as a homeschooler your child won't get into college or be able to win a scholarship?  You really think his chances are better in school where he has to compete with thirty other kids for the teacher's attention and where there are all sorts of other temptations to pry him away from his studies?  Do you believe he or she will be able to concentrate when they're suddenly thrust into a classroom with the other sex? (There's a lot to be said for all boy and all girl schools.)  Though your child may be strong in his convictions, do you think you are helping by suddenly exposing him to peer pressure and the easy availability to liquor, drugs, sex, and cigarettes?  Have schools become any less violent?  Are sports so important to you and your child that you would risk exposing them to all of this? Do you trust the teachers' values more than your own? After having homeschooled for all those years, when they're finally able to independently study and learn, you're ready to hang it all up and let the school take over and undo all the good habits they learned?

Remember why you began to homeschool.  Has that reason changed?

You **can** keep schooling that child.  You **are** smart enough. You've come up to challenges before and overcome them.  **You can do it now.**  "But I can't teach geometry, calculus, physics, or whatever else!"  And the list goes on.  No, you may not be able to teach these subjects, but what about someone else? There are so many people in our community that can do it and are willing to help.*  You just have to find them. Keep in mind that your child may be able to teach himself; they don't **always** need our help.  We tend to think we're indispensable, but if your child wants to learn something badly enough, he may be able to do so on his own.  Sometimes he needs only a bit of assistance.

For the past two years, we have had some wonderful people teaching our kids public speaking.  They're part of Toastmasters and were willing to share their expertise with our kids.  They seem to enjoy teaching them, and our kids love the challenge.  From public speaking, we branched out into debate.

I've found a wonderful video series for math called Chalkdust.  If you still don't understand after you've watched the video and read the lesson, you can email the teacher, or call, and he'll tell you what you're doing wrong.

There are wonderful science programs as well as labs available. There are even free high school courses on the Internet with virtual labs for science. (This is possible in Florida. I don't know if any of the other states offer this service.  This will become a diploma decreeing high school next year.)  When your child is about 15 years old he can enroll in a community college and take classes.  (Hopefully all the students in the class want to learn. I wouldn't leave my 15 year old there to socialize. I'd carefully monitor these classes and teachers.)

**Search for someone in the community who can help teach those subjects that you can't teach.**

Dr. Arthur Robinson (**Robinson Curriculum**) says that a homeschooled child **should** surpass his parents academically – this is possible and should be our ultimate goal. How does he go about doing this? The principal answer is loving to learn and knowing how to research areas of interest (this is what you have been instilling in your child since he was a toddler). Then he proceeds to teach himself. This can be done by having the best possible reading and research materials available and the parents' support in the various educational adventures he wishes to pursue. Our goal should be to have our kids working independently by the time they're in their teens. They should only come to us when special assistance is required.

If you've been homeschooling for a few years, your child should have developed some homeschool friendships. You should encourage these friendships and provide opportunities for them to get together and share their studies, such as: co-oping science labs, hosting a literature discussion, forming a debate group, and starting a homeschool or community newspaper, yearbook, or drama group. Don't try to do it all, but if a few parents would share the burden and take on hosting a group once a month, the kids would be meeting quite a few times.

Start a sports group. Be the coach or hire one. Compete with the local private schools. Where there's a will, there's a way!

No one said it would be easy, and why should it be? We weren't put here on earth to have an easy life. Life isn't fair, but if you think it's worth fighting for, do it. You're giving your kids the education of a lifetime which can't be duplicated anywhere. If the homeschooled kids, who I've seen graduate, are any indication of the movement as a whole, then we are bringing up well-rounded individuals. These kids have the potential to do anything because of the varied experiences shared growing up. They haven't been age-segregated for their entire lives; they've been immersed in their community. They are fighters and go-getters. They're smart and wise beyond their years. Colleges want them.

**It's worth the challenge and the fight!**

## REFLECTION:

You **can** homeschool through high school. Has your original reason for homeschooling suddenly vanished?

You child **is not** better off in a school institution. You can find others to help your child learn difficult subjects.  Think of at least one person you know who could help your child learn a subject.

What is your goal for this child - academia or heaven?

\* Last year my kids were co-oping a bird unit study with two other families. I called the local nature conservancy and asked whether they had any type of program on birds. They didn't, but they were more than glad to refer me to a local bird watching lady.  She volunteered to come to my house and present a slide show on the local bird life. A few weeks later, she took us out to the local conservancy and gave us a walking bird tour.  All this, for a mere phone call!

The trouble with a kitten is
THAT
Eventually it becomes a
CAT.

("The Kitten," by Ogden Nash)

## FURTHER READING:

**Robinson Self-Teaching Home-School Curriculum,** Oregon Institute of
Science And Medicine, 2251 Dick George Road, Cave Junction, OR
97523
This is a unique self-learning curriculum developed by the Robinson family consisting of 20 CD-Roms containing: a course of study, books, examinations, encyclopedia, dictionary, and vocabulary.
**Homeschooling For Excellence** by David & Micki Colfax (NY: Warner Books, 1988)
**And What About College?** By Cafi Cohen (MA: Holt Associates, Inc, 1997)

# CHAPTER
♥ 24 ♥

## THE JOURNEY'S END

Time flies and soon you will be coming to the journey's end – or will you? Is there a final destination?  We marry, start our family, decide to homeschool, and in the process create a lifestyle. We spend years disciplining and training our children, learning to organize our homes, budgeting our money, creating wonderful meals, collecting materials, analyzing curriculums, building our libraries, discussing and arguing learning styles, and suddenly...our babies are all grown up and gone.   Are you done? Are you at the end of your journey?

I think not.  Soon you'll find yourself helping your children set up their households and nurturing their little ones. Perhaps the second time around you'll have a more relaxed vision of education and actually start teaching their babies naturally, like God intended us to learn, with lots of love, and a good sense of adventure.

*And these words which I command you this day shall be upon your heart; and you shall teach them diligently to your children, and shall talk of them when you sit in your house, and when you walk by the way, and when you lie down, and when you rise.*                                      *Deuteronomy 6:6-7*

Parents never lose a job; they're parents for as long as they have children. And so...we'll continue to wander the by-roads helping teach along the way, shape character, and lead souls to heaven.

*A good man leaves an inheritance to his children's children...*
                                      *Proverbs 13:22*

Are we there yet? Never! The road just keeps on twisting and turning and never ending...

Our final destination?   Heaven!

Roads go ever on,
     Over rock and under tree,
By caves where never sun has shone,
     By streams that never find the sea;
Over snow by winter sown,
     And through the merry flowers of June,
Over grass and over stone,
     And under mountains in the moon.

Roads go ever ever on
     Under cloud and under star,
Yet feet that wandering have gone
     Turn at last to home afar.
Eyes that fire and sword have seen
     And horror in the halls of stone
Look at last on meadows green
     And trees and hills they long have known.

Taken from **The Hobbit** by J.R.R. Tolkien

# CAUTION:

# ACCIDENT UP AHEAD!

# BEWARE
# OF
# TRAFFIC JAM!

# ARE YOU READY TO CALL IT QUITS?

If you've read this entire book and are still considering putting your kids back into school - stop, look, and listen! Please!

**Why did you start to homeschool?**

- Because your child was attending school and **not** learning?

- Was there a serious learning problem **not** being addressed in school by the teacher?

- Was it because he or she was learning **too** quickly and sitting bored in class while the teacher patiently tried to teach the others?

- **Was** there a discipline problem in the classroom?

- Were you **afraid** for your child's safety?

- Was it the **lack of morality** that spurred you on?

- **Did** you have a problem with the health or sex ed class?

- Do you live in far off Alaska, in a jungle or the mountains, and aren't **close enough** to any school?

- If none of the above, was it because **God prevailed it upon your soul** that homeschooling was the path to bring up righteous children?

I'm sure that whatever your reason, it was a good one. In my opinion, any reason that brings the children back home to the nest is wonderful. The bottom line is that you love and care for your children. You and your spouse felt that it was your job to take over if your children were to receive a good upbringing and education. After making the decision, you were probably very scared, perhaps a bit excited, and certainly very cautious. I could just hear you saying, "I'll give it a year. I can't possibly do too much damage in a year." You looked at homeschooling either as a self-inflicted punishment or a great adventure. **However, you made this commitment because you love your child.**

Has any of this changed since you began?  Do you love your child any less?  Do you care about his future any less?  How then can you possibly consider quitting?  Ah...because reality hit you like a ton of bricks!  You saw that this was more work than you ever anticipated.  Well, let me ask you this:  When you were expecting your firstborn, weren't you both excited and scared at the same time?  You couldn't wait to have that little bundle of joy, but also you were trembling with worry and wondering how you would ever manage to take care of this baby. This precious gift would be your responsibility day and night for about eighteen years!

You then gave birth.  Weren't you even more scared, gazing into those angelic little eyes that stared back at you so trustingly?  What about those days when you didn't know if you would make it because you were so tired and so overwhelmed?  Those were the days that you may have literally flung that child into your husband's arms as he walked through the doorway after work.  What did this mean?  It didn't mean that you stopped loving the little tyke.  It meant that you were tired, perhaps alone, and needed help (any help) so desperately.

Homeschooling, the experience, is a lot like giving birth and caring for that newborn child.  You definitely go through much difficult labor and the job isn't over when the labor ends; it has just begun.  By far the biggest helping hand is to have a comforting shoulder to lean on so that you don't feel entirely alone and overwhelmed. This is exactly what this book is all about.  It's the support that is so sorely missing in this day and age when there doesn't seem to be any physical or spiritual help to be found.  It's meant to somehow help you find your place in a community that no longer exists. It's a guide to help each family create their own lifestyle and develop a community of friends.

If you find yourself ready to quit, try taking the following steps toward a better homeschooling path:

**First** realize that none of us can travel this path we've chosen alone.  We must find someone to share the burden with.  In my case, I rely on the grace of God.  There is no way humanly possible that I would be able to keep on going without the graces that the Lord pours down upon me daily.  Each one of us needs to share our burden with someone else.  If it's God, then pray without ceasing.  Begin your day with prayer and end it faithfully lavishing the Lord with your adoration and praise.   Rest assured that He is in control and always will be.  Offer your daily crosses up to God as sacrifices.  Each time you come up against a brick wall humbly say, "God, I offer this burden I must bear up to you. **Your** will be done."  Learn to ask the Lord for Him to make you **want** His will in your life.

**Second**, each of us must learn to share the responsibility of raising our children with our husbands.  God did not bless just you with that child; He blessed both of you.  Though your husband may not be able to help much in the day-to-day teaching, he can help you solve the daily problems, be they scholastic or behavioral.  When you learn to share with your spouse, those problems you've been having will not feel so insurmountable after all.  Your husband may have a very special knack for solving your problems.  Remember, he has more objectivity just because he's not in the trenches every day!

**Third**, work at developing an open line of communication with your kids based on trust, honesty, and lots and lots of love.  Make sure that you're the first one your kids come to when they're in trouble or need answers.  Don't let them bottle up hurts and anger. Make sure they value their siblings.

**Fourth**, find yourself a soul mate; someone else who's homeschooling and going on the same journey as you are.  It always helps to have a friend who has as many children as you do, approximately the same ages; or an older homeschooling mom who can be your mentor and loving shoulder to lean on.  Her children can possibly shepherd yours. Please remember, you can't do it alone. You must share your experiences with someone, or you'll explode like a bottle of soda water when it's shaken and released.

If you haven't realized it yet, relationships are crucial to successful homeschooling. You need:

- A close and prayerful relationship with your Creator

- A strong and healthy relationship with your adoring spouse

- A communicative and loving relationship with each of your children

- A trusting relationship with a friend or friends

If you take the time to develop these relationships, you are going to find yourself feeling more confident and in control and, most importantly, happy and content.

**Fifth**, simplify, simplify, and simplify again.  And again! **Simplify** your life by s...l...o...w... i...n...g   d...o...w...n.  Simplify your curriculum so that it doesn't overwhelm you. Simplify your house so that there's less to clean.  Delegate chores so that you're not trying to do it all.

**Finally, stop trying to be perfect.** Don't expect too much from yourself.  No one is perfect accept for our Lord, so don't try and think that you can ever possibly attain perfection.  Don't expect perfection from your children or husband, and don't be so demanding about the look of the house. You're busy raising and nurturing a family of souls. The house can wait till the babies are gone!

Instead of thinking of yourself, and how hard your present situation is, think of others first.  **Think of their feelings, their sorrows, their worries, their**

**discomforts... Ask them how they feel, what you can do for them.** This is exactly the opposite of what "the world" expects of us. The world wants us to think only of our own pleasures, but God's Word says, " *So whatever you wish that men would do to you, do so to them...*" *(Matthew 7:12)* When you put others first, when you truly live the Golden Rule, you may be pleasantly surprised at the returns you reap.

**Always remember to S...L...O...W D...O...W...N and have FUN!**

*Love is patient and kind; love is not jealous or boastful; it is not arrogant or rude. Love does not insist on its own way; it is not irritable or resentful; it does not rejoice at wrong, but rejoices in the right. Love bears all things, believes all things, hopes in all things, endures all things.* 1 Corinthians 13:4-7

# HOMESCHOOLING BY HEART SYNOPSIS
*"A Mom's Road Map"*

## WHERE IS YOUR HEART?

- IS YOUR HEART AT HOME WITH YOUR KIDS?
- DO YOU HAVE A "FIRE IN YOUR BELLY" TO HOMESCHOOL?
- CAN YOU VERBALIZE WHY YOU DECIDED TO HOMESCHOOL?
- ARE YOU READY TO WORK ON CREATING A FAMILY LIFESTYLE?
- DO YOU SEE MOTHERHOOD AS A VOCATION?
- ARE YOU READY TO SLOW DOWN AND SIMPLIFY?
- ARE YOU LIVING LIFE SPONTANEOUSLY OR INTENTIONALLY?
- IS THIS YOUR SEASON TO STAY HOME?
- HAVE YOU NURTURED YOUR RELATIONSHIPS: PLANTED AND WATERED YOUR COMMUNITY?
- DO YOU HAVE HOMESCHOOLING SUPPORT?
- TO WHOM DO YOU LOOK FOR SUPPORT?

## WHERE DOES THE JOURNEY BEGIN?

- PRAYER
- GOAL SETTING
- DISCIPLINE - HOLDING THEIR HEART
- ORGANIZATION & DE-CLUTTERING
- LEARN TO SCHEDULE: CALENDARS, COMMITMENTS
- ATTITUDE CHECK
- PLANNING MEALS
- SETTING A BUDGET AND TEACHING TO BUDGET

# THE JOURNEY

- WORK ON YOUR CHILDREN'S, AND YOUR OWN, CHARACTER
- ARE YOU CONCENTRATING ON INSTILLING THE LOVE OF LEARNING?
- SET A GOOD EXAMPLE - ALWAYS!
- NEVER PUSH A CHILD TO LEARN!
- ENCOURAGE INDEPENDENT LEARNERS
- ALWAYS HAVE FUN LEARNING
- BECOME AN "ENABLER"
- RELAX
- RAISE WISE CHILDREN
- INCLUDE YOUR TODDLERS IN YOUR ACTIVITIES

*Make school your life and life your school!*

# ARE YOU THERE YET?

- REMEMBER MOM - CONFIDENCE! IF YOU HAVE "A FIRE IN YOUR BELLY" FOR HOMESCHOOLING, YOU CAN DO IT!
- IF YOU FEEL THAT YOU'RE NOT CAPABLE OF TEACHING A CERTAIN SUBJECT, FIND A MENTOR OR OTHER ALTERNATIVE. WHERE THERE'S A WILL, THERE'S A WAY! DON'T GIVE UP JUST BECAUSE THE ROAD IS GETTING BUMPY!
- WHAT IS YOUR FINAL DESTINATION ANYWAY?

# CAUTION! ACCIDENT UP AHEAD! DELAYS! ARE YOU PREPARED?

- YOU CAN'T DO IT ALONE
- SHARE THE BURDEN
- COMMUNICATION LINES MUST BE OPEN
- DO YOU HAVE A SOUL MATE?
- S...L...O...W...   D...O...W...N ! AND SIMPLIFY!
- DON'T BE A PERFECTIONIST!

*Always remember to have fun and enjoy!*
*The love of learning will surely follow.*
*Homeschool By Heart*

### Epilogue

Finally I'm done. At least for today. Writing this book has been a great joy; it's made me focus in on what's truly important in my life. I've learned a lot about myself that I never took the opportunity to uncover; I've narrowed down my goals and seen that my aspirations are within reach. I've discovered that I can sit down and actually put my thoughts in writing to share with you.

As I wrote this book, I've had to make compromises - most involving my family. At the beginning it was easy to work at night when everyone was asleep. However, as my self-imposed deadline drew near, the book took on a life of its own and demanded that I show it more attention than I ever dreamed I'd need to. What I've found is that you can't do it all. You need to prioritize and make conscious decisions as to what needs to be accomplished and what doesn't. In order to make a project like this come to fruition, you need your entire family's cooperation, as well as many others close to you. Writing a book is not a solitary endeavor; it's most definitely a community affair (at least when you have a large and vibrant family).

My parting words to you are, once again, you can't do it alone. Rely on the grace of God, the mate He provided for you, your family, and all those around you. You need everyone's love and support to be able to successfully homeschool by heart!

Kristina

O Lord, you mete out peace to us,
For it is you who have accomplished all we have done.
Isaiah 26:12

Notes

Notes

Notes

# ORDER FORM

| QUANTITY | | PRICE | TOTAL |
|---|---|---|---|
| | HOMESCHOOLING BY HEART | 19.95 | |
| | | | |
| | | | |
| | | | |
| | SUB TOTAL: | | |
| | TAX (IF ORDERING IN FLORIDA): | | |
| | SHIPPING:     10% OF SUB TOTAL: | | |
| | TOTAL: | | |

NAME:

ADDRESS:

CITY & STATE:

ZIP CODE:

Please visit us at our virtual store

## Solomon's Secrets

Browse and buy your favorite
Odyssey Tapes
Usborne Books
Historical Novels
Biographies
and much more...
Check out our monthly sales

http://www.solomons-secrets.com